METAPHYSICS

THE BASICS

Metaphysics: The Basics is a concise and engaging introduction to the philosophical study of the world and universe in which we live. Concerned with questions about reality, existence, time, identity and change, metaphysics has long fascinated people but to the uninitiated some of the issues and problems can appear very complex. In this lively and lucid book, Michael Rea examines and explains key questions in the study of metaphysics such as:

- Can two things be in the same place at the same time?
- Do creatures of fiction exist?
- Are human beings free?
- Is time travel possible?
- Is there just one world or many worlds?

With a glossary of key terms and suggestions for further reading, the book considers key philosophical arguments around Metaphysics, making this an ideal starting point for anyone seeking a full intro-duction to the debates both within and about metaphysics.

Michael Rea is Professor of Philosophy at the University of Notre Dame. He is the editor of *Arguing about Metaphysics* (2009) and co-author of *Introduction to the Philosophy of Religion* (2008).

The Basics

METAPHYSICS

THE BASICS

Michael Rea

Routledge
Taylor & Francis Group

LONDON AND NEW YORK

First published 2014
by Routledge
2 Park Square, Milton Park, Abingdon, OX14 4RN

and by Routledge
711 Third Avenue, New York, NY 10017

Routledge is an imprint of the Taylor & Francis Group, an informa business

British Library Cataloguing in Publication Data
A catalogue record for this book is available from the British Library

Library of Congress Cataloging in Publication Data
Rea, Michael C. (Michael Cannon), 1968-
Metaphysics, the basics / Michael Rea. – 1 [edition].
(The basics)
Includes bibliographical references and index.
1. Metaphysics. I. Title.
BD131.R43 2014
110–dc23
2013035971

ISBN 978-0-415-57441-9 (hbk)
ISBN 978-0-415-57442-6 (pbk)
ISBN 978-1-315-79827-1 (ebk)

Typeset in Bembo
by Taylor and Francis Books

For Gretchen

CONTENTS

PREFACE

Western philosophy began with metaphysics. The earliest Greek philosophers were on a quest for the underlying natures of things. Some said everything is ultimately water; others said everything is fire; still others said that it is air. Pythagoras thought that everything was ultimately made up of mathematical objects (and *that* mystical view still has adherents even today). They also worried about change. The world is all in flux, observed Heraclitus—so much so that it is impossible to step into the same river twice. But what does *that* mean? You can step into the Nile twice; you can step into the Mississippi twice. So if it is really impossible to step into the same river twice, does that mean that there is something illusory about the Nile and the Mississippi, and perhaps about everything else that is changing? Parmenides said yes. Many in his wake decided that ultimate reality had to consist only of *unchanging* things. No more water, fire, and air; now it was ungenerated and indestructible atoms, or abstract ideas, or other esoteric things. And on and on.

Metaphysics in the twenty-first century deals with these questions and much, much more. It is a core area of philosophy and has flourished as such throughout most of the history of the discipline. And with good reason: Metaphysics deals with some of the deepest, most existentially important questions about human persons and the fundamental features of reality. Many of the questions that matter most to us—Can we survive death? Are we free? What is it to be a person? Do we have immaterial souls?—depend on decisions about matters metaphysical. Even the apparently esoteric answers described in the first paragraph to questions about change and the ultimate nature of things have proven important, exerting tremendous influence not only on the history of philosophy but on the history of theology as well, impacting even our very concept of God.

This book aims to provide an accessible introduction to the basics of metaphysics. Metaphysics is an abstract subject. Rarely does it make for breezy reading. But I have tried as much as possible to keep things simple, to avoid the jargon of the trade, and to expose the structure of the arguments under discussion so that readers can see with clarity what is going on. In some cases, the inclusion of technical terms was unavoidable. The first substantive occurrences of terms like **this** that recur multiple times in the text have been set in boldface and I have supplied definitions or explanations in the Glossary at the end. The Glossary does not add much beyond the definitions I supply in the text itself; but its purpose is to allow the reader to quickly access those definitions without having to look for them in the various chapters in which they are given.

The book begins with a chapter that explains what metaphysics is and what some of the main criticisms of metaphysics have been. Subsequent chapters focus on six topics that have been central to the discipline both throughout its history and in the contemporary literature. My hope is that this text will be of use not only to people who are looking to be introduced to some of the main problems and perspectives that have taken center stage in the contemporary literature in metaphysics, but also to people who just want to reflect on some of the great problems that have occupied the minds of great metaphysicians throughout the history of philosophy.

My approach, then, is *problem-based* rather than *figure-based*: I focus more on the problems that have occupied metaphysicians rather than on the metaphysicians themselves. But I have tried throughout to provide references both within the text and in the "Further Reading" that will guide the reader to some of the most important defenders (both contemporary and historical) of the perspectives developed herein.

Also, I should note that, following the general format for this series, I have not provided in-text citations for the philosophers

I discuss or the texts from which I quote throughout the book. Rather, in each chapter I have simply indicated whom I am discussing or quoting, and, where necessary, I have also given titles; then I have listed the works discussed or quoted from in the "Further Reading" section at the end. I have written this book so that a natural companion for it would be my edited textbook, *Arguing about Metaphysics* (also published by Routledge). The two books treat the same topics (except that the present volume includes a chapter on "substance," whereas *Arguing about Metaphysics* does not have a special section on that topic), and many of the specific articles discussed in this book are reprinted in *Arguing about Metaphysics*.

Chapter 4 of this book includes a few paragraphs from my introduction to *Material Constitution: A Reader* (Rowman & Littlefield, 1997) and other chapters include a few sentences or paragraphs from the introductory material in *Arguing About Metaphysics*. I thank the publishers for permission to reuse that material here. I am also grateful to several friends and colleagues who offered valuable help at various stages in the process of writing this book. The discussions of temporal experience and time travel in Chapter 3 were heavily influenced by discussions of papers written by me and by L. A. Paul in the Notre Dame Metaphysics and Philosophy of Religion Reading Group. Contributions to those discussions by Meghan Sullivan and Kenny Boyce were particularly helpful. Andrew Bailey provided me with very helpful comments on early drafts of the first three chapters, and Siobhán Poole reviewed the manuscript for the press and offered many suggestions for making things shorter and more accessible. Lindsay Rettler helped to proofread the final manuscript and prepared the index. For all of this I am very thankful. I am especially grateful to Alicia Finch and Jeff Snapper, both of whom commented on all of the chapters. Whatever its remaining failings might be, the book is much clearer and more accessible now thanks to their generously extensive and insightful comments. Finally, I am most grateful to my wife Chris and to my children, Aaron, Kristina, Gretchen, Matthias, and Penelope who graciously put up with me during those periods when the writing of this book dominated far too much of my work and free time.

INTRODUCTION

Most of us have questions about the world that science does not answer. Some of these are questions about how things *ought* to be, or about the concepts we use to talk about how things ought to be. Is it *wrong*, or just imprudent, to cheat on your exams? What is moral wrongness? What is a *just* society? How ought we to think? Is it *rational* to accept things on faith? What is knowledge? What is beauty? Set all of these questions aside; they are dealt with in fields like ethics, sociopolitical philosophy, epistemology, and aesthetics.

Others are questions about the principles of valid reasoning, the logical systems that aim to specify those principles, and the properties or concepts that are centrally involved in our formal languages. Set these aside too; they are dealt with in the fields of logic and philosophy of logic.

Still others are existence questions, possibility questions, questions about the intrinsic natures of things, or questions about the fundamental structure of the world. These are the sorts of questions with which this book is concerned.

For example: My words here are causing you to have certain thoughts. But what is the nature of causing? Is it some sort of necessary connection between objects or events? When a cause occurs does its effect *have* to follow afterward? If you are caused to do something, does that mean that you do not do it freely? For that matter, do you do anything freely, or is everything you do determined by the laws of nature? What does it even mean to say that you are free, or that there are such things as laws of nature? Is there a God? Do you have an immaterial soul? When you say "the number three," is there some actual thing that you are referring to that is prime, odd, and somehow in between two other things, namely the number two and the number four?

For some people, questions in metaphysics are conversation stoppers. Ask, over coffee, what it means to be free, and you might be answered with a roll of the eyes, or a profound, tightlipped, "meaningful nod." For others, however, they are scintillating puzzles—invitations to unravel a myriad conceptual knots in our commonsense and scientific ways of thinking about the world.

The eye-rollers tend to convey the impression that they have never even thought about metaphysical questions. The distributors of meaningful nods indicate by their nodding that *of course* we all know that metaphysical questions are profound but unanswerable. But in fact most people have at some point in their lives both thought about metaphysical questions and thought that those questions could be answered. Many of us begin reflecting on matters metaphysical in early childhood. We wonder what it could mean to say that God is everywhere. We wonder about the passage of time: If time moves, what does it move *in*? (Not in time, of course. But then what?) We wonder about ourselves: Do we control our thoughts? Can we exist outside our bodies? And so on.

In this first chapter, I have two goals: Firstly, to flesh out the characterization of metaphysics that I have already begun in these opening paragraphs; and, secondly, to explore and address three objections to the idea that human beings are capable of providing reasonably believable answers to metaphysical questions. Thus we begin by looking at the nature of metaphysics.

THE NATURE OF METAPHYSICS

Bookstores often have entire sections devoted to "metaphysics." They tend to be filled with books that deal with occult topics such as astrology, ghosts, psychic powers, the secret lives of plants, and the like. These issues are what folks in the general public recognize as falling under the label "metaphysics." So if you tell your dental hygienist or your prospective in-laws that you are studying metaphysics in college, they are all too likely to think that you are devoting your time and attention to something strange and frivolous rather than to a serious academic subject. But in fact these topics have very little to do with those studied by academic metaphysicians.

So what *can* we metaphysicians and students of metaphysics tell our friends and family about the subject to which we are devoting so much of our time? Here are a few common answers, followed by the one that I myself prefer.

BEING AS SUCH

Aristotle famously characterized metaphysics as the study of *being qua being*, or of *being as such*. A simpler way of putting the same idea is to say that metaphysics, according to Aristotle, is an investigation into the different kinds or categories of being. To understand what he had in mind, it is helpful to know that, as Aristotle saw things, terms like "being" or "existence" have a variety of different meanings. For example, what it is for a horse to exist is very different from what it is for a number to exist. You might think that this is just a funny way of expressing the commonsensical idea that a horse is a different kind of thing from a number. But that wouldn't be quite right. A horse is a different kind of thing from a cat; but what *existence* is for a horse is the same as what existence is for a cat. They have the same kind of being, even if they are not exactly the same kind of object. Numbers, on the other hand, besides being different kinds of objects from horses or cats, do not even *exist* in the same way. They have a very different kind of being.

Aristotle's idea was that "being" and related words (like "is" or "exists") mean one thing when predicated of a horse or a cat and something else when predicated of a number. The meanings are related to one another, but still different. We can understand this point by way of an analogy. Consider the word "healthy." We might say that a meal is healthy; we might also say that someone's complexion is healthy, or that she herself is healthy. It seems that "healthy" means something different in each of these three cases. The meanings are related, but they are still different. So, likewise, Aristotle thought, with words like "exists" or "is": They too vary in meaning, depending on the sort of thing to which they are applied.

According to Aristotle, then, the fundamental task of metaphysics is to discover and more richly understand the most general kinds or categories of being. In carrying out this task, what we are most interested in are the different meanings of the term "being" that correspond to the different categories. We are not so interested in what it is *to be a horse*, or *to be the number three*. Rather, we are interested in what it is *to be*, in each of its different senses. In other words, we are interested in being *as such*, and not in *beings* themselves and their particular distinguishing attributes.

The trouble with this characterization is that most philosophers nowadays think that there is a lot more to metaphysics than the study of being as such. Questions about the compatibility of freedom and **determinism**, or about the nature of the causal relation, for example, don't seem to be questions about being as such, but they are generally regarded as belonging to the domain of metaphysics. Moreover, this way of thinking about metaphysics isn't a recent development. It is how the field has been conceived for hundreds of years.

ULTIMATE REALITY

According to a more common characterization, metaphysics is the study of *what there is*, or of *what there REALLY is*, or of *ultimate reality*. But these characterizations too are less than helpful. Why think that it is in metaphysics rather than in botany or zoology or theoretical physics that we learn about "ultimate reality" or about "what there really is"? Why are we doing metaphysics when we ask whether there are numbers or sets but not when we ask whether there are unicorns? Why do questions about the nature of causation have more to do with ultimate reality than do questions about the function of a human heart, or about the defining characteristics of electrons? What does it even mean to make a distinction between what exists and what *really* exists, or between reality and *ultimate* reality?

We can get some insight into the idea underlying this characterization when we look at the difference between the way in which metaphysicians ask certain kinds of questions and the way in which scientists, mathematicians, or people in the ordinary business of life ask those same questions. Is there a table in this room? As an everyday sort of question, the answer is settled by a quick look around. We take for granted the idea that, as a general rule, table-experiences are caused by tables. So, after looking around, if we find ourselves with table-experiences, we say, "Yes, there is a table in this room."

If we are doing metaphysics, however, part of what we are calling into question is the assumption that our table-experiences are caused (or are in some other way dependent upon) objects answering to the general description of a *table*. We don't normally believe that *football teams* are large objects made up of players. We normally think that our football-team experiences are caused not by a single object but by a bunch of objects acting in concert. Why not say the same thing about (so-called) tables? In other words, when you have a table-experience, why suppose that there is a single object—a table—causing that experience? Why not suppose instead that *there is no table* but just a bunch of atoms arranged table-wise?

We can now begin to see why people say that metaphysics is concerned with questions about what *really* exists, or about what is *ultimately* real. "Is there a table in this room?" is naturally construed as an ordinary question with a straightforward answer. But if we ask, "Is there *really* a table in this room?" or "Are tables part of *ultimate* reality?," we signal our interest in some of the further, metaphysical questions raised at the end of the previous paragraph. Depending on how we answer these questions, we might conclude that the "straightforward" answer is false, even if it is perfectly appropriate for the ordinary business of life. Or, depending on our views about language, we might conclude that it is true but somehow not in conflict with the answer we give at the end of our metaphysical inquiry—just as we take there to be no conflict between the "ordinary" claim that the sun is setting over the mountain and the more scientifically informed claim that the Earth's rotation is causing the mountain to obscure our vision of the sun. Either way, the main point to note is that the questions we are interested in when we ask whether there is *really* a table in the room are not answered by science or observation alone. Instead, the answers depend upon the truth or falsity of more general metaphysical claims about what it takes to make several objects become parts of a larger whole, or about what it is to be a material object, and so on.

Still, as a general characterization of metaphysics, the idea that metaphysics is the *study of what really exists* falls short because it is incomplete. The question whether free will is compatible with determinism, for example, is a paradigmatic example of a question in metaphysics. But it is not naturally construed as a question about what really exists, or even as a question about ultimate reality.

THE FUNDAMENTAL LEVEL

There is a trend now among metaphysicians of saying that metaphysics is (or should be thought of as) the study of what is **fundamental**, or *basic*. This way of thinking about metaphysics has also been attributed to Aristotle, and it has been gaining traction since the publication of Jonathan Schaffer's influential paper, "On What Grounds What." Schaffer's paper opens by declaring his intention to revive a conception of metaphysics that differs from the one that he believes currently dominates the field. On the dominant conception, he says, "metaphysics is about what there is. Metaphysics so conceived is concerned with such questions as whether properties exist, whether meanings exist, and whether numbers exist." On the conception he aims to revive, metaphysics "does not bother asking whether properties, meanings, and numbers exist. Of course they do! The question is whether or not they are *fundamental*."

Fundamental things, if there are any, are the things out of which all others are made, or the things without which nothing else could even exist. They are the "grounding" entities, the things on which everything else in the world depends. For example: Thales famously said that everything is water. The view seems crazy if we think that what he meant was that, contrary to all appearances, there's no real difference between a baseball and a raindrop. But the standard way of understanding Thales' famous claim is as a claim about what is fundamental: The underlying stuff in the world is water; everything is ultimately made out of water; water is the fundamental stuff of the universe. Similarly, many people nowadays endorse **physicalism**, which can be roughly characterized as the view that everything is ultimately made up of properties and objects posited by our best theories in physics. This, too, is naturally understood as a thesis about what is fundamental.

The view that metaphysics is concerned with what is fundamental is obviously related to the idea that metaphysics is concerned with what "really" or "ultimately" exists. "Ultimate" is sometimes used as a near synonym for "fundamental," so it is easy to see why the idea that metaphysics is concerned with ultimate reality might be understood as the idea that metaphysics aims to discover what is fundamental. Similarly, a metaphysician who says, for example, that table-experiences are caused not by tables but simply by atoms arranged table-wise might express her view by saying, "There aren't *really* any tables." But since the very same metaphysician will probably, in the ordinary business of life, do things like ask her children to come sit at the table for dinner, we might think that all she means by saying that there aren't really any tables is that tables are not fundamental, that they are instead reducible to atoms or particles.

As with previous characterizations, however, the problem with this one is incompleteness. Metaphysics *is not* just about what is fundamental. Historically, the following questions have been almost universally acknowledged as falling within the domain of metaphysics:

- Is change really possible? If so, what does it mean to say that something has changed?
- Can the past be changed? How about the future?
- Is the passage of time possible? What is time, anyway?
- What is an event? Can the same event happen more than once? What is involved in one event's *causing* another?
- What are human minds? Are they immaterial thinking substances, or are they material objects (brains, perhaps?), or something else entirely?
- Are there any nonphysical things? If so, could they causally interact with physical things?
- Are human beings free? Is freedom even possible?
- Is it possible to live after death?
- Do human beings or human faculties have anything like a proper function?

None of these is plausibly construed as a question about what is fundamental.

I suspect that claims like "Metaphysics is about what is fundamental" are not usually intended to be taken strictly at face value.

They are most charitably construed as hyperbolic claims intended to push metaphysicians into a particular way of thinking about their discipline. The goal isn't to get metaphysicians to see questions like those just mentioned as falling outside their discipline but rather to get them to see questions about fundamentality and grounding as importantly *central* to their discipline.

Even so, I must still register skepticism. Why think that questions about what is fundamental are in any way more "central" or "important" than questions about human free agency, or the possibility of change? So far as I am aware, there is no argument to be had for the conclusion that they are. So it is hard to see why we should think anything more than that questions about fundamentality are *among* the questions of metaphysics—which, of course, no one would ever have denied.

THE FINAL CHARACTERIZATION

We do best to approach the question of what metaphysics is by first looking at what questions metaphysicians typically ask and then asking what, if anything, those questions share in common. We have already seen quite a few sample questions; here are a few more:

- When you assert something, is there some *thing* that you're asserting? If so, what kind of thing is it?
- When you talk about ways things could have been (e.g., "There's more than one way this class could turn out"), to what sorts of things (if any) does the word "ways" refer?
- What is the relation between an object and its properties? Are the properties of a thing parts of it? If so, then do objects have any other kinds of things as parts—say, a bare substratum that *has* all of the properties? If not, then are we supposed to imagine that properties are somehow external to the things that have them and are related to those things simply by resemblance or some other sort of relation?
- A gold statue is constituted by a lump of gold. The lump of gold still exists after it is melted down and reshaped, but the statue doesn't. So what is the relationship between the lump and the statue? Are they two different things in the same place at the same time? If not, then how do "they" have different survival conditions?

- Are there contingent beings, or is the way things are somehow the way things have to be? Is there a necessary being (a God, perhaps) who created all contingent things?

There are many more such questions, but these are sufficient to provide a feel for the sorts of issues with which metaphysicians typically concern themselves.

What do these questions have in common? I used to say that what they have in common is that they are nonscientific questions about what exists, and about the necessary connections among certain kinds of concepts—namely, those falling outside the domains of ethics, epistemology, logic, and sociopolitical theory. Although I still think that this is reasonably accurate, putting it this way suggests that there is no methodological continuity whatsoever between metaphysics and science. It also suggests that metaphysics is a sort of hodge-podge discipline, encompassing all and only questions that haven't been taken over by another subdiscipline. As my colleague Meghan Sullivan put it to me in conversation, this is a "garbage bag" conception of metaphysics; and, more importantly, it does not really capture what it is that *unifies* the discipline of metaphysics. It would be nice if we could do better.

What I am now inclined to say is that questions in metaphysics have the following in common: To answer them, one must make non**empirical** claims (i.e., claims that are not based on observation or experience) about what there is or could be, or about the nature or defining essence of some concrete thing, or about the proper analysis of concepts of a certain kind. What kind? Just about any kind other than those used specifically for the evaluation of the actions, beliefs, or reasoning processes of agents and the institutions created by agents. So, most moral and aesthetic concepts, a variety of social, psychological, legal, and political concepts, the concept of knowledge (which, under some analyses, includes the concept of "justification"), and many others will all be excluded from the purview of metaphysics. But not all evaluative concepts will be excluded. Metaphysicians might, for example, turn their attention to the analysis of non-moral goodness, proper function, or the sublime without leaving the domain of metaphysics.

This characterization adequately captures the fact that (a) metaphysics is a nonempirical (**a priori**) mode of inquiry; (b) it is partly about *what there is*; (c) it is partly about describing the essences or natures of things; and (d) it is *not* in the business of analyzing concepts that figure centrally in ethics, sociopolitical philosophy, epistemology, and aesthetics. (Sometimes you will hear philosophers talk, for example, about the "metaphysics of morals." In using terms like that, what they have in mind are nonscientific questions about the *existence* of certain kinds of moral properties or about the *consequences* that certain claims in the domain of ethics might have for broader metaphysical concerns; they do not have in mind the proper *analysis* of moral concepts.)

On this way of thinking about the discipline, metaphysics is not defined solely by its method, nor is it defined solely by its subject matter. Although I have not explicitly identified questions about "being as such" or about "what grounds what" as among those that are investigated by metaphysics, neither does this conception locate them outside the discipline. In fact, they do fall within the domain of metaphysics under this conception; for answering those sorts of questions will involve exactly what I have said that answering metaphysical questions will involve: One will have to make nonempirical claims about the natures of things, about the proper analysis of nonevaluative concepts, and about what there is.

People sometimes distinguish metaphysics from **ontology**, which is typically seen as a subfield within metaphysics. Ontology is commonly characterized as the study of *what there is*. Or, more precisely: It is the branch of study that focuses on *existence* claims of the sort studied by metaphysics and on the logical consequences thereof. So, metaphysical claims that tell us what exists or that tell us about the natures of things will generally belong to the domain of ontology, whereas metaphysical claims that simply tell us what there *could* be, or that give an analysis of some concept, generally won't.

I mentioned earlier that many people start asking metaphysical questions in early childhood. It is entirely natural to wonder, even at a very young age, about the nature of time, of the soul, of our own free agency, and so on. What might seem a bit surprising upon reflection, however, is that the drive to answer these questions persists well into adulthood. Why in the world would anyone (but a child) think that human beings are capable of answering questions that pertain to matters not only outside the grasp of our own sensory apparatus but beyond the reach of science altogether? Why think that human beings have any hope at all of answering *nonempirical* questions about what exists or about the fundamental natures of things?

AGAINST METAPHYSICS

The fact that metaphysics concerns itself with *nonempirical* questions about the character and makeup of the world has made many philosophers uneasy with the whole enterprise. The sciences enjoy a great deal of respect as fields of inquiry, and many think that the methods of science and those methods alone are the tools by which we ought to build our theories about the world. *A priori* theorizing about the world—the sort of theorizing that requires no lab equipment or experimental apparatus but just a rocking chair, a working brain, and a good chunk of time free for thinking—has long been viewed with skepticism. According to many philosophers, metaphysical theorizing is just idle tale-spinning.

One of the most well-known expressions of this sort of negative attitude toward metaphysics comes from David Hume (1711–1776). In Section XII of his *Enquiry Concerning Human Understanding*, Hume writes:

> If we take in our hand any volume; of divinity or school metaphysics, for instance; let us ask, Does it contain any abstract reasoning concerning quantity or number? No. Does it contain any experimental reasoning concerning matter of fact and existence? No. Commit it then to the flames: for it can contain nothing but sophistry and illusion.

Hume's attitude is characteristic of those in the **empiricist** tradition, those who treat empirical theorizing of the sort found in the sciences as the only way of acquiring reliable information about the world. Likewise, contemporary empiricists have had little better to say about metaphysics. Rudolf Carnap (1891–1970), for example, complained in his article "The Elimination of Metaphysics through Logical Analysis of Language" that metaphysicians are like "musicians without musical ability," the point being that metaphysical theories are devoid of cognitive content and (unlike good music) not even endowed with aesthetic value.

What we have here are two different but closely related concerns. The Humean concern can be fleshed out as follows. We have good reason to believe that the methods of science are reliable sources of information about the world. Those methods have enabled us to make striking and tangible improvements in our ability to predict and control our environment and also in our ability to develop useful and sometimes downright amazing pieces of technology. Matters are different in metaphysics, where the staple mode of inquiry is nothing more than *a priori*, **intuition**-based theorizing. Notably, metaphysics as a discipline doesn't make discernible progress in the way that the sciences do. In metaphysics, we find widespread and persistent theoretical disagreement, very few problems that the community of metaphysicians take to have been decisively solved, and no clearly measurable track record of success whatsoever. *One* conclusion one might draw from the difference is this: Unlike the methods of science, the methods of metaphysics show no sign of being reliable ways of increasing our knowledge about the world; thus, there is some reason to suspect that metaphysical theories are nothing more than "sophistry and illusion."

Carnap also privileges empirical investigation over *a priori* theorizing. But, from his point of view, the problem isn't simply that the methods of metaphysics are unreliable. On his view, the "questions" discussed by metaphysicians don't even rise to the level of being meaningful. Underlying this view is the idea that a question is meaningful only if it can be answered somehow by appeal to observation, empirical theory, or the meanings of the words in the question. In other words, the meaningful questions are the ones that science can answer and the ones that can be answered by appeal to **analytic** truths—sentences like "bachelors are unmarried," which are commonly said to be purely conceptual truths, expressible by sentences that are "true by definition," or such that their truth is grounded solely in the meanings of the terms involved. If the questions can't be answered in one of these ways, then they are meaningless; and if they can be so answered, then the *correct* answers are just the answers given by observation, empirical theory, or the relevant definitions. So, for Carnap, to ask, as the metaphysician does, whether the entities referred to in our empirically supported theories *really* exist is silly. Either the question is meaningful and *already settled* by whatever empirical evidence we have for the theory, or else it is meaningless and so a pseudo-question.

Let us consider an example. In mathematics we have axioms, definitions, and theorems that imply apparent existence claims like "There are two prime numbers between the numbers four and eight." Definitions explicitly provide the meanings of some of our mathematical terms; axioms implicitly supply meanings for other terms; theorems express the logical consequences of the axioms and definitions. Now, suppose someone asks, "Are there *really* two *things*—prime numbers—between two other things called 'the number four' and 'the number eight'?" As Carnap sees it, this question can be taken in one of two ways. It can be taken as a question *internal* to the mathematical enterprise, which is to say that it can be taken as nothing more than an ordinary mathematical question. Taken that way, the question is perhaps a bit puzzling, but the answer is obvious: "Yes, of course there are two prime numbers between four and eight!" The answer follows straightforwardly from the axioms, definitions, and theorems of our mathematical theory. It is, in other words, an analytic truth. Thus, the question is meaningful, and so likewise with other internal mathematical questions.

Alternatively, our question can be taken as an *external* question, asking *about the whole mathematical enterprise* whether apparent existence claims like "There are two prime numbers . . ." *really* commit us to believing in things like numbers. That question, Carnap says, is meaningless. We can give it meaning by taking it as an indirect way of asking whether it is a good idea to continue with our current systems of mathematical axioms, definitions, and theorems. This latter question is meaningful because it can be settled by re-examining the place of mathematical discourse in our overall body of scientific theory. We might ask, for example, whether our scientific theories might be more useful to us, or more successful at making verifiable predictions, if we were somehow to stop using current mathematical theories. These are empirical questions, and so they are meaningful. But to take the question of whether there really are numbers any other way, he thinks, makes no sense. For, in general, a question is intelligible only under the supposition that it is to be answered by way of empirical investigation; and this is precisely the supposition we rule out when we take ourselves to be asking an "external question."

Carnap's concern is motivated by strong assumptions about the conditions under which a question is meaningful. It also seems to assume that we can sensibly distinguish between analytic and nonanalytic truths. These assumptions are controversial. But "neo-Carnapian" critics of metaphysics have raised a very similar objection against metaphysics that does not depend on Carnap's assumptions. The objection starts with the observation that, regardless of *how* we know that there are two prime numbers between four and eight, the fact is that we *do* know it. It is an indisputable mathematical fact that there are two prime numbers between four and eight; and the following argument form is obviously valid:

1 There are two Fs between x and y.
2 Therefore: There are (at least) two Fs.
3 Therefore: Fs exist.

Thus, we can simply deduce from obvious, indisputable facts the conclusion that there are numbers. And the same might be said about questions like "Are there really tables?" or any of the other existence questions that metaphysicians like to ask.

Why, then, do philosophers continue to argue over questions like "Are there prime numbers," given that they have such easy answers? A common diagnosis is that parties to metaphysical disputes are simply using words differently both from ordinary speakers and from one another. So, for example, when Philosopher A says, "There are no prime numbers," and Philosopher B disputes her claim, both of them are using at least one of the terms in the disputed claim— probably either "there are" or "numbers"—differently from one another and from ordinary speakers for whom the truth of the claim is obvious. Notice that even where there are metaphysical disputes about the existence of things like tables or numbers, there is no sub-stantive dispute about the "underlying facts" that lead us to say things like "There are two prime numbers between four and eight" or "There are tables." Most philosophers who would deny that there are prime numbers *wouldn't* deny claims like "Five is prime," "Seven is prime," or "Five and seven are between four and eight." Likewise, philosophers who deny that there are tables will not hesitate to say there is matter arranged table-wise. Thus, many philosophers think that all of this evidence together suggests that the questions of metaphysics, even if not strictly meaningless, are at least not substantive.

The upshot of this third objection, then, is that metaphysicians in dispute with one another are like two people arguing over the question whether the crust left over from a piece of pizza itself counts as pizza. One says that something is pizza only if it has sauce, crust, and cheese; the other says that since the crust was part of the original pizza, one is still eating *pizza* even when one is down to eating nothing but the crust. There is obviously no real or interesting dispute here; it is just a silly difference about how to use the word "pizza." Settling the debate isn't a matter of looking into the fundamental nature of pizzahood, or of anything else. It is, rather, just a matter of taking a closer look at our language, or stipulating a particular way in which the term "pizza" is to be used henceforth. So, likewise, say the objectors, with metaphysical disputes about the existence of tables, numbers, and the like.

IN DEFENSE OF METAPHYSICS

We now have three related objections against metaphysics on the table. Firstly, the methods of metaphysics are not reliable means of discovering truths about the world; secondly, the questions of metaphysics are meaningless; and, thirdly, even if the questions of metaphysics aren't strictly meaningless, they are at least non-substantive, giving rise to mere verbal disputes. In light of these sorts of objections, it is easy to see why many people think that academic discussion of metaphysical topics is neither serious nor important.

Before considering answers to these objections, we should first observe one difference between the first objection and the second two. If the first objection is sound, then the *whole field* of metaphysics is indicted. Matters are less clear with the second two. We could perhaps acknowledge that certain disputes in ontology are mere verbal disputes without obviously calling the whole field of metaphysics into question. For the fact is metaphysicians examine and critically evaluate some of the most existentially important beliefs that human beings ever hold, beliefs that lie at the very heart of our conception of ourselves and our commonsense ways of thinking about the world. It matters very much to us whether we are free in a way that would allow us to be genuinely responsible for our actions, whether we might possibly survive death, whether there might be things—perhaps even intelligent and powerful things—beyond what we find in the material world, and so on. It would take substantial argument to show that these questions are meaningless, or that our disputes on such topics are mere verbal disputes.

But now what should we think of our three objections? Let us begin with the Humean objection. There are at least two ways of responding. First: The starting point for the objection is the fact that metaphysicians rely on **rational intuitions** (intellectual experiences of the sheer obviousness or necessary truth of various claims) in building their theories. But it is notoriously hard to produce an *argument* against the reliability of intuition as a source of evidence without *relying* on intuitions. Is persistent disagreement and ongoing failure to reach decisive solutions to the discipline's central puzzles and problems really evidence of general lack of progress? Is lack of *the sort of progress that one finds in the sciences* really evidence that the methods of a discipline are unreliable? These are philosophical questions, answerable only by way of the very methods on which metaphysicians rely, methods that include appeals to intuition as a source of evidence. Our answers to these questions will depend significantly on our intuitions about the nature of *progress* and about the conditions under which we ought to believe that a method of inquiry is unreliable. So, if one answers both questions affirmatively (which one must do in order to defend the main premises of the Humean objection), one successfully indicts rational intuition, but one also thereby indicts the very methods by which one reached the affirmative answers. Clearly that won't do. If, on the other hand, one answers the questions negatively, then the Humean objection cannot get off the ground.

In light of the reply just given, many contemporary metaphysicians have felt content simply to ignore objections arising out of the empiricist camp, at least until those objections can be made precise enough to be persuasive. It might be tempting to think that this reaction comes to nothing more than sticking one's head in the sand. Even if we grant that there is something self-defeating about a *philosophical* objection to the methods used in one of the core subfields of philosophy, can't we at least acknowledge that it's not *obvious* that the methods of metaphysics are reliable? And, if so, shouldn't metaphysicians be working hard to show that their methods are reliable? And isn't their failure to do so itself rather telling?

In a word, no. Indeed, the "head in the sand" response is exactly the reaction that many empiricists themselves have toward more general skeptical complaints, complaints that challenge the evidential value of sense perception, for example. When skeptics demand evidence for the reliability of our senses, empiricists generally take themselves to be justified in ignoring the demand. You can call it sticking your head in the sand, but to do so presupposes what most philosophers would not grant—namely, that the skeptic has issued a legitimate challenge that demands a response.

Contrary to this presupposition, most philosophers now think that we are entitled simply to trust our senses and that the demand for evidence that demonstrates them to be reliable cannot be met. If that is right, then shouldn't we be entitled simply to trust our rational intuitions as well? Many have thought so.

In this vein, consider what Thomas Reid (1710–1796) says in his *An Inquiry into the Human Mind*:

> The sceptic asks me, Why do you believe the existence of the external object which you perceive? This belief, sir, is none of my manufacture; it came from the mint of Nature; it bears her image and super-scription; and, if it is not right, the fault is not mine: I even took it upon trust, and without suspicion. Reason, says the sceptic, is the only judge of truth, and you ought to throw off every opinion and every belief that is not grounded on reason. Why, sir, should I believe the faculty of reason more than that of perception?—they came both out of the same shop, and were made by the same artist; and if he puts one piece of false ware into my hands, what should hinder him from putting another?

The point here is that reason (which includes rational intuition) and sense perception ought to be treated as on a par—at least initially, unless and until we get evidence that one or the other is untrustworthy. Why? Because whatever processes gave rise to the one almost certainly also gave rise to the other. Reid, of course, is defending the trustworthiness of sense perception, but exactly the same sort of speech might equally be made in defense of intuition. To be sure, those offering Reidian speeches on behalf of intuition-based theorizing must grant that there is more disagreement and less "progress" in metaphysics than in science. But many of us think that even once this difference is accounted for, the alleged reasons for abandoning metaphysics are far from compelling.

A second reaction to the Humean objection has been to take on the empiricist preference for empirically based theorizing, along with empiricist skepticism of appeals to rational intuition, and to try to do metaphysics in a way that is roughly continuous with science and that goes beyond science as little as possible. Those who identify with the tradition of philosophical naturalism manifest a deep skepticism about appeals to rational intuition. So they confine themselves to a sort of metaphysics that aims simply to fill explanatory gaps in our scientific theories and to draw out some of the interesting logical consequences of those theories. This reaction concedes a lot of territory to the objectors. But, if sound, it still leaves an important place in the overall project of human inquiry for the practice of metaphysics.

Initially, this way of thinking about metaphysics might seem puzzling. It looks like the philosophical naturalist agrees with Carnap in thinking that metaphysicians shouldn't be looking to answer questions that can't be answered by science. After all, we just said that the naturalist wants to go beyond science "as little as possible"; and, though it is surely a fine thing for metaphysicians to spend their time filling gaps in scientific theories and drawing out interesting logical consequences, it is not as if working scientists couldn't do those things for themselves. So, what *distinctive work* is left for the metaphysician to do? And why isn't the naturalist just a Carnapian in disguise?

Remember that Carnap's objection to metaphysics rested in part on a sharp distinction between analytic and nonanalytic truths and also on a particular view about the conditions under which a question or statement might be meaningful. But the distinction between analytic and nonanalytic truths is now widely regarded as suspect; and once that distinction is blown, Carnap's views about the conditions under which a question or statement is meaningful are also in trouble. After all, claims of mathematics and logic (to take just two examples) are meaningful but not directly empirically verifiable. For Carnap, this wasn't a problem because these claims could plausibly be regarded either as analytic truths or as truths derivable from some combination of analytic and empirically verifiable truths. Without the analytic/nonanalytic distinction, *this* reason for thinking that the claims are meaningful disappears. But it is hard to see any other way of guaranteeing their meaningfulness that wouldn't also open the door to saying that lots of other empirically unverifiable claims—including claims of metaphysics— are meaningful as well. These criticisms of Carnap were pressed most famously and strongly by W. V. Quine (1908–2000). Quine shared Carnap's commitment to science and to certain other principles of traditional **empiricism**. But he nevertheless thought that questions in ontology were meaningful and that philosophers could give them meaningful answers. This is one crucial difference between the naturalist and the Carnapian.

The difference between the Quinean and Carnapian perspectives on metaphysics depends partly on differences in their conception of how empirical evidence supports the various things that we believe. Like a lot of us, Carnap took it for granted that there is a reasonably sharp boundary, with no substantial middle ground, between claims that are empirically testable and claims that aren't. As he saw it, the empirically testable ones were the meaningful and scientifically respectable claims; the rest were either analytic truths or meaningless. Quine, however, thought that empirical evidence can provide support for a claim by supporting an *overall body of theory* that includes the claim in question as an integral part. So, for example, principles of mathematics and logic can be seen as *empirically* supported, even though they obviously aren't directly testable. This is because they are important parts of an overall web of belief which includes our best scientific theories and which enjoys, as a whole, a large measure of support from direct observation, experimental tests, and other empirical methods. For Quine, the idea that we can go through our total set of beliefs and sort them neatly into boxes marked EMPIRICALLY VERIFIABLE, ANALYTIC, and MEANINGLESS is wholly misguided. What we have instead is a web of beliefs which is continually revised in light of our experiences and which is more or less confirmed *as a whole* by the way in which the beliefs together cohere with one another and with our total experience.

Quine, unlike Carnap, is prepared to acknowledge that there are many scientifically respectable claims that are not empirically testable. Such claims, he says, fill in some of the gaps left by our scientific theories and sometimes lead to further hypotheses that can be tested. At any rate, the acceptable ones do this; and many of the claims made by metaphysicians can be seen as fitting this description. Moreover, since there is no sharp line between claims that are testable and claims that merely fill gaps in our theories, the boundary between science and metaphysics is likewise unclear. But that does not matter; for Quine has no interest in drawing sharp lines between philosophy and science. Quite the contrary: As a naturalist, he sees the disciplines as continuous with one another.

Thus far I have been explaining *why* Quine thinks that philosophers can answer questions in ontology. But that still leaves us with the question of *how* such questions are to be answered—especially since Quine himself is no fan of intuition-based theorizing. The answer is that we look to our best scientific theories and ask ourselves, "Which of the entities apparently referred to by these theories *have* to exist in order for the theory to be true?" So, for example, suppose our theory says the following:

T   The average family has a mother, a father, and 2.2 children.

The ontologist might ask, "Do there *have* to be such things as average families, and mothers, and fathers, and children in order for this theory to be true?" A fairly natural answer is to say that there *do* have to be mothers, fathers, and children, but there *doesn't* have to be any such thing as the average family. Why? Because it is fairly easy to *paraphrase* the sentence in a way that gets rid of apparent reference to average families, whereas it would be much harder to paraphrase away all apparent references to mothers, fathers, and children.

We can put all of this a bit more precisely as follows: Philosophers generally assume that claims like "Tables exist" or "There are tables" are logically equivalent to "Something is a table." Now, most commonsense and scientific theories (no matter how we express them) will include or logically imply a variety of claims that have this form:

E1   Something is an F,

where "F" stands in for some kind-term like "table" or "number." Quine thinks that if a theory implies a sentence with the same form as E, then that theory is *committed* to whatever must exist in order for that sentence to be true. So, for example, if T really implies that *something is an average family*, then our theory T is committed to the existence of average families. The question for the ontologist, then, is whether T really does imply that something is an average family. Most of us would say that it does not. According to Quine, the way to be sure that it does not is to try to express T in a different way, to paraphrase it. If we find that T can be stated without using terms that refer to average families, then we are entitled to say that T does not imply that something is an average family. If we fail in our efforts to find a suitable paraphrase, then we must admit that T is committed to average families after all.

It is easy to see how this way of thinking about ontology will enable us to ask and explore a wide variety of interesting questions. Our best mathematical theories tell us that there are two prime numbers between four and eight. So one apparent implication of those theories is E1:

E1 Something is a number.

Our best biological theories seem to tell us that spiders and insects share several features in common. So one apparent implication of those theories is E2:

E2 Something is a feature.

Are E1 and E2 *genuine* implications? For Quine, that all depends on whether there are acceptable paraphrases of the prime number sentence, or of the spider-insect sentence, that don't make reference to numbers or features. Are there such paraphrases? That is a hard question. Moreover, it is not at all clear that we would have to rely on anything as suspect as rational intuition in order to answer it. In any case, according to Quine, answering that question is precisely what it takes to find out whether our best confirmed theories are committed to things like numbers and features; and isn't it obvious that we should believe in the things to which our best theories are committed?

Before moving away from the Humean objection which has been our focus thus far, we should close this discussion of Quine by noting that, although Quine is a naturalist, Quine's approach to ontology has been embraced wholeheartedly by nonnaturalists as well. The basic idea underlying Quine's approach to ontology is entirely commonsensical: If you have a theory (supported by science, intuition, commonsense) that seems to imply that something is an F, you seem to face only three choices when pressed on the question as to whether you really believe in Fs:

1. Retract the claim that seems to imply that there are Fs.
2. Say that the implication is only apparent and supply a paraphrase that doesn't refer to Fs.
3. Accept the consequence of your theory and admit that you believe in Fs.

We have now finished dealing with the Humean objection. Moreover, we have already seen along the way how the second, Carnapian, objection might be dealt with. Thus, we shall now move on to the third objection: the neo-Carnapian concern that metaphysical debates are, at best, nothing more than mere verbal disputes.

As with the Humean objection, there are at least two ways of responding to the neo-Carnapian objection. One way is to try to stake out a middle ground between Carnap and Quine. One might take on board the idea that metaphysical questions are, in large part, questions about the meanings of our words but nevertheless maintain that at least some such questions are subject to genuine and substantive philosophical dispute. This middle position is defended by Amie Thomasson. Thomasson's views are generally characterized as neo-Carnapian because of obvious affinities that they bear with those of other neo-Carnapians. Despite this, I still think that it is fair to characterize her as offering a response to more extreme neo-Carnapians who think that all or virtually all metaphysical disputes are mere verbal disputes.

In the concluding chapter of her book, *Ordinary Objects*, Thomasson observes that contemporary philosophers tend to think of metaphysics as analogous to science. Theories are evaluated on the basis of criteria like simplicity and explanatory power; and there is every expectation that inquiry will ultimately lead to theories that force us to *revise* many of our previously held "pre-theoretical" beliefs. After all, there is no reason to think that our overall body of commonsense beliefs will be respected by the simplest and most explanatory theory. But, she argues, one of the lessons of her book is that this way of thinking about metaphysics is incorrect: Distinctively metaphysical questions are to be answered through a kind of conceptual analysis—an activity pursued via reflection on the meanings of our words—rather than through methods of the sort we find in science.

So, for example, suppose we are raising metaphysical questions about whether there are numbers, or tables. On Thomasson's view, the way to address these questions is to analyze our concepts of *number* and *table* and to determine the conditions under which those concepts would apply to something. Doing this is difficult, and the results may well be controversial. Thus, on her view, there is no reason to think that debates about the application conditions for our concepts of *number* and *table* will be meaningless, trivial, or merely verbal. But, she says, once a view has been reached about the application conditions for these concepts, the answers to questions like "Are there numbers?" or "Are there tables?" are straightforward: We simply look to see whether the application conditions are fulfilled.

Nevertheless, Thomasson does think that many of the "typical" debates in metaphysics *are* mere verbal disputes. The reason is that philosophers are not typically asking about the application conditions of particular terms like "number" or "table"; they are, rather, asking more general questions about what kinds of *things* or *objects* there are, and, on Thomasson's view, the terms "thing" and "object" are subject to a variety of different uses. The result, then, is that philosophers using the words "thing" and "object" in subtly different ways reach different conclusions about what kinds of things or objects there are. But, of course, in using their central terms in different ways, they end up talking past one another.

A second way of responding to the neo-Carnapian is to point out that the argument for thinking that metaphysical disputes either have easy answers or are mere verbal disputes itself depends on substantive metaphysical premises.

So, for example, suppose I reason thus:

1.1 There are two prime numbers between four and eight.
1.2 In general, if there are two Fs between some x and some y, then there are Fs.

1.3 Therefore: There are (at least) two numbers.

1.4 Therefore: Numbers exist.

The neo-Carnapian declares that this argument is straightforwardly valid and that the premises are clearly true; thus, the question "Are there numbers?" has an easy answer: "Yes, of *course* there are!" But not so fast. Just as the metaphysician asks, "Are there really numbers?," so too she might ask, "Are there really two prime numbers between four and eight?" Here the neo-Carnapian may roll her eyes and say, "Come on! Do you really mean to question our most basic and well-entrenched mathematical theories?" There is no reason why the metaphysician should be cowed by this response. After all, it is a substantive question whether the truth conditions for "There are two prime numbers between four and eight" require the existence of numbers.

A substantive question maybe, but must we think it is a substantive *metaphysical* question? Might it not be a substantive *linguistic* or *mathematical* question instead, one to be answered by examining the behavior of expressions like "There are" in English or in specifically mathematical contexts? Here I think that the answer is unequivocally and obviously "No." The reason is quite simple. Suppose linguistic or mathematical theory supplies you with an answer to a question of the form, "Are there Fs?" Now consider the question whether the answer thus supplied is *really* correct— whether, in other words, there *really are* Fs. This is clearly a different question from the first one. Carnap, as we know, would have dismissed it as meaningless. But what sets the neo-Carnapians apart from Carnap himself is the refusal to join Carnap in this dismissal. But the question cannot be construed as just another linguistic or mathematical question either, for otherwise it would not be a different question. So it is a substantive question in metaphysics.

CONCLUSION

In this chapter, I have considered a variety of different characterizations of metaphysics and defended one that I think captures what is generally going on in the field. Again: Metaphysics is the attempt to answer questions that can only be fully answered by making nonempirical claims about what there is or could be, or about the nature or defining essence of some concrete thing, or about the proper analysis of concepts other than those used specifically for the evaluation of agents and their institutions. I have also explored and responded to three different objections against metaphysics: the Humean complaint that metaphysicians rely illegitimately on rational intuitions, the Carnapian complaint that metaphysical questions are meaningless, and the neo-Carnapian complaint that metaphysical disputes either have easy or trivial answers or are nothing more than mere verbal disputes. Not everyone will be convinced by the responses I have given; nor, indeed, can *all* of the responses be endorsed at once, since different responses embody different visions about how exactly metaphysics is to be done. In what follows, I shall presuppose that at least one of the responses has been successful, that the typical debates in metaphysics are substantive, and that rational intuition is a perfectly legitimate source of evidence for premises in arguments for metaphysical conclusions. Beyond these presuppositions, I suspect that whatever else I shall say will be neutral between the various different visions of metaphysics and its methods that are represented here.

FURTHER READING

The opening books of Aristotle's *Categories* and *Metaphysics* provide his own characterization of metaphysics. A good single source for discussion and display of the other conceptions of metaphysics discussed in this chapter is David Chalmers, David Manley, and Ryan Wasserman, eds., *Metametaphysics: New Essays in the Foundations of Ontology* (Oxford: Oxford University Press, 2009), hereafter cited simply as *Metametaphysics*.

I mentioned several philosophers who take metaphysics to be the study of what is fundamental. A good starting place for this view is Jonathan Schaffer, "On What Grounds What," in *Metametaphysics*. Interested readers will also want to see L. A. Paul, "Building the World From Its Fundamental Constituents," *Philosophical Studies*, vol. 158 (2012): 221–256 and Theodore Sider, *Writing the Book of the World* (New York: Clarendon Press, 2011). As we saw, Schaffer denies that metaphysics is most centrally about "what there is"; but, as we also saw, some think that questions about what there is are best construed as questions about what is fundamental. On this, see Ross

P. Cameron, "Truthmakers and Ontological Commitment: Or How to Deal with Complex Objects and Mathematical Ontology Without Getting Into Trouble," *Philosophical Studies*, vol. 140 (2008): 1–18; and "How to Have a Radically Minimal Ontology," *Philosophical Studies*, vol. 151 (2010): 249–264.

The edition of Hume's *Enquiry* which I cited in the course of discussing objections against metaphysics is: *An Enquiry Concerning Human Understanding; [with] A Letter from a Gentleman to His Friend in Edinburgh; [and] An Abstract of a Treatise of Human Nature*, 2nd edn. (Indianapolis, IN: Hackett Publishing Company, 1993). A recent book that objects to traditional metaphysics in the same spirit as Hume did is James Ladyman and Don Ross, *Every Thing Must Go: Metaphysics Naturalized* (Oxford: Oxford University Press, 2009).

In discussing Carnap's objection against metaphysics, I cited his "The Elimination of Metaphysics Through Logical Analysis of Language," in A. J. Ayer (ed.), *Logical Postivism* (New York: Simon & Schuster), pp. 60–81; but the more important source for the views I attributed to him is his "Empiricism, Semantics, and Ontology" in *Meaning and Necessity: A Study in Semantics and Modal Logic* (Chicago, IL: University of Chicago Press, 1956), pp. 205–221. For discussion of Carnap's views and more detailed and sophisticated treatment of the Quinean response to Carnap, see Huw Price, "Metaphysics after Carnap: The Ghost who Walks?" in *Metametaphysics*, pp. 320–346, and Stephen Yablo "Does Ontology Reston a Mistake?" *Aristotelian Society Supplementary Volume* (1998), pp. 229–261. The paper by Yablo also provides a neo-Carnapian perspective on metaphysics. For other neo-Carnapian perspectives, see the contributions by Eli Hirsch, Thomas Hofweber, and Amie Thomasson to the *Metametaphysics* volume, as well as Amie Thomasson's book, *Ordinary Objects* (Oxford: Oxford University Press, 2007).

For Quine's conception of metaphysics, I think that the best place to start is W. V. Quine, "Naturalism; Or, Living Within One's Means," *Dialectica* vol. 49, (1995): 251–263. But readers will also want to look at his "On What There Is," reprinted in Michael Rea, *Arguing About Metaphysics* (London and New York: Routledge, 2009), and Peter van Inwagen, "Being, Existence, and Ontological Commitment," in *Metametaphysics*. Quine's article demonstrates his approach to answering metaphysical questions, and van Inwagen's article explains that approach.

I cited a passage from Reid's *Inquiry into the Human Mind* in defense of the evidential value of intuition. That can be found in Thomas Reid, *Inquiry and Essays*, edited by R. E. Beanblossom and K. Lehrer (Indianapolis, IN: Hackett Publishing Company, 1983), pp. 168–169. For contemporary defenses of the evidential value of intuition, see George Bealer, "The Incoherence of Empiricism," *Aristotelian Society Supplementary Volume* (1992), pp. 99–138, and Joel Pust, "Against Explanationist Skepticism Regarding Philosophical Intuitions," *Philosophical Studies* vol. 106 (2001), pp. 227–258.

2

ON WHAT THERE IS

The ontological question, according to Quine, asks "What is there?" Biologists, chemists, physicists, zoologists, and many others supply us with some provisional answers: There are trees, molecules, bosons, horses, and so on. Reasoning about our commonsense beliefs can supply us with further answers. Ontologists look more deeply into such provisional answers and ask which of them are true and which only appear to be true.

One might wonder why we should *want* to do **ontology**. It is annoying to respond to a question like "Where are my keys?" by saying, "Well, how do you even know you have keys? Do keys *really* exist?" Commonsense belief in the reality of keys is *useful*. It helps get us around in the world. It is "empirically adequate"; it is not the sort of belief that will be seriously called into question by observation or experiment. But if empirically adequate beliefs about what exists are all that we need to get around in the world, why should we try to look any deeper?

The answer is that sometimes ontological questions do bear on matters of great concern. Though it is hard to see how questions about the reality of keys make a difference to anything we care about, it is not at all hard to see the importance of questions like "Is there a God?" or "Do I have a soul that can survive the death of my body?" or "Am I free?" or "Do my commonsense intuitions about what exists in the world and about what the world is like lead me badly astray?" Our answers to these questions will be intimately connected with various ontological questions. Sometimes ontological questions *are* the questions we care about. Sometimes they bear only indirectly on the questions we care about. Either way, they are still important.

Suppose you think that there are immaterial souls and that they are invisible and not physically located in spacetime. Someone might tell you that it is unreasonable to believe in things like that. Can you sensibly reply that it is reasonable to believe in numbers and say that numbers are like that? That depends on whether it is reasonable to believe that there *really are* numbers. Similarly, as we shall see in a later chapter, it is remarkably easy to show that commonsense beliefs about material objects lead us into contradictions. Learning this, one might just shrug it off and concede that our commonsense conceptual framework is an incoherent mess. Many of us, however, would prefer to see whether we can avoid such contradictions by thinking harder and more carefully about what really exists. It is disturbing to think that our commonsense intuitions are wildly unreliable. So many philosophers have been interested in examining those intuitions to see just how much commonsense ontology can be saved. Sometimes the result of this process is that we reach conclusions like "There are no nonliving composite objects," which then have implications for questions about whether our keys or our dining-room furniture really exist. So, even if those latter questions are not, all by themselves, of philosophical interest, they come to be of interest because of their connection to other questions which are of deeper and more lasting philosophical import.

As a general rule, people seem to avoid believing in things that seem weird, especially things that cannot in principle be detected by sensory experience or instruments, and things belief in which leads to paradox. I suspect that this general preference goes some distance toward explaining why, in contemporary ontology, questions about the existence of abstract objects, nonexistent objects, creatures of fiction, God, souls, and composite material objects of various kinds have tended to dominate the literature. Abstract objects are things like the number two, the set of all horses, beauty, and so on. They are the sorts of things that cannot even in principle be detected by sensory experience or instruments. (We see beautiful things, not beauty itself; we see horses, but not sets thereof, and so on.) If they exist at all, they are immaterial, (probably) have no location in spacetime, and lack causal powers. They are weird. Many philosophers do not wish to believe in them. Belief in God and souls has seemed problematic for similar reasons, though God and souls are usually classed as concrete objects by virtue of their alleged causal powers. Creatures of fiction and nonexistent objects are not only weird but paradoxical. For example, we seem often to talk about such things. Peter Parker (a.k.a. Spiderman) works at the *Daily Bugle* and engineered his own web-shooters. But neither Parker nor the *Daily Bugle* nor Spiderman's web-shooters exist. How could *both* of the previous two sentences be true? Ponce de León spent a good deal of his life searching for the Fountain of Youth, which seems to imply that he spent a good deal of time searching for a *thing* that *does not exist*. But it sounds contradictory to say that there is a thing that does not exist. Composite material objects also present us with paradoxes—enough, in fact, that some philosophers have decided that the best overall response is simply to deny the existence of composite objects altogether.

In the present chapter, we shall focus primarily on questions about the existence of (certain kinds of) abstract and nonexistent objects.

PRELIMINARIES

As we have already seen, it is helpful to think of ontology as examining what we say loosely speaking and in the ordinary business of life, and as trying to figure out which of those claims are true *strictly speaking*, for purposes of philosophical theory. Much of what the ontologist tries to do is to distinguish the genuine logical consequences of things that we believe from merely apparent logical consequences. (For example, if we say that there is more than one way to skin a cat, do we *really* mean to say that there are these things, *ways to skin a cat*, such that the number of those things is greater than one? Is that a true logical consequence of what we are saying when we utter that cliché?) In carrying out this enterprise, a big part of what we are trying to do is to figure out which of the words we use correspond to things in the world and which do not.

Consequently, some of the technical vocabulary in the sections that follow has been developed with the goal of clearly distinguishing *linguistic items*—bits of language—from *things in the world* that correspond to those bits of language. Here I want to comment just briefly on some of the more important items in this vocabulary.

Let us begin with the distinction between terms and referents. A term is a word or phrase that refers to something; a referent is a thing to which the term refers. "Socrates" is a term; Socrates (the man) is the referent of that term. "The author of *Metaphysics: The Basics*" is a term; I am the referent of that term. "Spiderman" is a term. It is an interesting philosophical question whether that term has any referent.

We should also distinguish types from tokens. I have two quarters in my desk drawer. Each is a token of a common type. I said that "Spiderman" is a term, but notice that the actual marks on the page are just a token of a common type. (One token of that term occurs in the previous paragraph and another token occurs in the present one. If you read the term out loud, you will produce another token of that term.) It is important to keep in mind that words for linguistic items—words like "term," "word," "sentence," and so on—can refer *either* to tokens or to types. The types, presumably, are abstract objects that have instances; the instances are just the tokens.

Some terms are predicates, like "is wise." So, predicates, like terms, are linguistic items. Predicates have extensions, where the extension of a predicate is the class of things that satisfy the predicate. Some predicates (like "is a true contradiction") cannot be satisfied; these have the null class (i.e., the class that has no members) as their extension. A class is a collection of objects, and no two classes have exactly the same objects as members. A set is a class that conforms to further axioms that do not necessarily govern classes. For the most part, the differences between classes and sets do not matter here. But since *class* is the broader category, and because the differences between classes and sets do start to matter as one digs deeper into the details of some of the theories we shall be discussing, I will mostly use the term "class" rather than "set" throughout this chapter.

Predicates are commonly regarded as having properties and relations as their referents. So, for example, "is wise" is commonly regarded as referring to *wisdom* and "is paired with" is commonly regarded as referring to the relation of pairing. Properties and relations are sometimes treated as the same kind of thing, where a relation is a property that requires more than one thing in order for it to be exemplified. Wisdom, for example, can be exemplified by just one thing; the pairing relation applies only to pairs of things. The things related by a relation are called the **relata** of the relation.

Sentences are linguistic items too. We don't normally say that they have referents, but many philosophers do believe that typical declarative sentences (and maybe others as well) express things in the way that predicates or names do. The things that they express are called propositions. Confusingly, some philosophers in the past have used the word "proposition" to mean something like "sentence type." We shall not be using the term in this way. Also confusingly, some philosophers identify propositions with *meanings*, whereas others do not. These are controversies that we will mostly ignore.

PROPOSITIONS

One cannot get very far in contemporary metaphysics without encountering talk about propositions, states of affairs, and properties. For many philosophers, these sorts of things are among the most basic building blocks of reality. So having some understanding of them, and of the motivations for believing in them, is crucial for understanding a wide variety of other metaphysical theories. In this section, we focus on propositions.

Friedrich Nietzsche famously said that God is dead. He said it, but he didn't use those words. Nietzsche wrote in German. So his actual words were "Gott ist todt." Nevertheless, we legitimately attribute to him the saying that God is dead because "Gott ist todt" and "God is dead" are just different sentences that say the same thing. Moreover, not only can we say in different languages that God is dead, but speakers of different languages—even those wholly unacquainted with the German language—can believe or disbelieve it, fear or hope for it, regard it as profound or stupid, and so on. Not so, however, with the sentences that express Nietzsche's claim. The sentence "Gott ist todt" cannot itself be said in English. Nor can it be believed or disbelieved, loved or hated, and so on, by someone who has no acquaintance with the German language. What this means, then, is that the German sentence, "Gott ist todt," is one thing, and *what the sentence expresses* is something completely different.

We have now identified a role: being something that is expressed by sentences in different languages, that can be asserted or denied, believed or disbelieved, feared or hoped for, desired or dreaded, and so on. The entities that supposedly fill this role are what philosophers call *propositions*. Propositions have also traditionally been thought of as the fundamental bearers of truth and falsity. What this means is that they are the sorts of things that can be true or false, and everything else that can be true or false derives its truth or falsity from the proposition it expresses. So this is another role that propositions are supposed to play. Combining the two roles, we might say that propositions are supposed to be the referents of "that-clauses." (A *that-clause* is any noun phrase beginning with "that.") One can assert *that God is dead*, hope *that God is dead*, say in German *that God is dead*; and it can be true or false *that God is dead*. In each case, "that God is dead" names the proposition that God is dead—or so say the believers in propositions. Asking whether there are propositions, then, amounts to asking whether anything occupies the roles we have just identified. Asking what propositions are amounts to asking about the nature of whatever it is that occupies those roles.

One might wonder what it means to say that a proposition is an object of attitudes like fear, hope, and so on. After all, nobody is afraid of a proposition; likewise, nobody hopes for one. Here it is helpful to distinguish between two senses of "object of fear." If you are afraid of a rattlesnake in your garden, the snake is an object of your fear in one sense: You fear *it*, or something that it will do to you. This is not the sense in which propositions are objects of fear. Propositions are objects of fear in the sense that they are the *contents* of our fears. If you fear *that the snake will bite you*, the proposition that the snake will bite you is the content of your fear; it is just what you would express if you were to describe in detail exactly what it is that you fear. So, likewise, they are the contents of our hopes, beliefs, and other such attitudes.

The idea that propositions are objects of attitudes like belief, desire, and so on, makes good sense out of a variety of things that we are inclined to say. For example, suppose Alice has been studying late all week with Brian, whom Alice's roommate (Christy) wants to date. Alice hopes, and Christy fears, that Brian would like to date Alice. As it happens, Brian's friends all *believe* that he would like to date Alice. But their beliefs are false: Brian would really prefer to date Christy. It is only natural in this case to say that *what Alice hopes* is at the same time *what Christy fears* and *what Brian's friends all (falsely) believe*. It is hard to make sense of this unless we assume that there is a common object—the proposition that Brian would like to date Alice—toward which Alice's hope and Christy's fear are directed. Likewise, it is hard to make sense of the idea that this common object is *believed* by many people unless we suppose that it is the sort of thing that can be true or false. (Things that cannot have a truth value—things like clouds or prime numbers— cannot be believed.) Once we admit that it is that sort of thing, it is natural to say that the beliefs of Brian's friends are false *because* the proposition is false; not the other way around. So there seems to be good reason for thinking the roles we have identified are occupied by propositions.

But what are propositions? What is their nature? Given their intimate connection with sentences and beliefs, they would have to be things that could be true or false; they would also have to be things that could stand in logical relations to one another. What you say can be *conjoined* with what I say; it can either be *consistent with* or *contradict* something I believe; it might *entail* something I believe; and so on. All of this suggests (but does not guarantee) that propositions have something like a linguistic structure: logical form, parts or **constituents** corresponding to subject and predicate, and so on.

There are, in short, three ways in which one might think of propositions: (1) as mental items (beliefs, maybe); (2) as linguistic items; or (3) as abstract objects of some sort. One serious problem with the first two options is that there might never have been any creatures with the capacity for thought or language. But surely in that case it would have been *true* that there are no thinking creatures; that $2 + 2 = 4$; that contradictions can't be true, and so on—and this despite the fact that there would be no bits of language. So, if propositions are the fundamental bearers of truth and falsity, they cannot be linguistic items, nor can they be creaturely mental states. One could say that propositions are divine thoughts, but this view commits one to belief in God, which is a commitment many philosophers would be reluctant to take on simply to accommodate a theory of propositions.

We can now see why those who object to abstract objects in general typically also object to propositions. Since there might never have been any concrete things (other than God, perhaps), propositions cannot be identified with anything concrete (outside of God). But thinking of propositions as wholly unique abstract objects is also problematic. Earlier we said that the sentences "God is dead" and "Gott ist todt" *express the same thing*. But how can we possibly know this if propositions are neither concrete objects nor abstract objects of some very familiar sort (like classes, or sets)? If all we know is that propositions are some perhaps very unfamiliar kind of abstract object, we will have no reason to think that we have any real clue as to what rules govern their behavior.

Partly because of this, it is rare now to treat propositions as being wholly different from other kinds of abstract object such as states of affairs, properties, relations, and classes. More often, people to try to assimilate some of these things to one another. Among the more common theories of propositions, two come to the fore. The first identifies them with *states of affairs*. The second puts them in the same category as *properties*, either identifying them with properties of a certain kind or else treating properties and propositions as different species of a common genus.

STATES OF AFFAIRS

A **state of affairs** is a circumstance, a situation, or a way things are. Saying this, however, does not tell us much about what states of affairs are like. It does not tell us much about their intrinsic nature. The two most well-developed conceptions of states of affairs are those of Roderick Chisholm and David Armstrong.

According to Chisholm, states of affairs are necessarily existing abstract entities. They are divided, broadly speaking, into two classes: those that occur and those that do not. My being a philosopher is among those that occur. My running a marathon in less than ninety minutes is, sadly, among those that do not. The latter state of affairs *exists*. I can think about it, talk about it, try (in vain) to bring it about, and so on. It just isn't among the things that have happened or will ever happen in our world's history.

The distinction between *occurring* and *not occurring* mirrors the distinction between *being true* and *being false*. My being a philosopher is among the states of affairs that occur; correspondingly, the proposition that I am a philosopher is true. My running a marathon in less than ninety minutes is among those that do not occur; correspondingly, the proposition that I have, or someday will, run a marathon in less than ninety minutes is false. More generally, it seems that for every state of affairs that occurs at some time or other, there is a corresponding true proposition, and, likewise, for every state of affairs that never occurs, there is a corresponding false proposition. To this extent, then, states of affairs resemble propositions.

There is another point of resemblance. Consider again attitudes like hope and fear. Earlier we said that propositions function as the objects of our hopes and fears, but it makes equally good sense to suppose that states of affairs do. What Alice hopes for and Christy fears, we might say, is nothing more or less than *Brian's preferring to date Alice*. We didn't consider this proposal earlier, because we had not yet introduced anything that might serve as the referent of the phrase "Brian's preferring to date Alice." But now that states of affairs are on the table, we do have a referent. We might say that *Brian's preferring to date Alice* is the name of a state of affairs—one that exists but does not occur. Since it exists, it can be an object of fear and hope. Moreover, it seems that for every proposition that serves as the object of some attitude like fear, hope, or belief, there will be a corresponding state of affairs that is equally suited to be an object of the same attitude.

Chisholm embraces the idea that states of affairs are the things that we hope for, fear, believe or deny to be the case. Indeed, on Chisholm's view, the defining characteristic of states of affairs is that they are capable of *being accepted*. But now it is hard to see any good reason for thinking of propositions as distinct from states of affairs. Both are abstract (assuming, again, that we cannot sensibly identify propositions with mental states or linguistic items); both are objects of propositional attitudes; and it is hard to appreciate any real distinction between "occurring" and "being true" or between "not occurring" and "being false." So, why not just say that propositions and states of affairs are identical to one another?

In fact, Chisholm does say that all propositions are states of affairs. In particular, he says that they are *eternally occurring states of affairs*.

On his view, many states of affairs (e.g., Sally's *eating dinner*) occur at some times but not others; but propositions, he thinks, are either always true or always false. Thus, every proposition is a state of affairs on his view, but not vice versa. So, whereas there is no proposition corresponding to *Sally's eating dinner*, there is a proposition corresponding to *Sally's eating dinner at t*, which occurs either always or never. Accordingly, the proposition that Sally eats dinner at *t* is either eternally true or eternally false.

The view that propositions do not change their truth values is controversial. Those who allow that propositions can change their truth values will have a hard time spotting any relevant difference between propositions and states of affairs. But, in fact, most philosophers side with Chisholm. One reason is that formal logic is simplified if we assume that propositions have their truth values eternally. Another reason has to do with general metaphysical problems about change over time, some of which will be explored in Chapter 4.

The fact that Chisholm's theory of states of affairs makes it easy to identify propositions with states of affairs is one of its advantages. Even so, Chisholm's theory will not be in the least bit attractive to people who want either to eliminate abstract objects from their ontology altogether or to identify all abstract objects with classes. One option for those in this latter category is simply to deny the existence of states of affairs. Another is to identify states of affairs with properties or classes. A further strategy would be to identify states of affairs with concrete objects of some sort. This is the approach taken by David Armstrong.

Like Chisholm, Armstrong thinks of states of affairs as the sorts of things that might be named by phrases like *Aristotle's being a philosopher* or *the cat's napping in the sun* or *Christy's liking Brian*. Unlike Chisholm, he thinks of them as concrete entities that have **substances** and attributes as constituents. Familiar particulars—you, me, horses, trees, and so on—are states of affairs, according to Armstrong; and, indeed, he describes the whole world as a "world of states of affairs." In saying this, he does not just mean that the world is populated by states of affairs but that states of affairs are the fundamental building blocks of the world.

This latter claim might seem to be at odds with the idea that states of affairs have substances and attributes as constituents. After all, if the world is built up out of states of affairs, and substances and attributes are the constituents of states of affairs, then isn't the world *really* built up out of substances and attributes? Not quite. But here we need to say a bit about substances, attributes, and Armstrong's understanding of how exactly they figure into states of affairs.

Very roughly, the distinction between attributes and substances is just the distinction between properties (like *being blue*) and things that *have* properties. Philosophers sometimes use the term "attribute" instead of "property" to signal their adherence to a particular understanding of what properties are like; but I shall use it as synonymous with "property." For Armstrong, attributes are **immanent universals**. To say that they are immanent is to say that they are located in spacetime, in the objects that instantiate them. To say that they are universal is to say that they are instantiated by many objects at once and therefore wholly located in many places at once (unlike particulars). As for substances, it is a bit tricky to say what these are supposed to be for Armstrong. On the one hand, there is good reason to think that substances are just things like you and me. After all, I have attributes; so do you. So we are clearly things that have properties. On the other hand, it seems rather strange to suppose that *I* am the thing that underlies *all* of my properties. Suppose you strip away properties like *being a philosopher, having mass, being human, having a body*, and so on. What would be left? Certainly not *me*. It seems, instead, that either nothing would be left—in which case there are no substances, but only bundles of properties—or else all that would be left is what philosophers call a "bare particular." In light of this, it is tempting to think of Armstrong's "substances" as bare particulars—sort of like pincushions to which all of the attributes are pinned.

Armstrong is sometimes interpreted as a bare-particular theorist. Interestingly, his understanding of the way in which substances and attributes are blended in states of affairs calls into question the idea that his substances are just bare particulars. In laying out his view, Armstrong distinguishes between **thin particulars** and **thick particulars**. The thick particular is a state of affairs, specifically, one which has only non-relational properties as constituents. (**Relational properties** are properties that involve relations to other things—e.g., *being ten feet away from a horse* or *having three sides*. Non-relational properties are, sensibly enough, properties that do not involve relations.) The thin particular is an object—so, again, a state of affairs—*considered in abstraction from its properties. Both* count as substances, according to Armstrong. The thin particular is a constituent in a state of affairs; the thick particular *has* both the thin particular and its properties as constituents. Note, too, that just as a thin particular is a state of affairs considered in abstraction from its properties, so too a universal is (according to Armstrong) "everything that is left in [a] state of affairs after the particular particulars involved in the state of affairs have been abstracted away in thought."

So, for example, consider the state of affairs that consists in Christy's liking Brian. This is a complex state of affairs which includes at least two others: Christy and Brian. The relation *loving* will be a universal, and it is "what is left" when we consider the state of affairs in abstraction from Christy and Brian. Christy and Brian, of course, will be thick particulars. (Christy's liking Brian won't be a particular because it includes a relation among its constituents.) Christy's thin particular will be Christy considered in abstraction from *all* of her properties, so, whatever is left when we remove (in thought) Christy's humanity, her mass, her hair color, her various relational properties (such as *liking Brian*), and so on.

In light of all of this, we can now start to see why I say that Armstrong's theory identifies states of affairs, rather than their constituents, as the basic building blocks of reality. The constituents of states of affairs have, on Armstrong's view, no *independent* existence. One never finds thin particulars standing bare without any properties. Likewise, there are no free-standing, uninstantiated universals, no properties existing apart from any property-bearers. Particulars and universals come only in packages, bound together in states of affairs.

The trouble is that this very feature of Armstrong's theory raises serious questions about the claim that states of affairs have substances as constituents and, indeed, about the claim that they have any constituents at all. If states of affairs are the fundamental entities, then they, not their constituents, would seem to be the things that have the independence requisite for counting as substances. More importantly, it is hard to see how states of affairs as Armstrong characterizes them can even be said to *have* constituents. What is Christy, *considered as the liker of Brian*? Just Christy. What is Christy, *considered as a woman*? Just Christy. What is Christy, *considered as a student*? Still Christy. So what is Christy *considered apart from all of her properties*? Again, Christy. But *Christy* is not a thin particular that exists as a mere constituent of Christy. Christy is, if anything, a thick particular. So, it looks as if *there is no thin particular*. Likewise, what is left after we have abstracted away all of the particulars involved in Christy? Well, if the line of reasoning we have just gone through is sound, the only particular involved in Christy is *Christy*, and to consider Christy in abstraction from Christy is to consider nothing at all. So it looks as if there are no universals either. But then it looks as if Armstrong's characterization of states of affairs as substance–attribute complexes can't possibly be correct. For, contrary to what Armstrong says, his view implies that there is nothing contained within a state of affairs answering to the description of either a (thin) substance or a universal.

PROPERTIES

Traditionally, the landscape of views about the nature of properties has been divided into two broad categories: *realist* views and *nominalist* views. In what follows, I will briefly characterize the distinction between realism and nominalism and then identify some of the most important versions of each.

In philosophical lingo, **realism** about such-and-suches is usually the view that *there are* such-and-suches and that something's being a such-and-such doesn't depend on human beliefs, opinions, or concepts. So, for example, most of us are not realists about *leprechauns*, nor are we realists about *obnoxious behaviors*. In the case of leprechauns, we are not realists because we believe that there are none. In the case of obnoxious behaviors, we all know that there are such things (most of us have engaged in them), but we are not realists about them because we see that whether something counts as obnoxious depends on whether people find it offensive. If belching loudly in the middle of a wedding ceremony were generally taken as a sign of respect, it would probably no longer count as obnoxious.

On the traditional conception, properties (if they exist at all) are **universals**, which are abstract objects of a certain kind. And universals (if they exist at all) do not depend for their existence or nature on human beliefs, concepts, or opinions. Accordingly, *realism* *about properties* is typically identified with the view that there are universals. For purposes here, I will characterize the alternative view, **nominalism**, as the thesis that universals do not exist. This is a slightly nonstandard characterization, but I adopt it for the sake of simplifying our discussion. More commonly, nominalism is identified either with the view that everything is particular (i.e., there are no universals) or with the view that everything is concrete (i.e., there are no abstract objects). Since both imply that there are no universals, my own characterization covers the territory that is relevant for this section.

Philosophical arguments aside, nominalism is an attractive position. The idea of an abstract object is hard to wrap one's mind around. They are not like us, or like anything else we encounter in nature. They do not *affect* us in any way, so they are even unlike the invisible immaterial things that many of us believe in—God, for example, or souls. For this reason, as Peter van Inwagen points out, it seems that it would be better not to believe in them if we could avoid doing so. Our overall theory of the world would be simpler, more elegant, and easier to understand if we did not have to suppose that, in addition to the category of familiar concrete entities, there is a radically different category of abstract objects.

Much the same can be said about the idea of a *universal*. Universals are supposed to be objects that somehow lack particularity. But what could it possibly mean to lack particularity? There are no very helpful answers to this question. Universals are sometimes said to be *present in* many things at once. But what does that mean? They are not in material objects in the way that, say, water is in a cup. They are not ingredients, like tomatoes and basil in pizza sauce. They are not shared among objects as parts can be. So, again, what could we mean by saying that they are *in* the objects that exemplify them? As we noted in our discussion of Armstrong, we might observe that universals, in contrast to particulars, *have instances*. Universals are *exemplified*, whereas particulars are not. But this observation does not help much either. It seems that all we really know about having instances is that it is what universals do. Likewise with being exemplified. So, to say that universals, but not particulars, have instances, or are exemplified, is just to say that universals, but not particulars, do whatever it is that universals do. We might as well say that universals, but not particulars, are brillig, and that being brillig is the defining attribute of a universal. We learn nothing from this. So, just as it would be nice if we could avoid believing in a category of abstract objects, it would also be nice if we could avoid believing in a category of universals.

It is, unfortunately, remarkably difficult to avoid believing in abstract universals. The reason, in short, is that it is hard to account for commonsense ways of talking about properties without endorsing realism. We often talk about different kinds of objects sharing features in common. We can pick out our favorite attributes of things. We compare different kinds of attributes in a way that seems to presuppose their reality (e.g., "Bourne's amnesia lends him a human vulnerability that helps to offset his machine-like fighting prowess"). And so on. It is generally thought that if only we can provide a satisfying account of attribute agreement (of specific facts like *x and y both have the property F*, as well as of general facts like *x and y share a feature in common*), we will then also have the resources to account for all of our other commonsense ways of thinking and talking about properties. The challenge to provide an account like this is *the problem of universals*. The particular difficulty that nominalists face is that it is hard to construe all of our talk about features as ultimately being talk about concrete objects and classes (the sorts of things nominalists typically favor). So, say the realists, we ought to give up on nominalism and accept that what we refer to by names like "features," "attributes," and so on, are abstract objects belonging to a special, hard-to-define category of their own. That category, of course, is just the category of *universal*.

To appreciate the force of this argument, it will help to take a brief look at some of the main varieties of nominalism. The first thing to note, however, is that *every* version of nominalism either denies that there are properties or identifies them with abstract objects of some sort—usually classes of objects or classes of abstract particularized properties called **tropes** (e.g., *the particular tomato-basil flavor of this spoonful of pizza sauce*). So, if you want to avoid believing in abstract objects altogether, you should say that there are no properties. Good luck with that. The most viable versions of nominalism are ones that admit the existence of properties but deny that properties are universals.

There are three versions of nominalism worth highlighting: class nominalism, trope nominalism, and resemblance nominalism. These do not exhaust the territory, but, at the moment, they seem to be the most popular alternatives to realism. We can characterize each of these views by saying briefly how it fills in the blanks in each of the following statements:

1 Properties are identical with _____.
2 There is a property that x and y have in common if, and only if____.
3 Something has (e.g.) the property *being human* if, and only if____.

In discussing each view, I shall also highlight some of its most salient problems.

Class nominalism maintains, as the label suggests, that properties are classes. Everyone can agree that every predicate is associated with a class of objects—the predicate's extension. (As was mentioned earlier, not every predicate can be satisfied. Those that cannot be have the null class as their extension.) A natural thought for a nominalist, then, is that the property expressed by a predicate *is* the predicate's extension. A natural further thought is that classes that aren't the extension of any predicate nonetheless count as properties too, since, after all, they *could* be associated with pre-dicates if only language were to develop in a certain way. So, class nominalists typically believe in a vast array of properties but reduce them all to classes. According to class nominalism, then, the prop-erty *being human* is the class of all human beings, and something has that property if, and only if, it is a member of the class. Two objects have a property in common on this view if, and only if, there is a class of which both are members.

One of the main attractions of this view is that it identifies prop-erties with abstract objects of a sort that even most nominalists agree that we simply cannot do without. Although many philosophers have wanted to do away with abstract objects entirely, it is widely held that one must at least admit the existence of classes. If one *must* posit abstract objects, so the reasoning goes, then at least we should try to minimize the varieties of abstracta that we posit and stick, if at all possible, to ones (like classes) that are fairly well understood.

There is an obvious problem with class nominalism as I have just presented it, however. As was noted earlier, no two classes have exactly the same members. So, if a property is nothing other than the class of its instances, then it follows that no two properties have all of the same instances. So, for example, if I were to collect all of the ivory-billed woodpeckers in my backyard and chase out all of the other birds, then the class of ivory-billed woodpeckers would be identical to the class of birds in my backyard. According to class nominalism, then, the *property* of being an ivory-billed woodpecker would be identical to the property of being a bird in my backyard. But, of course, that is absurd. Worse, as soon as the ivory-billed woodpecker becomes extinct, it looks as if class nominalism will imply that the property of being an ivory-billed woodpecker is identical to the null class which, in turn, is identical to the property of being a dinosaur (since, of course, the class of all dinosaurs is also the null class). But clearly the property of being an ivory-billed woodpecker is different from the property of being a dinosaur.

We might try to avoid this problem, and others, by identifying a property with the class whose members are all of its *past*, *present*, and *future* instances. Suppose this move is successful. Still, we face another, very similar, problem, one posed by properties that have never been and will never be exemplified. Nothing is (or ever will be) a unicorn, a fairy, or a mountain made of gold. Thus, class nominalism will identify all of the following properties with the null class, and so with one another: *being a unicorn*, *being a fairy* and *being a mountain made of gold*. But surely being a unicorn is not the same property as being a mountain made of gold.

There is one more step we can take, however, to minimize the class nominalist's problems. David Lewis argues that in addition to the actual world (which comprises all past, present, and future objects), there are infinitely many concrete *possible worlds*. (By "possible," here and throughout the book, except where otherwise indicated, I mean **metaphysically possible**.) According to Lewis, a possible world is a universe-sized concrete object. He thinks that for every comprehensive way that a universe *could* be, there is a universe spatiotemporally unrelated to our own where things *are* that way. This implies that there are infinitely many universe-sized concrete objects, all spatiotemporally disconnected from our own universe, and that some of these universes are very similar to ours except in minor details, whereas others are vastly and even bizarrely different. Everything that can exist does exist somewhere in the space of possible worlds. Thus, just as the class of human beings has members, so too the class of unicorns, the class of fairies, and the class of mountains made of gold have members. So we can avoid the aforementioned problems by identifying a property not with the class of all of its *actual* (past, present, and future) instances but with the class of all of its *possible* instances. The property *being human*, for example, is just the class that includes every human being from every possible world. The property *being a unicorn* is the class that includes every unicorn from every possible world. And so on.

One advantage to Lewis's view is that it identifies *propositions* with classes. On Lewis's view, every proposition is identical to the property of being a world in which that proposition is true. (Well, almost. Certain special kinds of propositions require special treatment. But we shall ignore those complications here.) So every proposition is a property, and every property is a class. For example, the proposition that you are studying metaphysics is just the property *being a world where you are studying metaphysics*, which, in turn, is just the class that includes every world in which you are studying metaphysics. This is a nice and tidy view in which apparently disparate kinds of abstract objects are reduced to a single kind: classes.

But tidiness comes at a price. For starters, note that you can accept Lewis's view only if you believe that there are unicorns, golden mountains, leprechauns, and the like. You do not have to believe that there are such things in *our* universe, of course; but Lewis's view implies that such things do exist, albeit in a way that is spatiotemporally unrelated to us. Do you believe in such things? If not, look elsewhere for a theory of properties. If so, consider the further consequences of Lewis's view and see whether you can accept those as well.

Like other versions of class nominalism, Lewis's view maintains that necessarily coextensive predicates (i.e., predicates that are necessarily such as to have the same extension) express the same property. For example, since it is a necessary truth that every three-angled figure is a three-sided figure, and vice versa, the class of all possible triangular things is identical with the class of all possible trilateral things. So, Lewis's view implies that the property of being triangular is identical to the property of being trilateral. So far, one might not be too concerned. This consequence is, at any rate, not nearly as bad as saying that *being an ivory-billed woodpecker* is the same property as *being a bird in my backyard*. But the problem worsens when we turn our attention to predicates that cannot possibly be satisfied. These will all have the null class as their extension, so they will all express the same property.

Moreover, since Lewis's view implies that every sentence that cannot possibly be true also expresses the null class, it turns out that every unsatisfiable predicate expresses the same thing as every sentence that can't possibly be true. So Lewis's view implies (for example) that the property *being both a man and a sugar cube* is identical to the property *being a gold mountain made entirely of water* and to the proposition expressed by "Bill is a married bachelor."

Finally, since necessary truths are propositions that are true in all possible worlds, Lewis's view implies that if a sentence expresses a necessary truth, the proposition it expresses is the class of all possible worlds. So "2 + 2 = 4" expresses the same proposition as "It is morally wrong to torture small children for fun," and this proposition, oddly enough, is identical to the property of *being a possible world*. Add all of these costs together, and it is easy to see why Lewis's brand of class nominalism—which seems to be the most viable brand—is widely rejected.

There is one further objection against class nominalism that we should discuss before moving on, because it helps to make our transition to resemblance nominalism. According to class nominalism, having a property is *simply* a matter of belonging to a certain class. There is nothing in the story that indicates *why* one class rather than another is associated with a given predicate. A realist might say that the class of humans is the extension of the predicate "is human" because *all of the members of that class instantiate a common universal—the one we call "humanity."* But the class nominalist has no explanation to offer. This is puzzling.

Resemblance nominalism does not suffer from this problem. According to the resemblance nominalist, attribute agreement is explained ultimately by appeal to a primitive (unanalyzable) resemblance relation. If there are properties, then they are classes whose members resemble one another, or certain paradigms. The nature of the property is defined by the paradigms or by the nature of the resemblance among the members of the class. So, some resemblance nominalists will say that something has, e.g., the property *being human* if, and only if, it resembles paradigm human beings or, if there are no paradigms, resembles everything else that belongs to the class of all human beings. There is a property that two things have in common if, and only if, those two things are members of a common resemblance class.

Another advantage to resemblance nominalism is that it avoids the problem of uninstantiated and necessarily instantiated properties. Although every predicate will have an extension, there is no pressure to say that all predicates express properties, since there is no guarantee that the members of every predicate-extension will genuinely resemble one another. Not only is this advantageous from the point of view of trying to avoid problems associated with uninstantiated and necessarily instantiated properties, but it is also advantageous insofar as it allows the resemblance nominalist to endorse what is known as a *sparse* theory of properties. A sparse theory of properties maintains that relatively few predicates correspond to properties. The motivation for such a theory is just the idea that not every predicate corresponds to a genuine mode of resemblance. For example, infinitely many predicates are satisfied by both goats and microwave ovens. Goats and microwaves are such that seven is a number, they are not trees, etc. But it would be odd to say that, by virtue of this fact, a goat and a microwave *resemble* one another. One way of explaining why this is odd is to say that *being such that seven is a number* and *being a non-tree* are not genuine modes of resemblance—they are not real properties. One who endorses this sort of view will say that a great many predicates (not just the paradoxical ones) fail to express properties; hence, the description of such a view as a "sparse" theory of properties. Again, one advantage to resemblance nominalism is that it can accommodate such a view.

But, as one might expect, there are also significant problems. Firstly, note that we still face the problem of *coextensive* properties. The resemblance class that includes all and only triangles is (of necessity) identical to the resemblance class that includes all and only trilaterals; so resemblance nominalism has no way of distinguishing these two properties. But, intuitively, the property of having three *sides* is distinct from the property of having three *angles*.

Secondly, we might well ask where the paradigms are. Who are the paradigm humans, for example? What are the paradigm red things? Any answer, it seems, will be hopelessly arbitrary. For this reason, resemblance nominalists now typically refrain from saying that property-having depends on resemblance to paradigms; rather, they say that having a property is simply a matter of belonging to a resemblance class. For example, being human is not a matter of resembling paradigm humans but is, rather, a matter of belonging to a certain class of things (the class of human beings), all of whom resemble one another.

Thirdly, there is the so-called problem of *imperfect community*. It seems possible for there to be resemblance classes whose members share no common property. For example, suppose the only properties are F, G, and H, and the only objects are a, b, and c. Suppose, further, that a has properties F and G, b has properties G and H, and c has properties F and H. Here, a, b, and c form a resemblance class; each resembles the other two. But there is no property that all three have in common. It is open to the resemblance nominalist to insist that cases like this are impossible; and it is, admittedly, hard to think of uncontroversial real-world examples. But many will find the response intuitively unsatisfying. It seems as though such cases *are* possible, but resemblance nominalism does not seem to allow for them. What we want, of course, is a way of distinguishing different ways in which objects resemble one another: a and b resemble one another in one way; b and c resemble one another in another way. We could do this by supposing that there are a great many different resemblance relations (one for each property). So, in other words, we might say that a G-resembles b but F-resembles c, and b and c H-resemble one another. But having to say something like this seems to greatly diminish the attractiveness of resemblance nominalism, and it is hard to see other viable options.

Finally, we turn to *trope nominalism*. Trope nominalism identifies properties with sums or classes of tropes. Tropes, as I said earlier, are supposed to be abstract particular entities like *the particular whiteness of my shirt*, *Socrates' humanity*, and so on. Tropes are typically referred to as "property-instances," presumably because they are tokens of particular property types. (Just as a particular quarter in my desk drawer is a token of the type *quarter*, so too the particular tomato-basil flavor of a spoonful of pizza sauce is a token of the type *tomato-basil flavor*.) Furthermore, trope theorists typically say that familiar objects are somehow built up out of tropes.

So, something has, for example, the property *being human* if, and only if, it has a *humanity* trope among its constituents. What it is for two objects to share a property in common—being the same color, for example—is just for each object to have a constituent—a trope—that *perfectly resembles* a corresponding constituent of the other object.

Trope theory avoids the problems associated with class nominalism in much the same way that resemblance nominalism does. Trope theorists face no pressure to admit the existence of uninstantiated properties, since there is no reason to think that every predicate extension will have members that all share a property in common. Moreover, trope theory also avoids the main problems associated with resemblance nominalism. Necessarily coextensive properties can be distinguished by appeal to differences among tropes. For example, we have no good reason to think that a three-sidedness trope would perfectly resemble any triangularity trope; so there is no obvious obstacle to insisting that they would differ from one another. Likewise, since properties are classes of perfectly resembling tropes, there is no problem specifying paradigms, nor is there any apparent way of generating a problem of imperfect community.

So trope theory has some real advantages. Like the other versions of nominalism, it also has some serious drawbacks. For example, consider the properties of tropes. Tropes obviously have properties: *Being abstract* and *being particular* are the most notable. But it would be absurd to say that all tropes have *abstractness* and *particularity* tropes as parts. For one thing, tropes are supposed to be pure property-instances; they don't have parts. Moreover, it seems odd to say (as we would have to) that abstractness and particularity tropes themselves have abstractness and particularity tropes as parts. Indeed, this would imply that every abstractness trope is infinitely complex: It would have an abstractness trope as a part which, in turn, would have another abstractness trope as a part, and so on.

Of course, I have already acknowledged that trope theorists need not say that every predicate corresponds to a property. Why not apply that strategy here and deny that "is abstract" and "is particular" express properties of tropes? The answer is that if one did so, then one might as well deny the existence of properties altogether. As we have already noted, some predicates—e.g., "is such that the moon exists and $2 + 2 = 22$" or "is a unicorn"—do not seem to pick out genuine modes of resemblance among things. It makes sense to deny that such predicates express properties. But tropes *do* resemble one another by being abstract and particular; indeed, the kind is defined by way of the predicates "is abstract" and "is particular." We can thus sensibly deny that those predicates express properties only if we can sensibly deny that *any* predicates that pick out genuine modes of resemblance express properties. One can try to give up on properties altogether; but, as we noted earlier, there seems to be little reason for optimism that such a strategy can work.

There is another problem for trope theory worth mentioning as well. Consider the particular whiteness of my shirt. Call that trope "T1." According to trope theory, my shirt counts as white by virtue of having T1 as a part. But now consider two other objects: the left half of my shirt and the right half. These are distinct objects that resemble one another perfectly with regard to their whiteness. Each, then, must have its own distinct whiteness trope, T2 and T3, both of which will perfectly resemble T1. Now consider four other objects, namely the top and bottom halves of the left and right halves of my shirt. Each of *these* objects is white too and so each will have a whiteness trope distinct from T1–T3. In the region occupied by my shirt there will be a myriad perfectly resembling and substantially overlapping whiteness tropes. But what grounds, really, do we have for believing in T1 anymore? Trope theory posits T1 to explain *the whiteness of my shirt*, but my perception of whiteness in the region occupied by my shirt, as well as the resemblance between what I see when I look at the shirt and what I see when I look at other white shirts, is perfectly explained by the presence of the myriad "smaller" whiteness tropes that are present in the smallest white portions of my shirt. T1 is explanatorily and perceptually redundant. Moreover, the same goes for T2, T3, and, indeed, for every whiteness trope that overlaps the smallest whiteness tropes present in the region occupied by my shirt. So it seems that we should not believe in T1, T2, and so on. But if there is no such thing as *the particular whiteness of my shirt*, then, according to trope theory, my shirt is not white. So the problem comes to this: It seems as if my shirt can be white simply by having a sufficiently large number of small parts that each have their own whiteness tropes; but trope theory insists that *nothing* is white unless it has its own distinct whiteness trope.

Here, as with the other two varieties of nominalism, I do not take myself to have given an exhaustive list of objections, and neither do I take the objections to be decisive. But the objections are serious enough and the responses baroque enough that realism deserves a serious hearing. The main problem with realism seems just to be the outright weirdness and elusiveness of the universal–particular distinction. However, when we compare this weirdness with the weirdness of saying that the null class is both a property and a proposition, or that there are infinitely many distinct resemblance relations, or that there are tropes that somehow entirely lack properties, it is not so clear that realism comes up with the short end of the stick.

As with nominalism, realism comes in several varieties. But here we can be much more brief, for the varieties are easily characterized by reference to three main decision points, and there is no need to identify multiple distinct problems with each version of realism. For, again, the main problem for all versions is essentially the same: All are committed to a universal–particular distinction, and to the view that the category of universal and the category of particular both have instances.

The first decision point concerns the question whether universals are *immanent* or *transcendent*. Plato, Bertrand Russell, and many others think of universals as transcendent in the following sense: They are wholly outside space and time, and they are not in any way "present in" the objects that exemplify them. Often the term "participation" is used to characterize the relationship between particulars and transcendent universals; often, too, people draw a sharp distinction between "exemplification" and "instantiation" (the former being the relation between particulars and transcendent universals, and the latter being the relation between particulars and immanent universals). But it is not clear that there is any substantive content to terms like "participation" and "exemplification" beyond their contrast with terms that are supposed to indicate the *inherence* of universals in particulars. As you might guess from what has just been said, believers in immanent universals think that universals are somehow present in their instances. Some go so far as to say that they are parts of their instances. Aristotle is among the defenders of immanent universals, and, as we have already seen, so is David Armstrong.

The second decision point concerns an issue that also arises in connection with nominalism: Do we endorse a **sparse theory of properties** or an *abundant* or *plentiful* one? That is, do we endorse a restrictive view about which predicates correspond to properties, or do we say that just about every meaningful predicate expresses a property? Peter van Inwagen, for example, opts for an abundant theory. According to van Inwagen, properties are *assertibles*, things that can be said of other things. Since every meaningful predicate expresses something that can be said of something else—that's just what predicates do, after all—it turns out, on his view, that every such predicate expresses a property. David Armstrong, on the other hand, believes that quite a lot of predicates fail to express universals. His view, rather, is that universals constitute the "genuine" modes of resemblance among objects, and the mere fact that two objects satisfy the same predicate by no means guarantees that the two objects genuinely resemble one another. Returning to an earlier example: You and the number 77 both satisfy the predicate "is such that the moon exists and 2 + 2 = 22." Does it follow from the fact that you both satisfy this predicate that you *resemble* the number 77? Armstrong and many others will say, "No": You and the number 77 are not similar at all.

Lastly, we need to decide whether we believe in *unexemplified* or *uninstantiated* universals. Obviously this decision is related to our previous one. If, for example, we endorse a view like van Inwagen's, we can hardly avoid saying that there are unexemplified properties. For, after all, among the things that can be said of me are *that I am a unicorn*, *that I am a round square*, and so on. Of course, these things are falsely said of me (if said at all); but they can be said of me nonetheless. Others, however, Aristotle and Armstrong among them, endorse a *principle of instantiation*, according to which there are no uninstantiated universals. On this view, then, "is a unicorn" does not express a universal, even though it would have done so, had there been unicorns. One consequence of this view is that most universals exist contingently, contrary to what many realists are inclined to think. If there had been no elephants, for example, and it seems that there could easily not have been, then there would have been no property of *being an elephant*. One attractive feature of this view is that it allows us to say that universals depend in an important way on the things that have them, rather than the other way around.

NONEXISTENT OBJECTS AND CREATURES OF FICTION

We come, finally, to nonexistent objects and creatures of fiction. We often seem to talk about such things; there seem, in fact, to be a wide variety of truths about such things. Santa Claus dresses in red; the Easter Bunny does not. Wood nymphs are generally more beautiful than sirens, but sirens have voices to die for. Tyrion Lannister and Katniss Everdeen are more complicated characters than Elrond Half-Elven or Molly Millions. Jason Bourne's amnesia lends him a human vulnerability that helps to offset his machine-like fighting prowess. Jack Reacher and Jack Bauer resemble one another in their ruthlessly utilitarian approach to threat management. And so on. Each of these claims seems *true*. But how can they be true if the names embedded in them do not refer? The claim that Katniss Everdeen is a more complicated character than Molly Millions, for example, seems to be *about* both Katniss and Molly. But how could it be so if Katniss and Molly do not exist and are not even characters in the same fiction?

Let us begin with nonexistent objects. The main motivation for believing that there are things that do not exist is, as I have just noted, that we seem to refer to such things. So, one way to settle the question is to determine whether we ought to take this appearance at face value. If there is good reason to doubt that we ever refer to things that do not exist, then the motivation for believing in nonexistent objects is lost.

We can begin to make some progress by noting a distinction between two kinds of claims: specific non-existence claims, on the one hand, and a general claim to the effect that there are non-existent things. Claim 2.1 below is a claim of the first sort, whereas 2.2 is a claim of the second sort:

2.1 Pegasus is nonexistent.
2.2 There is something, x, such that x is nonexistent.

It is easy to see why the truth of 2.1 would give rise to the appearance that we sometimes refer to things that do not exist. As I have already noted, many sentences (including 2.1) seem to refer to Pegasus; and yet Pegasus does not exist. The problem, though, is that there is good reason to doubt that 2.2 follows from 2.1, and so there is good reason to doubt that we ever refer to things that do not exist.

To appreciate the reasons for doubting that 2.2 follows from 2.1, it will help to say just a little bit about standard predicate logic. In general, from a sentence of the form "*a* is F" (where "*a*" is a name like "Pegasus" and "F" is a predicate like "is a horse"), one is allowed to infer a sentence of the form "*There is something, x, such that x is F*" or "*There exists an x such that x is F*." That is why 2.2 *seems* to follow from 2.1. But there is a complication. The italicized words in each of the latter two sentences are standardly regarded as equivalent acceptable readings of a logical symbol, "∃," known as the *existential quantifier*. In standard predicate logic, if you want to express the claim that something is a horse, that horses exist, that there are horses, or anything else relevantly like that, you would simply write "∃x(x is a horse)," or "∃xHx," where "Hx" abbreviates "x is a horse." In other words, the following sentences are equivalent: "∃x(x is a horse)," "∃xHx," "Something is a horse," "There are horses," and "Horses exist." So standard predicate logic makes no distinction between *being* and *existence*. Saying that there *are* horses is the same as saying that horses *exist*. Accordingly, most contemporary philosophers recognize no such distinction either. To say that there *is* something that does not exist is, therefore, to say something contradictory.

So here is our situation: 2.1 looks like a sentence of the form "*a* is nonexistent." As we have already seen, however, we are allowed to infer from this the sentence "∃x(x is nonexistent)." But the sentence "∃x(x is nonexistent)" *cannot possibly be true* on the standard interpretation of the quantifier. So, 2.2 cannot possibly be true. We therefore have three options:

1. We can say that Pegasus exists.
2. We can make a distinction between being and existence, and then revise our interpretation of the quantifier. Doing this would open up the possibility that 2.2 expresses a truth.
3. We can deny that 2.1 is to be taken at face value. We might say that, although it *seems* to be a claim of the form "*a* is nonexistent," what we *really* mean to say when we affirm sentences like 2.1 is something with a different logical form, something

that doesn't imply anything so bizarre as 2.2. (This is just an application of the Quinean approach to matters of ontology that we saw in Chapter 1.)

Setting aside the question whether Pegasus might be a creature of fiction, option 1 is obviously a nonstarter. Option 2 means allowing that there *are* some things that don't exist, which sounds incoherent. So most philosophers take option 3. W. V. Quine's suggestion in his famous paper, "On What There Is" is that we can think of *being Socrates* (say) as a kind of activity that something does; and we can then introduce a new verb—*socratizing*—for that activity. To say that Socrates exists, then, would be equivalent to saying that something socratizes. Likewise, to say that Pegasus does not exist would be equivalent to saying that *nothing pegasizes*. But, just as one can't infer a claim like 2.2 from the claim that nothing runs, or nothing sits, or nothing plays soccer, so too one can't infer a claim like 2.2 from the claim that nothing pegasizes. For, "Nothing pegasizes" does not have the *form* "*a* is F," and without that form 2.2 cannot be validly inferred from it. Problem solved.

Alternatively, one might think of *being Socrates* in just the way that property realists think of ordinary predications. So, just as *being red* is equivalent to *having the property redness*, so too *being Socrates* might be equivalent to *having the property socrateity*. In that case, to say that Socrates exists would be equivalent to saying that something exemplifies socrateity. Likewise, saying that Pegasus does not exist would be equivalent to saying that nothing exemplifies pegasity.

Note that we avoid commitment to nonexistent objects only by finding suitable *paraphrases* of 2.1, paraphrases about which we can say, "This sentence, rather than 2.1, captures the *true* logical form of what I was trying to say in uttering 2.1." Note, too, that the price of avoiding commitment to nonexistent objects seems to be commitment to bizarre activities (like pegasizing) or bizarre properties (like pegasity). If we can be content with such commitments, then there will be little else to push us in the direction of belief in nonexistent things. If, on the other hand, we find the bizarreness of such things to be too much to swallow, then perhaps we ought to follow philosophers like Terence Parsons and Richard Routley in developing full-blown theories of nonexistent objects.

Let us turn now to creatures of fiction. One might think that in dealing with the problem of nonexistent objects we will automatically settle all questions about creatures of fiction. After all, aren't creatures of fiction nothing more or less than specific, interesting examples of nonexistent objects? If we reject the latter, don't we automatically reject the former? In a word, no. Some philosophers insist that there are no nonexistent things but nevertheless admit the existence of creatures of fiction. (In so doing, of course, they deny that creatures of fiction are nonexistent things.) The reason, in short, is that it is harder to paraphrase claims that seem to be about creatures of fiction than it is to paraphrase claims that seem to be about nonexistent objects that are not parts of any particular fiction.

Consider again the case of robustly drawn creatures of fiction—Katniss Everdeen and Molly Millions, for example. Although we can all agree that Molly and Katniss are not real people, it is nevertheless easy to cite a great many facts about them, both individually and in comparison with one another. Both are science-fiction heroines; both are strong female characters who are able to physically dominate many of the men with whom they come into conflict; both are troubled in various ways; only one (Molly) is a character from the cyberpunk subgenre; only one (Katniss) is a minor; and so on. We can compare their skills and their armaments; we can sensibly ask which would be a better companion or partner in various scenarios; we can speculate about who might win in a fight. It is hard to see how all of this could possibly make sense unless Katniss and Molly *exist*. It is hard to see how we could paraphrase these claims in such a way as to say everything we mean while doing away with all of the troubling implications (like *something is identical to Katniss Everdeen* or *something is a creature of fiction*). Similar remarks might be made about Jacks Bauer and Reacher. How could one paraphrase claims about the ways in which they are similar without doing so in a way that presupposes their existence? So, at least initially, we should be open to the idea that fictional characters are to be treated differently from nonexistent objects.

Let us sharpen the problem by looking at two particular examples, one that compares two fictional characters by name and another that talks very generally about creatures of fiction without mentioning any by name:

2.3 Katniss Everdeen is younger than Molly Millions, not nearly as well armed, and exists in an entirely different universe.

2.4 The protagonists of Tolkien novels are much more like mythical heroes than like cyberpunk antiheroes.

Each of these sentences, like 2.2, *apparently* implies the existence of things (Katniss, Molly, protagonists of Tolkien novels, mythical heroes, and cyberpunk antiheroes) that we commonsensically take not to exist. But how could we possibly paraphrase sentences like 2.3 and 2.4 so as to avoid commitment to such things? It does not seem that we can use the devices of inventing verbs (*katnissizing*, *mollyizing*, etc.) or names for properties (*katnissity*, *mollicity*, etc.) to help us; for it seems quite clear that, whatever we might think about claims like "Katniss does not exist," 2.3 and 2.4 at any rate are *not* about the property of katnissity nor are they about the activity of katnissizing. The reason, importantly, is that the property (if there is one) isn't exemplified, and the activity (if there is one) is not engaged in by anything; so it would be false to say, for example, that something with the property of katnissity is poorly armed.

I will leave it as a challenge to the reader to find suitable paraphrases of 2.3 and 2.4 that do not somehow imply claims like the following:

2.5 $\exists x(x = \text{Katniss Everdeen})$
2.6 $\exists x(x \text{ is a Tolkien character})$

If, as is extremely likely, we all fail to find suitable paraphrases, it seems that we face just the same two alternative options we faced in the case of Pegasus:

1. Admit that Katniss Everdeen, Molly Millions, Tolkien characters, and so on all exist.
2. Interpret the quantifier as expressing *being* rather than *existence* and say that Katniss, Molly, Tolkien characters, and the like, are all nonexistent objects.

If we take the first option, we face the burden of explaining how the claim that Tolkien characters exist is consistent with the commonsense truism that Aragorn, Elrond, elves and hobbits generally, and so on, *do not exist*. There are interesting ways of discharging that burden, but to go into them would take us much too far afield. Instead, I want to close by highlighting one other concern for the view that creatures of fiction exist. The concern is that there is no principled way of drawing boundaries between *creatures of fiction* (which, now, we are saying *do* exist) and anything else that we might take not to exist. The reason, in short, is that there are no clear standards for what counts as "creating a fiction."

Quine's "On What There Is" includes an example involving a "round square cupola on top of the Berkeley tower." Intuitively, such a thing does not exist. But if we had a novel that featured a round square cupola on top of the Berkeley tower, such a thing would be a creature of fiction and, on the present view, would exist. But why should writing a *novel* that makes mention of a round square cupola suffice for the creation (or discovery) of such an item, when writing a *philosophy article* that makes mention of the same sort of thing would not suffice? Similarly, why should writing a movie script that makes mention of fictional microbes like midichlorians suffice for the creation of such things, whereas writing a (false) chemical theory about, say, phlogiston wouldn't? Why should introducing a character like Katniss Everdeen in the context of a novel suffice for the creation of something, whereas introducing a character like Pegasus in a religious myth wouldn't? I can see no sensible answers to these questions. Maybe, then, the cases of fictional characters and nonexistent objects are not to be handled so differently after all.

So we end this chapter having discussed a variety of things that many of us would prefer not to believe in—propositions, states of affairs, abstract universals, nonexistent things, creatures of fiction—that philosophers have nonetheless found good reasons for believing in. My goal has not been to convince anyone that she *should* believe in these things. Rather, my goal has simply been to help us get a clearer picture of *why* philosophers are inclined to believe in and argue about such strange entities. The answer, in short, is that ridding ourselves of them often comes at the price of giving up very commonsensical claims, and believing them sometimes for good reason seems like the best of a bad lot of alternatives.

FURTHER READING

An excellent starting place for some of the issues in philosophy of language about meaning and reference that were touched on in the section entitled "Preliminaries" is Jeff Speaks's encyclopedia article, "Theories of Meaning," in *The Stanford Encyclopedia of Philosophy*, ed. Edward N. Zalta, 2011, available online at http://plato.stanford.edu/archives/sum2011/entries/meaning/.

The theories about propositions, properties, and states of affairs that were attributed to David Armstrong, Roderick Chisholm, and David Lewis can all be found in the following works by those philosophers: D. M. Armstrong, *A World of States of Affairs* (Cambridge: Cambridge University Press, 1997); Roderick M. Chisholm, *Person and Object: A Metaphysical Study* (La Salle, IL: Open Court, 1976); David K. Lewis, *On the Plurality of Worlds* (Oxford: Blackwell, 1986). David Lewis, whose work is discussed in most of the chapters of this book, was one of the most influential and systematic metaphysicians of the twentieth century. A good resource for understanding his overall system is Daniel Nolan's, *David Lewis* (Montreal: McGill-Queen's Univ Press, 2005).

In the section on propositions, I raised a question about whether it makes sense to treat propositions as objects of attitudes like fear and hope. For more detailed discussion of that issue, see Trenton Merricks, "Propositional Attitudes?," *Proceedings of the Aristotelian Society*, vol. 109 (2009), pp. 207–232. On the subject of structured propositions, I have learned a great deal from Lorraine Keller, *Whence Structured Propositions?* (PhD thesis, University of Notre Dame, 2012).

For a very accessible book-length treatment of the issues about properties discussed in this chapter, see D. M. Armstrong, *Universals: An Opinionated Introduction* (Boulder, CO: Westview Press, 1989). Bertrand Russell's, "The World of Universals," in *The Problems of Philosophy* (Oxford: Clarendon Press, 1912, pp. 91–100) is a classic statement of realism about universals. Peter van Inwagen's "Theory of Properties" (from which I quoted in this chapter) and David Armstrong's "A World of States of Affairs" (not to be confused with his book of the same title) also develop realist views about properties, and both are anthologized in *Arguing about Metaphysics*. Henry Fitzgerald's "Nominalist Things," also anthologized in *Arguing about*

Metaphysics, provides a lighthearted characterization of the distinction between "nominalist-friendly" objects and the sorts of things that only a realist would believe in. Classic statements of resemblance nominalism and trope theory can be found, respectively, in H. H. Price, "Universals and Resemblances," in *Thinking and Experience* (Cambridge, MA: Harvard University Press, 1953, pp. 7–32) and D. C. Williams, "The Elements of Being," *Review of Metaphysics*, vol. 7 (1953), pp. 3–18, 171–192.

I cited two articles that defend belief in nonexistent objects: Terence Parsons, "Are There Nonexistent Objects?" *American Philosophical Quarterly*, vol. 19 (1982), pp. 365–371; and Richard Routley, "On What There Is Not," anthologized in *Arguing about Metaphysics*. On creatures of fiction, see David Lewis, "Truth in Fiction," reprinted in *Arguing about Metaphysics*, as well as Peter van Inwagen, "Creatures of Fiction," *American Philosophical Quarterly*, vol. 14 (1977), pp. 299–308; and Stuart Brock, "The Creationist Fiction: The Case against Creationism about Fictional Characters," *Philosophical Review*, vol. 119 (2010), pp. 337–364. For discussion and display of the methodological issues that arose during that discussion, see Quine's "On What There Is," and David Lewis and Stephanie Lewis's engaging paper, "Holes," both reprinted in *Arguing about Metaphysics*. See also Peter van Inwagen's "Being, Existence, and Ontological Commitment," in the *Metametaphysics*.

3

TIME AND TIME TRAVEL

In an oft-quoted passage, St. Augustine remarks, "So what is time? If no one asks me, I know; if I want to explain it to someone who asks me, I do not know." We know time experientially. There is probably no more fundamental or constant aspect of our experience than our sense of time and its passage. Knowing it experientially is one thing. Understanding it is another.

Time slips away, and the future has yet to come. So it is natural to think that there is, quite literally, nothing but the present. But the present is so incredibly "thin" that it seems hardly big enough to contain all the richness of thought and experience and activity that occupies our minds and lives at any given moment. Could it really be that all there ever is to a high-school prom, or a college football game, or a bloody war is the thinnest slice of instantaneous action? Is there nothing more to time itself than an eternal succession of tiny slivers of temporality? Or are past and future more like distant places that not only exist but are even accessible, if only we had the right technology?

The first step toward understanding time is to say something about the nature of *times* and about what the terms "past," "present," and "future" refer to. The next step is to look at what reasons we might have for and against the claim that past and future times (or, as I shall prefer to put it, past and future objects and events) do not exist. Discussing this question will, in turn, raise questions about the *passage* of time. What, exactly, does it mean to say that time passes? *Can* time pass? Following our discussion of these issues, we shall take up the topic of time travel.

TIMES

Says Qoheleth, "For everything there is a season, and a time for every matter under heaven: a time to be born, and a time to die" (*Ecclesiastes*, 3:1–2, NRSV translation). Ordinary speech, as well as much poetry, is replete with reference to times. What are these things?

There are three main ways of thinking about the nature of times. On one way of thinking, times are events. Some people think of events as abstract entities. For purposes here, however, we shall assume they are concrete. We can watch them happen, participate in them, cause them, and be affected by them. They are wars and weddings, games and celebrations, births and deaths. They exist precisely when they happen. Some exist only for an instant; others last through the centuries. Now consider some arbitrary event: the beginning of your own very existence, for example. Let us suppose that this event happens instantaneously, rather than gradually, over some duration. Now consider every event that was simultaneous with that one (in some particular **frame of reference**). Now consider the grand event that is the **sum** of all of those smaller ones. That grand event is a time. (I assume here that for any two events, there is exactly one further event that is their sum. So, for example, in addition to the football game down at the stadium and the tailgate barbecue in the parking lot, there is also an event consisting of *both* the game and the barbecue.)

We can represent this view graphically as follows. Consider Figure 1.

The horizontal axis represents space; the vertical axis represents time; the dots represent particular instantaneous events happening at each time; and the open space on the graph represents **spacetime** itself. The view that times are events would identify the time *t1* with the sum of *everything* that is happening at the *t1* coordinate. So *t1* will include *a* and *b* as parts. If, as many physicists believe, there is stuff going on even in what we ordinarily think of as "empty" space, we could shade in all of the open space on the graph and *t1*

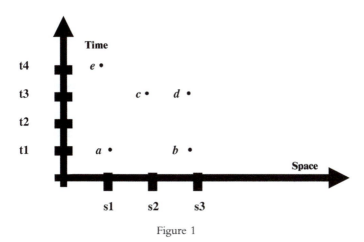

Figure 1

would include those events as well. It will also include other events that are only implicitly represented on the graph, such as the event of *spaces* s1 *and* s2 *being empty* and *a's occurring at such-and-such distance from* b.

Notice that if times are events, it follows that past and future times exist only if past and future events exist. Indeed, it also follows that if the time of your birth exists, then your birth itself exists (since your birth is a part of that time). Likewise, if future times exist, then all of the events that happen at those times exist as well.

Another way of thinking about times is to think of them as abstract states of affairs. Corresponding to every event is a state of affairs that obtains if, and only if, the event is happening. The occurrence of the event, we might say, *is* the obtaining of the state of affairs. (But, again, the event, unlike the state of affairs, exists *only* when the event is happening.) So too, then, with times: Corresponding to each grand event that we have been calling a "concrete time" will be an abstract state of affairs. We might choose to identify the time with the state of affairs rather than with the event.

As we have seen, it is common to think that states of affairs exist necessarily if they exist at all. Given this, treating times as states of affairs settles the question whether past and future times exist. (Of course they do.) But it still leaves open the more interesting question of whether past and future *events* exist.

Finally, one might think of times as *locations*, like points or planes in space. Consider our graph again. The view that times are locations would say one of two things:

1. Times are not to be identified with particular events, or states of affairs, or any other existing thing. Rather, existing *at a time* is a matter of standing in certain "earlier than" and "later than" relationships to other things. So, for example, existing *at t2* is a matter of being a little earlier than *c* and *d*, earlier still than *e*, a little later than *a* and *b*, and so on.
2. There is something in reality that corresponds to the blank paper on which the graph is drawn, a collection of empty "places" where events or the substance of spacetime itself can be inserted. A *time* is a particular region within that collection of empty places, a region like the empty lines demarcated by the labels "*t1*," "*t2*," and so on, on the graph.

I do not wish to advocate here for any particular view about the nature of times. What I do wish to note is that what one thinks about the nature of *time itself* will depend upon which of the aforementioned views one endorses. Likewise, what one thinks about what "past," "present," and "future" refer to will also depend upon what one thinks about times. If times are concrete events, then the past comprises just those grand events that happened prior to the present moment, and time itself is the sum of whatever grand events exist. If times are abstract states of affairs, then time will also be some sort of abstract thing, perhaps a total world history. The past, on this view, will be a partial world history: the state of affairs that includes everything that has ever happened up to the present moment. Likewise for the future.

For the remainder of this book, we will assume that times are concrete events.

PAST, PRESENT, AND FUTURE

Let us begin by considering the "ontological status" of non-present objects and events. Are there such things? On the one hand, it is hard to believe that events in the past and the future—your birth, your death, the age of the dinosaurs—are somehow "just as real" as events in the present. Where, after all, would such things be? On the other hand, it seems obvious that we can *remember, talk about, study*, and stand in all manner of other relations to merely past objects and events. (Some people still remember World War II, for example; others merely study it; I am presently writing a sentence about it.) But, as I noted in the previous chapter, it is hard to see how one can stand in relations to things that do not exist.

Some philosophers believe that there are no merely past or merely future things. They endorse *presentism*, the view that it always has been and always will be the case that whatever exists *presently* exists. Presentism might seem to be a truism. After all, "exists" is a present-tense verb, so *of course* whatever exists presently exists. Merely past things exist*ed*; things lying in the distant future *will* exist. To say that they *do* exist, then, might seem to reflect a failure to understand tense. But to think in this way is to miss the point of the debate between presentists and their rivals. Notice that in explaining why presentism might seem to be a truism, I made free use of expressions like "merely past things" and "things lying in the distant future." From the presentist's point of view, these are not referring expressions. Nothing lies in the distant future, and nothing is merely past. Strictly speaking, then, it is not true (according to a presentist) that merely past things existed, since there is not, never has been, and never will be anything referred to by the description "merely past thing." This, then, is something that presentists and their opponents can disagree about, which goes to show that presentism is not a truism after all.

The denial of presentism is *four-dimensionalism*, which we shall characterize simply as the thesis that presentism is false. Four-dimensionalism is currently the majority view among those writing in the field, in no small part because it is the view that many think fits best with our most successful theories in physics. In particular, most philosophers endorse a version of four-dimensionalism known as *eternalism*, the view that everything that ever did exist or ever will exist *does* exist.

"Scientific people," says the Time Traveler in H. G. Wells's *The Time Machine*, "know very well that Time is only a kind of Space." In the story, this remark comes toward the end of a brief parlor lecture wherein the Time Traveler argues that reality is extended in four dimensions, not three, and that the so-called temporal dimension is *not* fundamentally different from the so-called spatial dimensions. The idea, then, is that the universe is not a three-dimensional spatial volume that "moves" through time from one moment to the next; rather, it is a four-dimensionally extended block whose total volume *includes* its entire history. This is not to say that eternalism is inconsistent with the idea that time somehow passes. If the idea that time passes is itself consistent, then there is no special reason to think that eternalism precludes the passage of time. Rather, the point is that eternalism implies that the universe as a whole doesn't *move through* time; instead, the universe itself has a temporal dimension, just as it has spatial dimensions. (However, relativity theory is typically understood to imply that there are many equally good ways of dividing spacetime into its spatial and temporal dimensions.)

Although eternalism is the most popular version of four-dimensionalism, it is not the only version. Among the other versions are views according to which our universe is a *growing block* or a *shrinking block*. According to the former, only the past and the present exist, and the block of reality continues to grow as new times come into existence and existing times change from being present to being past. According to the latter, only the present and the future exist, and the block of reality continues to shrink as times cease to exist. There are still other varieties as well, but for the remainder of this section we shall leave them all aside. From here on, when I talk about considerations for and against four-dimensionalism, it shall be eternalism that is primarily in view, though readers should bear in mind that many of these considerations will apply equally to the other varieties of four-dimensionalism.

As we have seen, the Time Traveler cited *science* in support of his claim that "Time is only a kind of Space." Interestingly, *The Time Machine* was written in 1895, ten years before the special theory of relativity revolutionized our understanding of space and time. Nevertheless, Einstein's theory lends support to the thesis that space and time as we know them in experience are in fact mere appearances of a more fundamental reality—namely, spacetime. The *locus classicus* for the claim that special relativity supports this latter thesis is H. Minkowski's "Space and Time," which opens with the famous remark that "Henceforth, space by itself, and time by itself, are doomed to fade away into mere shadows, and only a kind of union of the two will preserve an independent reality." General relativity, proposed in 1916, likewise lends support to the thesis that there is no fundamental difference between space and time. Unsurprisingly, then, it is standard for descriptions of the geometry of spacetime to treat past and future events (within a frame of reference) as relevantly like distant places—existing elsewhere, but no less real than events happening here and now.

Some have made stronger claims on behalf of eternalism, arguing that its denial is outright inconsistent with our best scientific theories. These stronger claims, however, are generally regarded as having been discredited. Nevertheless, there are other considerations that speak in favor of eternalism. I shall focus on two.

The first, which I have already mentioned, is the so-called "problem of cross-time relations." It is hard to see how we can refer to and stand in other relations with objects and persons in the past and future unless such things exist. How can I remember my wedding if my wedding does not exist and, therefore, cannot be the object of any memory? How can I admire the bird who struggled so fiercely to escape the clutches of my cat when the bird no longer exists to be an object of my admiration? How can I sensibly think that my present acts can have future consequences if I insist that nothing but *present* events are available to stand in the *is caused by* relation to my actions? Indeed, we can convert these rhetorical questions into straightforward arguments for the existence of past and future objects and events:

3.1 I remember my wedding day, and I admire the bird who struggled with my cat.
3.2 Therefore: There is an x such that I remember x, and x is identical to my wedding day; and there is a y such that I admire y, and y is identical to the bird who struggled with my cat.
3.3 Therefore: My wedding day exists, and the bird who struggled with my cat exists.

From 3.3 and the fact that neither my wedding day nor the bird *now* exist, it follows that at least one merely past event and at least one merely past object exist. Likewise, we can argue for the existence of future events as follows:

3.4 My present acts are causes of events that are not happening now but will happen in the future.

3.5 Therefore: There are events x and y such that x is a present act of mine, y is an event that is not happening now but will happen in the future, and x is a cause of y.

3.6 Therefore: An event that is not happening now but will happen in the future exists.

From 3.6 it follows that there exists at least one merely future event.

One lesson from the first two chapters of this book is that we should be very suspicious of "cheap arguments" like these. True enough, they are straightforward. But, as we have seen, there are arguments like these to be had for the existence of all manner of things that we do not want to believe in. The challenge, then, for those who do not want to believe in past times is to explain why the first premise in each argument is false, or why the second does not follow from the first, or why the third does not follow from the second. I will take these strategies in reverse order, and I will restrict my focus to the first of the two arguments.

To deny the inference from 3.2 to 3.3 is to say that "There is something identical to my wedding day" does not imply that my wedding day exists, and that "There is something identical to the bird who struggled with my cat" does not imply that said bird exists. We have already explored this sort of move in Chapter 2, and there is nothing further to say about it here.

The better option, it seems to me, is to deny that 3.2 follows from 3.1. To do this is to say, in effect, that memory and admiration do not require *objects*. Perhaps what it is to *remember my wedding day* is for me to have a certain kind of mental imagery that stands at the end of a particular causal chain that began on my wedding day. Perhaps what it is for me to admire the bird who struggled with my cat is for me to have feelings of admiration that stand at the end of a causal chain that began with my initial observations of the bird. If all of this is correct, then remembering my wedding day does not involve standing in relations to my wedding day, and so it doesn't require the existence of my wedding day. All it requires is that my wedding day exist*ed*, and that it gave rise to a causal sequence culminating in particular mental imagery that I now have. Likewise for admiration of the bird.

The problem with this reply is that it relies on the possibility of diachronic (cross-time) causation, that is, causation between things existing at two different times. For the reply to work, there needs to be a causal *chain* moving forward in time from my wedding day to my present mental imagery, or from the event of the bird's struggle to my present feelings of admiration. But if such causal chains can exist only if past events exist, then the reply we are considering is useless.

The third alternative, then, is to deny the data: Contrary to appearances, I *do not remember my wedding day*; and, contrary to appearances, I *do not admire the bird*. In light of what has just been said about the second reply, it should be clear that, in the end, proponents of this reply will also have to deny the possibility of diachronic causal relations.

The other primary (nonscientific) motivation for eternalism comes from reflection on the apparent impossibility of temporal passage. On the other hand, reflection on the apparent *experience* of temporal passage provides one of the primary motivations for rejecting a "static" eternalist theory of time in favor of "dynamic" rival theories, like presentism and the growing-block theory. (Dynamic eternalism is also an option, although not a popular one.) I shall take up both of these issues in the next section.

TEMPORAL PASSAGE

In his famous article, "The Myth of Passage," D. C. Williams observes that the "most substantial and incorrigible" motivation for believing in the passage of time is the felt experience of temporal passage:

> It is simply that we *find* passage, that we are immediately and poignantly involved in the jerk and whoosh of process, the felt flow of one movement into the next. Here is the focus of being. Here is the shore whence the youngster watches the golden mornings swing toward him like serried bright breakers from the ocean of the future. Here is the flood on which the oldster wakes in the night to shudder at its swollen black torrent cascading him into the abyss.

Williams himself does not believe that time passes; so, strictly speaking, he should not concede that we *find* passage. For we can find only that which is real. Nor, likewise, should we open debate about the reality of temporal passage with the claim that we *experience* passage. For we can experience only that which is real. Instead, we should follow Laurie Paul's more careful mode of expression and ask not what we ought to believe in light of the experience *of* passage but rather what we ought to believe in light of the experience *as of* passage, thus leaving open the question whether our experience is veridical.

Static eternalism is the thesis that eternalism is true and time does not pass. *Dynamic eternalism* is the thesis that eternalism is true but time does pass—presentness moves along the temporal dimension rather like a spotlight moving along a wall. The question I want to ask now is whether our experience as of passage provides strong evidence that time passes. If it does, then it provides strong evidence against static eternalism.

Philosophical arguments against the reality of temporal passage imply that our experiences as of passage are illusory. It may be hard to give these arguments much credence if we have no independent reason for thinking that we might be susceptible to the illusion of passage and no explanation of how such an illusion might arise. Under such circumstances, one quite naturally weighs the evidence coming from constant experience more heavily than the evidence coming from philosophical intuition. However, Laurie Paul observes that it is already a well-known empirical fact that human beings are *susceptible* to illusions of motion, and she argues that the illusion of passage might arise in a way very similar to that in which some of these other illusions arise. If she is right, then the hypothesis that our temporal experience is illusory is a live option. If it is a live option, then the philosophical arguments against the reality of passage should carry more weight.

There are various well-known perceptual illusions in which subjects have experiences as of motion where in fact there is none (or, at any rate, none of the sort they seem to be experiencing). For example, in a string of lights, where each light is successively turned on and then off, we will have an experience as of the light racing along the string. On a computer monitor, if different dots are rapidly shown in succession in different places along a straight line, we will have an experience as of a dot moving across the screen. Paul also notes that films, time-lapse photography, and flip-books also provide us with illusions of motion. These cases alone suffice to establish the claim that we are susceptible to illusions of motion. And, according to Paul, empirical research on similar cases helps to provide an explanation of how the illusions might arise—an explanation which, she argues, sheds light on how we might have illusory experience as of temporal passage.

According to Paul, empirical research indicates that what happens in these cases is something like the following. *First*, the brain processes our experiences of the relevant static images (successive flashing dots or the pictures on the pages of a flip-book); *then*, afterwards, it mistakenly represents them as a single *continuously moving* image rather than as multiple static images occurring in sequence. If that is right, then the experience as of motion seems not to involve or require the continuous perception of motion; rather, motion can be represented "all at once" in a static brain state that is itself the product of prior sensory processing. So, the illusion of motion can arise in the cases just described precisely because the continuous perception of motion is not required for the representation of motion.

Paul's suggestion, then, is that the illusion of temporal passage might arise in a similar way. Suppose, as many eternalists would maintain, that at every moment *m* of your brain's existence there exists a distinct "brain-stage," a part of your temporally extended brain that exists at, and only at, that single moment *m*. (The idea that there might be temporal stages of four-dimensionally extended material objects like brains will be taken up in more detail in the next chapter.) Then what *might* take place is something like the following: First, a series of brain stages might together realize all of the various steps involved in *processing* sensory input from two discrete times; then another brain stage (or series of brain stages) might mistakenly represent that sensory input as being the product of a moving sequence of events which includes the "jerk and whoosh" of temporal passage.

This is hardly a complete or uncontroversial account of how the illusion of temporal passage might arise. But the availability of this sort of empirically grounded sketch of an explanation makes it difficult simply to dismiss out of hand the idea that our temporal experience might be illusory. It is at this point, then, that philosophical arguments against the possibility of temporal passage come to have real bite.

The problem, in short, is that it is hard to see what temporal passage could possibly amount to. Words like "flow" and "passage" suggest a kind of movement. A very natural thought is that the passage of time is the movement of "presentness" along a timeline— the "moving spotlight" idea mentioned earlier. This is not the only way to think of temporal passage, of course. Indeed, only eternalists could think of it this way, since only eternalists believe in anything remotely like a *timeline* along which presentness might *move*. But, before, introducing the other main way of thinking about temporal passage, let us pause for a moment to reflect on this one.

There is a venerable argument, due to J. M. E. McTaggart, that purports to show that temporal passage construed in the way just described is impossible. To understand McTaggart's argument, it helps to have in hand some of his terminology. A series of events whose members have properties like *being past*, *being present*, and *being future* is called an **A-series**. Accordingly, the properties themselves are commonly called A-properties. A **B-series** is a series of events whose members are ordered by simultaneity and temporal priority (earlier-than and later-than) relations. The relations themselves are commonly called B-relations. Any A-series is also a B-series, but not vice versa.

McTaggart assumed—and most philosophers are willing to grant—that if time exists at all, then time is *at least* a B-series. The question, then, is whether time must also be an A-series. Accordingly, philosophers typically say that an **A-theory of time** is one according to which time, if it exists at all, is both an A-series and a B-series, and a **B-theory of time** is one according to which time, if it exists at all, is just a B-series. McTaggart was an A-theorist. He thought—and argued—that time *cannot* be just a B-series. However, he also thought that an A-series is impossible. His argument for that conclusion is his famous argument against the possibility of temporal passage. If the argument is sound and the A-theory is right, then the ultimate conclusion of his paper is established: Time is unreal.

Simplified a great deal, McTaggart's argument against temporal passage starts like this:

3.7 Suppose (for *reductio ad absurdum*) that an A-series exists.
3.8 If an A-series exists, then events change their A-properties.

3.9 If events change their A-properties, then one of the following is true about *every* event *e*:
   (a) *e is* future and *will be* present, and then past.
   (b) *e is* past and *was* future, and then present.
   (c) *e is* present, *was* future, and *will be* past.

So far so good. But then McTaggart makes a surprising move: He suggests that if 3.9 is true, then *every* event has *every* A-property. Reconstructing the reasoning behind this move has proven to be extraordinarily difficult, but my own view is that McTaggart gets to his conclusion by way of the following assumption:

3.10 For any object x and property ϕ, if x is, was, or will be ϕ, then x is ϕ.

If 3.10 is true, then, for example, if *e will be* past, *e is* past. So if an event *e* is present and will be past, then it is both present and past. If it was future and is present, then it is both present and future. So it follows from 3.8–3.10 that every event *e is* future, *is* present, and *is* past—that is, every event has every A-property. Thus, the argument continues:

3.11 Therefore: If an A-series exists, every event has every A-property (from 3.8–3.10).

Together with 3.7, 3.11 implies that every event has every A-property. But it is obvious that no event can have more than one A-property. Thus, we reach a contradiction, thereby reducing 3.7 to absurdity. So, since the supposition that an A-series exists leads to a contradiction, it cannot be true. An A-series, therefore, is impossible.

The crucial premise in the argument is 3.10. At first glance, the premise seems obviously false. Why think that, in general, if something *was* ϕ, then it *is* ϕ? Beauty fades; so it hardly follows from the fact that someone *was* beautiful that he or she *is* beautiful. Things deteriorate; so it hardly follows from the fact that the building *was* sturdy that it *is* sturdy. Who in their right mind would affirm 3.10?

Answer: an eternalist. Indeed, the premise seems irresistible if one is an eternalist. According to the eternalist, every event that ever did exist or will exist does exist. Notice that the phrase "does exist" is used here in a tenseless way. Nobody would say that merely past or merely future events *presently* exist. But eternalists (and growing-block theorists) still say that they exist. That makes sense only if "exist" can be used in an untensed way. Once we see this, it is much easier to appreciate why the eternalist would affirm 3.10.

For clarity's sake, in the remainder of this section let us signal important tenseless uses of words by formatting them in small capitals. Premise 3.10 should then be rewritten as follows:

3.10 For *any* object x and property φ, if *x* is, was, or will be φ, then x IS φ.

(Other premises will have to be rewritten as well, but let us restrict our focus to 3.10.) We can now understand the eternalist's reasoning as follows. Suppose *e* was present but is now past. Whatever did, does, or will exist EXISTS. So the event *e*'s *being present* EXISTS. But, of course, that event EXISTS only if *e* is present. So, given eternalism, if *e* *was* present, then *e* IS present. But nothing in this reasoning depends on peculiarities about *e*, presentness, or the past tense (as opposed to the future tense). So we can generalize: For *any* object *x* and property φ, if *x* is, was, or will be φ, then *x* IS φ. Hence 3.10 is true.

That is one reason for affirming 3.10. Here is another (related) reason, which does not appeal directly to eternalism but rather rests on a particular analysis of tense. McTaggart seems to think that to say that *x* will be φ is to say that there IS a moment of future time at which the event of *x*'s *being* φ IS happening. Likewise with past-tense claims. But if that is right, then if *e* will be past, *e* IS past; if *e* was future, *e* IS future; and so on.

How might we respond to these defenses of 3.10? One way is to suppose that the "moment of future time" at which *e*'s *being past* occurs is a moment in some other time-like series. Thus, we might say something like this: There are locations, T1 and T2, in another temporal series (call it "hypertime") such that *t1* is the present moment at T1 and *t2* is the present moment at T2 (see Figure 3.2).

The basic idea here is that T1, T2, etc., are coordinates in *another* temporal series and that the "timeline" of our universe exists in its entirety at each of those coordinates, differing at each coordinate

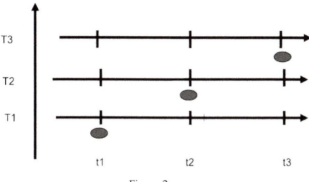

Figure 2

only with respect to which events are present. In Figure 2, the dot represents where *presentness* is located at each hypertime.

On this picture, then, the passage of *time* (i.e., passage within the *t-series*) consists in presentness changing its location on the t-series from one hypertime to the next. In Figure 3.2, for example, it seems true that, at T1, *t1* is present but will be past, whereas at T2, *t1* was present and is past.

This response helps us to see how one might accept McTaggart's analysis of tense without accepting 3.10, but it does so only at the cost of leading us into an infinite regress. To see why, consider this question: Is there such a thing as the *passage of hypertime*? Or is a B-theory true for hypertime? If we affirm a B-theory for hypertime, then it looks as if 3.10 will still be true. Look again at Figure 3.2. Suppose that time passes in the *t*-series but not in the T-series, and suppose we are presently located at T1. Still, if the T-series is a B-series, T2 and T3 EXIST, as does everything that HAPPENS at those times. So our problem remains. On the other hand, if we affirm an A-theory for hypertime, then won't we have to believe in a third time series, hyper-hypertime, in order to make sense of passage in hypertime? An infinite regress looms, which would clearly be a disaster.

My own view is that, given the truth of four-dimensionalism, McTaggart's argument is decisive. If four-dimensionalism is true, time does not pass. One of McTaggart's contemporaries, however, famously disagreed. C. D. Broad, a growing-block theorist, declared

McTaggart's argument to be "a howler." Broad insisted that McTaggart failed to see that temporal passage consists in the *absolute generation of new events*. If he is right about the nature of temporal passage, then McTaggart has indeed made a mistake in analyzing future-tense claims in the way suggested above. But by accepting the growing-block theory, it looks as if Broad has solved, at most, only half of the problem. For the growing-block theorist maintains that past events EXIST. And, if they do, then a suitably modified version of McTaggart's argument will show (absurdly) that every event has *two* A-properties: being past and being present.

So, I think that the objections to 3.10 thus far considered are failures. Astute readers will notice, however, that if 3.10 is true, it is not just change in A-properties that will be problematic but *any change whatsoever*. There is, then, a much more general problem lurking in the neighborhood, and four-dimensionalists will have to find a way to grapple with it.

Ultimately, then, I think that McTaggart's argument is sound under the assumption that four-dimensionalism is true. What this means is that dynamic versions of four-dimensionalism—dynamic eternalism with its moving-spotlight theory of temporal passage, the growing-block theory, the shrinking-block theory, and so on—are unworkable. In light of this, it is easy to see why the *experience* of temporal passage would be taken as evidence in support of presentism. But taking it so presupposes that presentists have a workable reply to McTaggart's argument. Is this correct?

Yes and no. Like Broad, the presentist will say that McTaggart has overlooked the possibility that temporal passage consists in the absolute generation of new times. Unlike Broad, the presentist will *deny* that there is any A-series of events. For presentists do not believe that there *ever* exists a temporally ordered *series* of events at all. Rather, temporal passage consists in the ongoing generation *and destruction* of times. So, interestingly, presentists can accept McTaggart's argument for the conclusion that *there is no A-series*, and they can insist that the whole problem arises out of treating temporal passage as change in the members of a series of events rather than as the ongoing generation and destruction of times.

Be that as it may, presentists are still generally considered A-theorists, and this for two reasons. Firstly, on some ways of thinking about times and events, it does turn out that presentists believe in an A-series. For example, if times are abstract, then every time that ever did or will obtain exists; and those times change their A-properties. Secondly, even if the only A-property, strictly speaking, is *presentness*, it is not unreasonable to think that coming into and passing out of existence are a way for a time to "change" its A-property. And, clearly enough, so long as a presentist accepts 3.10, it will be easy to show that her view is inconsistent with temporal passage. For if presentism is true and time passes, at least one of the following claims must be true about some particular event *e*:

3.12 *e was* present, but *is* not present.
3.13 The proposition that *e* is present *was* true but *is* not true.
3.14 A sentence saying that *e* is present *was* true but is not true.

Any of these claims, however, in conjunction with 3.10 will imply that *e* IS present and that *e* IS not present, which is contradictory. The only non-superficial reply for a presentist to make to the argument, then, is to reject 3.10.

Rejecting 3.10 is a pretty obvious move for a presentist to make in any case. Why would she even consider accepting it? Consider the claim that *e was* present. Unlike the eternalist, the presentist does not believe that the event of *e's being present* EXISTS; so there is no reason for the presentist to think that *e* IS present.

Keep in mind, however, that whatever else a presentist says about McTaggart's argument, she is ultimately committed to the view that events, even times, are continually coming into and passing out of existence. But this is deeply puzzling. What could it possibly mean, given presentism, to say that some particular event, or time, *did* exist or soon *will not* exist? How can we understand the tense in these claims? There seem to be only two options: One is to accept McTaggart's analysis of tense. But we have already seen that this way lie problems. The other option is to say nothing, to insist that tense is sufficiently well understood that no account of it is needed. This is not an incoherent position, but it leaves the phenomenon of temporal passage shrouded in mystery. Those who cannot abide the mystery will see in McTaggart's argument strong evidence for the conclusion that presentism is false and time does not pass.

TIME TRAVEL

Time travel is a staple of contemporary science fiction, and the philosophically puzzling features of time travel are precisely those features that make for the most interesting science-fiction stories. Nothing in contemporary physics seems to rule out the possibility of time travel. Nevertheless, many have thought that philosophical considerations do. In this closing section, I would like to consider and reject three reasons for thinking that time travel is impossible.

The first is related to our discussion about non-present times. Many have thought that presentism is inconsistent with the possibility of time travel. Suppose they are right. If presentism is true, this is a reason to reject the possibility of time travel. Then again, if time travel is possible, this is a reason to reject presentism.

The second concerns the famous "grandfather paradox." It seems clear that nobody can go back in time and kill her own grandfather before her grandfather has had the opportunity to sire children. For if one did do this, one would never come into existence to make the journey. But this is very strange. What would prevent one from doing such a thing? There is no known law of nature that prohibits it. Contrary to what is sometimes presupposed in time-travel fiction, there are no "logic police" running around trying to ensure that time travelers do not bring about incoherent states of affairs. So it looks as if the possibility of time travel implies that there are constraints on the behavior of time travelers that admit of no natural explanation.

The third issue pertains to backward causation. If time travel is possible, then some causes come *after* their effects. (For example, suppose you travel back to 1900 and then think of some events in your own childhood. Those events are among the causes of your mental states in 1900; and yet they will not occur until many years later.) Worse, if time travel is possible, then so are causal loops—causal chains that loop around on themselves, so that some events in the chain lie in their own causal history. But many people think that backward causation and causal loops are impossible. If they are, then time travel is impossible as well.

I shall discuss each of these issues in turn.

The idea that presentism is inconsistent with time travel is intuitively quite compelling. How can one travel to the past if, as presentism affirms, there is no past to which to travel? The argument implicit in this question has been formulated by Simon Keller and Michael Nelson as follows:

3.15 Travel requires a departure point and a destination.
3.16 If presentism is true, there are no destinations for time travel.
3.17 Presentism is true.
3.18 Therefore, time travel is impossible.

Keller and Nelson refer to this argument, appropriately enough, as the "Nowhere Argument."

Our first clue that something may be amiss with this argument should be the fact that even ordinary temporal passage (e.g., the passage of time from your starting this sentence to finishing it) is a kind of "time travel." Says the presentist, there are no future events or times, but there *will* be, and we will somehow manage to make our way from one to the next. If this is true, then the Nowhere Argument is unsound. Still, a presentist might think that time travel to the *past* poses a special problem. The reason is that even if 3.15 is false, the following premise seems quite plausible:

3.19 Travel to a destination *d* is possible only if *d* *will* exist when one arrives.

Moreover:

3.20 Presentism implies that no past time (no time with the property *being past*) *will* exist.

On the supposition that presentism is true, these premises imply that travel to the past is impossible.

Despite its plausibility, I think that there is reason to question 3.19. It makes sense to suppose that travel requires that one's destination *will* exist so long as one is also supposing that travel is a process that carries one forward in time. If we bracket that assumption and allow that some journeys might go backward in time, it is hard to see why we should continue to think that travel requires that the destination *will* exist. Shouldn't we rather say that travel to a location simply requires that the location exist when we arrive? If we do say this, then the revised Nowhere Argument is defused.

So the Nowhere Argument looks unpromising, as Keller and Nelson themselves point out. Moreover, there is a positive argument to be had for the conclusion that time travel is consistent with presentism. The positive argument is this: We can tell stories that are best characterized as time-travel stories but which say nothing that seems to imply the denial of presentism. (Keller and Nelson offer further motivations for thinking that presentists should believe in time travel but this is the only one I will discuss here.)

Consider the following story. Clare has a simple goal: to get rich. Her plan is to make two journeys. One trip will take her to December 1979, about six months after she was born, to make a $10,000 investment in Eaton Vance stock, the top-performing stock between 1979 and 2005, the year when she began work on her time machine. The other trip will take her to 2005 to cash in the stock and put the proceeds in an offshore bank account. (According to the *Eaton Vance Corporation 2004 Annual Report*, her 1979 investment would be worth over $10 million by 2005.) She has very good reason to believe that her journey will be—or has been—successful. In February 2005, while still in graduate school, she received a package which contained (a) all of the paperwork, ostensibly signed by herself only a week before, for the offshore account; (b) a complete explanation of her time-travel journeys and their outcome; and (c) detailed plans for building the time machine in which the journeys would be made. She knew that it could be a hoax; indeed, she suspected as much at first. But as she read through the detailed notes on the time-travel journey, written in her own hand and bearing on every page the unmistakable traces of her very own dry and self-deprecating sense of humor, she was soon a true believer. In short order, she quit her job and withdrew a not inconsequential sum of money from the offshore account to fund what would become an eight-year project of building her time machine according to the specs she had been given. She also began the challenging task of rounding up $10,000 in pre-1979 US currency.

As with most time-travel fiction, this story narrates some events leading up to a time-travel journey, then "follows" the central character through the journey and back to the present. But if such journeys *really happened*, the relevant events would simply unfold in a linear way from the earliest moment in the overall sequence to the latest. Thus, the story (narrated in the present tense) would unfold as follows: At some point in 1979, a woman named "Clare" appears (perhaps in a strange vehicle, or holding an odd-looking device) out of nowhere, carrying a bag filled with $10,000 in 1979 currency. She sets up an investment account in her own name, invests the money, and then disappears. (Meanwhile, elsewhere, there is a little baby named Clare who shares all of her DNA with this mysterious woman.) In February 2005, an extremely similar-looking woman, also named Clare (and with all the same DNA and memories as the one who showed up in 1979), appears out of nowhere and cashes in the investment. She then writes a note to another woman, younger but otherwise very similar, also named Clare, and sharing all of her DNA. She remembers *being* this younger woman and thinks of her as her younger self. The younger woman receives the note, and ... etc. In 2013, a woman named Clare, looking just like the woman who showed up in 1979 and 2005, and sharing all of that woman's DNA, activates a machine that she believes is a time-travel device that will take her back to 1979...

Nothing in the story obviously contradicts presentism; nor, it seems, do we contradict presentism if we *add* to the story the claim that, in fact, the woman who shows up in 1979 is the *same person* as the baby mentioned in the story, the woman who writes the note in 2005, the woman who receives the note in 2005, and the woman who steps into the time machine in 2013. That is, we can assume the story to be a true time-travel story without presupposing that, when 1979 was present, any twenty-first century object or event existed; and we can also assume it to be true without presupposing that events from the year 1979 exist. This is not to say that time-travel stories will always be free of problems. For example, our story implies that adult-Clare and baby-Clare were, in 1979, the *very same person* but, on the other hand, *in different places at the same time*. That seems weird. But problems like this are not peculiar to time-travel stories told under the supposition that presentism is true; rather, they have to be dealt with by *anyone* who believes in time travel.

Presentism all by itself, then, offers no clear reason for rejecting the possibility of time travel. But what about the famous "grandfather paradox"? Imagine that, rather than attempting a journey to 1979 in order to implement a scheme to get rich, Clare sets out on a journey to 1925 (when her grandfather was an infant) on a mission to murder her grandfather before he had the opportunity to sire children. Can she do it? On the one hand, she clearly cannot. If Grandfather is murdered before he sires children, Clare is never born; if she is never born, she never travels to murder him; but, according to our story, she *does* travel to murder him; thus we have a contradiction. On the other hand, if we build enough information into the story, it seems that she clearly *can* murder him. Imagine that she is an elite Navy Seals operative, traveling back to 1925 with the very best equipment that money can buy. She finds her grandfather sound asleep, all alone in a farmhouse in the middle of nowhere, recovering from an accident that has left him almost entirely physically incapacitated. It seems that if anyone can do anything at all, Clare can kill her grandfather. The "paradox," then, is the fact that both claims about what Clare can and cannot do seem equally compelling; yet it seems that only one of them can be true.

David Lewis solves the paradox by denying that only one of the claims can be true. According to Lewis, ability claims are context-sensitive. Relative to what we know about Clare's abilities, equipment, and other conditions, Clare *can* kill her grandfather. Relative to what we know about the total story, including the fact that Grandfather survives to sire one of Clare's parents—Clare *cannot* kill her grandfather. Hold one set of facts firmly in your mind and you will agree that she can; hold the other set of facts firmly in your mind and you will agree that she cannot.

I think that Lewis's response is successful at least to this extent: It shows us that there is no genuine *paradox*, that is, no pair of absolutely contradictory claims that we have equally good reason to affirm. For, as he explains it, the claim that Clare can kill her grandfather doesn't really contradict the claim that she can't. The one claim talks about her abilities relative to one set of facts; the other talks about her abilities relative to another set of facts. However, I do not think that Lewis's response does justice to the depth of the puzzle.

Consider another example from Lewis: I *can* read French (i.e., I have the ability to learn the language). But don't ask me to help you get around the streets of Paris, for I *cannot* read French (i.e., I have no present knowledge of the language). Here too we have context sensitivity in our use of the word "can." But here (and in other such examples where we aren't even tempted to say that we face a paradox) our puzzlement vanishes when we say more clearly what we mean by each of the apparently contradictory ability claims. I lack the necessary skills and knowledge to read French, but I have the right sorts of cognitive capacities, opportunities, and so on to acquire the necessary skills and knowledge. This is not even a little bit puzzling. When we try to do the same in the case of the Grandfather Paradox, however, the puzzle does not disappear. Clare does have the necessary skills and so on to kill Grandfather, and there are no obstacles to her doing so. But it is impossible that she do so. *This fact is what is puzzling.*

The problem, fundamentally, is that we seem to be confronted with a brute (unexplained) physical impossibility, and one which seems, oddly, to involve just a single individual. Of course, in one sense there is an explanation: A scenario in which someone kills her own, actual grandfather before he sires children is absolutely metaphysically impossible; if Clare were to kill this man, her actual grandfather, she would be in such a scenario; therefore, it is impossible that Clare kill this man. The trouble is that absolutely none of the other *indicators* of impossibility is present in the scenario. It seems that anyone else in the same position as Clare *could have* killed her grandfather. What, then, is so special about Clare?

In reply, there seem to be two ways to go, short of trying to rest content with the absence of further explanation. One way is to try to dissolve the puzzle by arguing that not only is Clare unable to kill Grandfather but *no one* would have been able to do so. This solves the problem by showing that the impossibility in question is "principled"; it is not confined to just one individual. The other way is to try to show that the alleged impossibility is not genuine: that, in fact, the past can be changed and Grandfather can be killed, even by Clare. My own preference is to go the first route, arguing that, between the earliest arrival point and latest departure point of a time-travel journey, nobody is free. Others prefer the second route. For purposes here, we shall rest content having identified the two routes and will move on to the next topic.

So, leaving the Grandfather Paradox, we come at last to the question of backward causation and causal loops. A causal loop is a series of events such that each event in the series lies in its own causal history: Each event in a loop helps to cause *itself*. Indeed, some of the most interesting time-travel stories present us with *objects* whose very existence is loopy. The object has no beginning in time and no end, and each "stage" of the object's career lies in its own causal history.

In Robert Silverberg's "Absolutely Inflexible," for example, we find a time machine whose entire career is a causal loop. In the story, a time machine is given to Mahler, the story's protagonist, by a time traveler who has been taken prisoner and put in a space suit for purposes of contamination avoidance. The time traveler seems to recognize him, but Mahler cannot identify the time traveler, in part because his visage is obscured by the helmet of the space suit. In short order, Mahler initiates a time-travel journey during which he receives a severe beating, and at the end of which he is returned to a time shortly before the time when he was given the time machine. Upon his return, he is taken prisoner, put into a space suit so as to prevent him from contaminating others with any germs he might be carrying, and dragged before the magistrate . . . himself, to whom he gives the time machine. The *machine itself* has no life outside of this sequence of events. It is given to Mahler and taken on a journey which ends precisely where it started, with its being given to Mahler. It has no origin and no end. It exists in a causal loop.

Causal loops are deeply puzzling; many think that they are impossible. Some think that they are impossible because backward causation in general is impossible. But (unrestricted) time travel to the past is possible only if both backward causation *and* causal loops are possible. If you can travel to the past, and if there are no restrictions on where you can go in the past, then you can travel to places and times that allow you to do things that lie in the causal history of your own time-travel journey. In such a case, every event in the journey will lie in its own causal history, and so some effects will be temporally prior to their causes.

Are causal loops, or backward causation more generally, impossible? Here I shall consider just two arguments for the conclusion that they are. The first is a direct attack on the possibility of backward causation and rules out causal loops simply because the latter are possible only if the former is. (The argument is due to D. H. Mellor. The example that follows is not quite Mellor's; it is an adaptation of Mellor's which incorporates elements from Ted

Chiang's science-fiction story, "What's Expected of Us.") The second is an argument due to Aaron Segal and rules out causal loops alone on the grounds that their existence is conceptually impossible.

Suppose I have a device in my office that (I claim) sends a signal, at the press of a button, one hour into the past to another device in the fire pit in my backyard, one that produces a spark that will ignite whatever fuel I have stacked up on the grate in my fire pit. I demonstrate my device as follows: First, I load up the grate with wood and a bit of gasoline. We then watch for a few moments, and, lo and behold, the device ignites the fire. Let the ignition time be t. A short time later, we take a walk to my office, wait until exactly one hour past t, and I press the button. Thus my demonstration. Will you be convinced?

According to Mellor, the button-pressing event can be a cause of the earlier fire only if there is a non-coincidental, non-artificial positive correlation between the pushing of the button at one time and the igniter's emitting a spark one hour earlier. But, he says, it is *impossible* that there be any such correlation. Why, we might ask? Notably, Mellor does not demonstrate the impossibility. Rather, he simply invites us to imagine trying to test for such a correlation. As he imagines it, we would *always* be able to falsify the correlation. That is, we would always be able to act so as to make it the case that the correlation does not hold. Suppose we load up the grate with fuel and we watch as a fire starts at noon. Instead of walking to the office and pushing the button, we could set out to falsify the correlation and simply stay home from the office. Or, in an effort to be more thorough, we could go to the office and stand guard outside to ensure that no one pushes the button at 1 P.M. Or we could rush to the office and push the button repeatedly before noon and then destroy it before 1 P.M. Or... it seems there are all manner of things we could do to try to falsify the correlation.

Not every case of backwards causation would be so easily tested, and Mellor has given no argument for the claim that unfalsified claims of backward causal correlations could not possibly be true. Still, I take it that his general idea is this: In cases we would know how to investigate, falsification is easy—absurdly easy. This fact by itself gives us reason to believe that the necessary correlations are impossible.

But not so fast. Consider again the claim that, in the cases we would know how to investigate, *falsification is easy*. What evidence, really, do we have that this is true? None, it seems, apart from (a) the fact that we have never observed the right sort of correlation between future causes and past effects, and (b) the *assumption* that, in fact, there simply could not be any such correlation. If we set aside (b), it is hard to see why we should agree that, of necessity, it would be easy to falsify *any* alleged backward causal correlation. Indeed, it is not hard to imagine having real trouble falsifying some such correlation. Suppose that every time we make, and carry out, a definite plan to go push the button at 1 P.M., a fire starts at noon. Every time we post guards outside the door, no fire starts. Occasionally, we observe a fire to start in the absence of any plan on our part, and we find, invariably, that the button is pushed at 1 P.M.—perhaps by a maintenance worker, or inadvertently by us. We rig up a device to drop a weight onto the button at random intervals and to record each time the weight is dropped; we set video cameras on the fire pit, post sentries around the pit and on the office door, and then wait—only to discover, once we check our video and our office records, that multiple fires started throughout the day exactly one hour before the weight was dropped onto the button. And so on. Obviously the fact that we can imagine all of this does not establish that backward causation is possible, but it does serve to undermine key premises in Mellor's argument for the conclusion that it is impossible.

What about causal loops? There can be no doubt that causal loops—and especially object loops (objects whose entire history consists in a causal loop)—are highly improbable. Consider Mahler's time machine, for example. Suppose that when Mahler receives it from himself, it is in pristine condition—not even a scratch—and is composed of certain particles. Between the time Mahler receives it from himself and the time when he hands it over to himself, whatever happens to the time machine in terms of nicks, scratches, minor alterations in its composition, and so on will have to be undone. If it is scratched on the time-travel journey, the scratch will have to be removed by the journey's end. If, as he touches the machine, certain particles are sloughed off, *those very particles* will have to be put back *in precisely the locations they were in when Mahler received the machine* by the journey's end. Massive improbability indeed! But so far this is no reason to think that causal loops are impossible.

Still, there is the following conceptual problem. The causal relation is commonly taken to be **irreflexive** and **transitive**. To say that it is irreflexive is to say that nothing is a cause of itself: For any event *e*, *e* itself is not among the causes of *e*. To say that it is transitive is to say that if *e1* is a cause of *e2* and *e2* is a cause of *e3*, then *e1* is a cause of *e3*. But if both of these things are true of the causal relation, then causal loops are impossible. Again, a causal loop is a casual chain in which at least one of the events in the chain lies in its own causal history. So, for example, suppose we have a causal chain such that *e1* causes *e2*, which causes *e3*, which causes *e4*, which causes *e1*. By transitivity, it follows that *e1* is a cause of *e1*, which violates irreflexivity. So argues Aaron Segal.

How serious is this problem for those of us who would like to believe in the possibility of causal loops? Ultimately, I think that it is not serious at all. Self-causation is surely rare, surely improbable, but I see no reason to think that it is ruled out by the very concept of a cause. Although the world of fiction is filled with impossible stories, stories that straightforwardly violate *conceptual* truths are rare, and they would, in any case, strike us immediately as incoherent. (Just imagine trying to get your mind around a romance story in which a woman has an affair with a married bachelor.) But time-travel stories that incorporate causal loops are ubiquitous; and, though some are manifestly incoherent, not nearly all of them strike us this way. This is very surprising if our concept of causation rules out causal loops in the way that our concept of bachelorhood rules out the possibility of married or female bachelors. Although this is not proof that the objectors are incorrect, it at least provides grounds for insisting that they argue, rather than merely assert, that "our" concept of causation includes transitivity and irreflexivity. So far as I am aware, no convincing argument for this conclusion has yet been given.

FURTHER READING

The opening quotation from St. Augustine's *Confessions* comes from the translation in Arthur Hyman, James J. Walsh, and Thomas Williams, eds., *Philosophy in the Middle Ages: The Christian, Islamic, and Jewish Traditions*, 3rd edn. (Indianapolis, IN: Hackett Publishing Company, 2010).

On the question whether merely past or merely future times exist, see Thomas M. Crisp's "Presentism" and my own "Four-Dimensionalism," both in Michael J. Loux and Dean W. Zimmerman, eds., *The Oxford Handbook of Metaphysics* (Oxford: Oxford University Press, 2003), pp. 211–245 and 246–280. Both handbook articles contain copious further references to the literature on presentism and four-dimensionalism. The Time Traveler's speech from H. G. Wells's *The Time Machine* is reprinted in *Arguing about Metaphysics*, along with excerpts from Alan Lightman's provocative *Einstein's Dreams*. For H. Minkowski's comments about the relationship between space and time (quoted earlier in the chapter), see his "Space and Time," in *The Principle of Relativity*, ed. H. A. Lorentz et al. (New York: Dover, 1908), pp. 73–91. For an important recent challenge to the idea that debates like this one can be settled by appeal to physics, see Bradley Monton, "Prolegomena to Any Future Physics-Based Metaphysics," *Oxford Studies in Philosophy of Religion*, vol. 3 (2011), pp. 142–65.

On the passage of time, two classic articles are D. C. Williams, "The Myth of Passage," reprinted in *Arguing about Metaphysics*; and J. M. E. McTaggart, "The Unreality of Time," *Mind*, vol. 17 (1908), pp. 457–474. Paul Horwich's "The Metaphysics of Now," reprinted in *Arguing about Metaphysics*, presents a reconstruction of McTaggart's argument. C. D. Broad's reply to McTaggart's argument is in the section entitled "McTaggart on the Unreality of Time," in his *Examination of McTaggart's Philosophy* (Cambridge: Cambridge University Press, 1938), vol. II, part 1. The article by L. A. Paul on temporal experience that I discussed at some length is her "Temporal Experience," *Journal of Philosophy*, vol. 107 (2010), pp. 333–359. (The quotation from Williams that I used is from pp. 335–356 of her article.)

On the subject of time travel, David Lewis's "The Paradoxes of Time Travel," *American Philosophical Quarterly*, vol. 13 (1976), pp. 145–152, is an absolute must-read. I also referred to S. Keller and M. Nelson, "Presentists Should Believe in Time-Travel," *Australasian Journal of Philosophy*, vol. 79 (2001), pp. 333–345. *Arguing about Metaphysics* reprints a couple of excellent short stories that illustrate the idea of a causal loop: Robert Heinlein's

"—All You Zombies—" and Robert Silverberg's "Absolutely Inflexible." I also mentioned Ted Chiang's story, "What's Expected of Us," which is also reprinted there. D. H. Mellor's argument against causal loops is to be found in his *Real Time II* (London and New York: Routledge, 1998). Also on causal loops, see Aaron Segal, "Half-hearted Humeanism," *Oxford Studies in Metaphysics*, vol. 9 (forthcoming), and Richard Hanley, "No End in Sight: Causal Loops in Philosophy, Physics and Fiction," *Synthese*, vol. 141 (2004), pp. 123–152. Hanley defends at length the idea that causal loops are merely improbable, not impossible. On changing the past, see Peter van Inwagen, "Changing the Past," *Oxford Studies in Metaphysics*, vol. 5 (2010), pp. 3–28, and the reply by Hud Hudson and Ryan Wasserman, "Van Inwagen on Time Travel and Changing the Past," *Oxford Studies in Metaphysics*, vol. 5 (2010), pp. 41–49. My own view that nobody is free between the earliest arrival point and the latest departure point of a time-travel journey is defended in my "Time Travellers Are Not Free" (forthcoming).

CHANGE AND IDENTITY

Central to our commonsense view of the world is the idea that familiar objects can persist through a wide variety of changes. People grow up; trees drop their leaves in the fall and have them restored in the spring; caterpillars become butterflies. But no matter how obvious—indeed, trite—such claims might seem, the phenomenon of change is fraught with serious difficulties.

In this chapter, we take up four of the most important and apparently intractable arguments against change and identity over time that have occupied philosophers for the past two millennia. We begin with an argument against the reality of change that is due to the pre-Socratic Greek philosopher Parmenides, followed by three arguments against the reality of motion that were given by his famous disciple, Zeno. The arguments of these philosophers exerted a powerful influence on the shape of Western philosophy. Many in their wake were captivated by the idea that the changing world of sensory experience is but a mere shadow or reflection of a more fundamental, more deeply real world of *unchanging* things. Next, we discuss a contemporary argument for the claim that no object can change its **intrinsic properties**. Thirdly, we discuss a family of puzzles that crop up under the assumption that different kinds of things can survive different kinds of changes in their *parts*. Finally, we focus on the special problems that arise when we consider how *persons* can survive changes in their properties or parts.

PARMENIDES ON CHANGE

Parmenides of Elea, who lived during the sixth and fifth centuries BCE, is generally regarded as the most important and influential of the pre-Socratic philosophers. His philosophical views were articulated in a poem, large fragments of which have been preserved through the writings of other philosophers. In the poem, Parmenides describes his journey to meet a goddess who reveals to him two paths of inquiry: the Way of Truth and the Way of Mortal Opinion. Those who follow the latter fall into all manner of "erroneous" beliefs that most of us would regard as plain common sense: The world is filled with many different things, these things come into existence and pass out of existence, they change, they move, and so on. On the Way of Truth, however, one finds arguments for the conclusion that all of these commonsense beliefs are mere illusions. Parmenides endorsed a version of what is now known as "Eleatic Monism," the view that there exists exactly one thing that is ungenerated (it did not come into existence), indestructible (it cannot go out of existence), does not change or move, and is undivided in time and space (it has no spatial gaps or holes within itself, and there are no gaps between the times at which it exists either). Parmenides' monistic worldview was developed and defended by his followers, especially Zeno and Melissus. Our concern in this section is with the arguments against change and motion.

Parmenides held that whatever exists is wholly unchanging. His defense of this view rests on the idea that *non*existence is unintelligible. According to Parmenides, it is impossible to talk about or even to think about what does not exist. The reason, presumably, is that what does not exist is not available to be an object of thought or discourse. Thus, what does not exist cannot be an object of inquiry; nor can it be referred to by the subject term of any sentence. But then it looks as if nonexistence claims—claims like "Santa Claus does not exist"—cannot possibly be true. This is the first major step in his argument against change.

The next step should be easy to guess: Generation and destruction involve nonexistence. Suppose that Parmenides himself came into existence at some time. This supposition pretty obviously implies that there once was a time when Parmenides did not exist. But, if Parmenides is right, the proposition that *Parmenides does not exist* cannot possibly be true. Thus, the supposition that there once was a time when Parmenides did not exist must be false. Thus, Parmenides is ungenerated. Similar reasoning rules out the possibility of Parmenides passing out of existence; thus, he cannot be destroyed.

Parmenides seems to have thought that all change involves generation and destruction. Suppose that Parmenides stands up. This change in Parmenides occurs when the event *Parmenides standing* is generated and the event *Parmenides sitting* is destroyed. Likewise, Parmenides changes from not cheering to cheering when the event *Parmenides cheering* is generated and the event *Parmenides standing quietly* is destroyed. But generation and destruction are impossible. Thus, these changes cannot possibly occur. Likewise for any change whatsoever.

Parmenides' arguments rest on the thesis that nonexistence claims cannot be true. In Chapter 2, we discussed some of the main reasons one might have for endorsing this thesis, along with the major strategies for resisting it. To recap briefly: Suppose we say that Pegasus does not exist. This seems to imply that *there is something that does not exist*. But, assuming *being* and *existence* are the same thing, this latter claim is self-contradictory. One way to avoid the contradiction is to admit that Pegasus exists. Another is to sever the link between being and existence. A third is to reinterpret the claim that Pegasus does not exist as saying something like *nothing Pegasizes*. There are other solutions in the contemporary literature as well, most exploring the semantics of "empty names" (names that seem not to refer to anything). By and large, these solutions can be seen as instances of the "reinterpretation" strategy. Importantly, however, none of these solutions has immediate intuitive appeal. The basic problem that Parmenides has handed down to us is a formidable one.

Zeno of Elea lived in the fifth century BCE and has passed on to us a variety of puzzles aimed at defending various theses of Eleatic monism. Here we shall focus on three of his paradoxes aimed at demonstrating the impossibility of motion. Zeno did not deny the *appearance* of motion. His point was simply that the appearance is misleading: Ultimate reality does not include motion.

Whereas Parmenides' arguments traded on the unintelligibility of nonexistence, Zeno's exploit the puzzling nature of the infinite. Zeno assumes that space and time are continuous: They are composed of unextended points or, in the case of time, instants, and between any two points or instants there are infinitely many other points or instants. The main idea underlying the first two paradoxes is that motion from point A to point B requires that the mover first touch the midpoint between A and B. The main idea underlying the third paradox is that nothing is in motion at an instant.

With this in mind, consider first the Traveler Paradox. Suppose that in a finite period of time T, Frodo travels a finite distance (from the Shire to Rivendell). Before reaching Rivendell, Frodo will have to reach the midpoint between the Shire and Rivendell (Weathertop); and before reaching Weathertop, Frodo will have to reach the midpoint between the Shire and Weathertop (somewhere outside of Bree); and . . . *ad infinitum.* So there will be an infinity of midpoints that Frodo will have to reach before he gets to any particular destination. But it is impossible to reach an infinite number of points in a finite period of time. So, in general, motion is impossible.

It may be tempting to respond by saying that the argument falsely presupposes that Frodo would have to *touch* every point along his path between the Shire and Rivendell in order to get to Rivendell. But, small as he is, Frodo is too big to do that. He won't touch every point; he will merely "cross" every point—which, one might think, is less problematic. But we can reframe the problem as follows. Consider a cube sliding across a desk. As the cube slides, so does the two-dimensional surface. Presumably the two-dimensional surface is of the right size to "touch" literally every point along the distance from one end of the desk to the other. But, of course, the surface can't do that.

The Paradox of Achilles and the Tortoise is similar: In order for the faster runner to catch the slower runner, the faster runner must first reach the point from which the slower runner started. But by the time Achilles gets to the tortoise's starting point (call it S1), the tortoise will have moved on to a new "starting point" (S2). So now, once he has reached S1, Achilles can catch the tortoise only if he first reaches S2—by which point the tortoise will again have moved on to a new starting point (S3)—and so on, *ad infinitum.*

As with the Traveler Paradox, the Paradox of Achilles and the Tortoise exploits the apparent fact that some tasks are such that, in order to perform them, one must be able to perform what contemporary philosophers and mathematicians call a *supertask*. In his *Stanford Encyclopedia of Philosophy* article on supertasks, J. P. Laraudogoitia defines a supertask as "an infinite sequence of actions or operations carried out in a finite interval of time." Some believe that supertasks are impossible and deny the apparent fact that we would have to be able to perform them in order to move from one point to another; others believe that they are possible and provide explanations as to how they might be so.

The third puzzle about motion handed down to us from Zeno is the Paradox of the Arrow. This one trades on the continuity of time rather than the continuity of space. Begin by considering the world at an instant (i.e., a point in time). Nothing moves at an instant: Motion takes place over time. Now, consider a flying arrow. Since nothing moves at an instant, it seems that, at every instant at which it exists, the arrow will have to be stationary. But if the arrow is stationary at every instant of its existence, it is not moving—and so it is not flying. Hence our paradox. Unlike the other two paradoxes, this one arises out of the fairly intuitive idea that a dynamic universe cannot be built from merely static instants. Solving the paradox in a satisfying way thus requires us either to deny that time is continuous or to arrive at an understanding of motion that helps us to see how *being in motion* is a property that something like an arrow can have even at an instant.

THE PROBLEM OF TEMPORARY INTRINSICS

Eleatic arguments against change and motion gripped the ancient world and exerted heavy influence on subsequent metaphysical theorizing. But they are hardly the only puzzles about change with which a metaphysician must contend. Another puzzle, one which has garnered a great deal of attention in the contemporary philosophical literature, is the so-called "problem of temporary intrinsics," a puzzle that raises difficult questions about the possibility of intrinsic change.

Intrinsic properties are attributes which something can have regardless of what the rest of the world is like. For example, *being bipedal* is intrinsic, because having it depends only on how one's own parts are arranged and not on what anything outside of one happens to be like. *Being married* or *being the only biped in the world* are not intrinsic, because having those properties depends to some extent on what the rest of the world is like. Being married requires the existence of someone else, and it requires furthermore that you have a particular sort of relationship to that person. Being the only biped requires the nonexistence of other bipeds.

With this in mind, consider an ordinary case of intrinsic change: Homer is sitting at *t1*, and so at that time has a *bent* shape. He stands up at *t2*, and so at that time has a *straight* shape. We can begin to see the problem by considering a spatial analogy. Think of places like the Notre Dame football stadium, the White House, or the Redondo Beach pier. If Homer is sitting in the Notre Dame football stadium, then Homer is sitting, period. If Homer's sitting is part of an event that we might describe as *everything happening at the Redondo Beach pier*, then Homer is sitting, period. In general, what occurs *at a place* occurs, period. Why should times be any different? But if we say that matters are not different in the case of times, then we will endorse the view that whatever occurs *at a time* occurs, period. So if Homer is bent at *t1*, then Homer is bent, period. And if Homer is straight at *t2*, then Homer is straight, period. But now we have our problem. Our principle, together with the supposition that Homer changes, has led us to affirm that Homer is both bent and straight, period—which is impossible.

The idea that what occurs at a place occurs, *period*, can be formulated more generally and precisely as follows:

4.1. For any x and t, if x is Φ at t, then x is Φ.

We discussed a similar principle (3.10) in Chapter 3. (Note that I have not reinstituted the policy of formatting tenseless uses of verbs in small capitals. I assume that by now context should make it clear when that is intended.) When we discussed 3.10, we saw that eternalists have persuasive reasons for accepting it, whereas presentists do not. The same is true here, and for similar reasons. Suppose x is Φ at t. Eternalism implies that x exists and t exists; so it seems also to imply that the event x's being Φ exists. But if x's being Φ exists, x is Φ. To say otherwise makes no sense. So if eternalism is true, 4.1 is true. Similar reasoning will show that other versions of four-dimensionalism imply somewhat modified versions of 4.1, but to simplify our discussion we shall leave those aside and focus our attention on (static) eternalism as the most viable brand of four-dimensionalism.

Whereas eternalists are committed to 4.1, presentists can reject it. They will sensibly interpret the claim that x is Φ at t as an imprecise way of saying either that x was Φ when t was present or that x will be Φ when t is present (depending on whether t is supposed to be a past or a future time). Interpreted that way, 4.1 is virtually equivalent to 3.10, which, as we saw in Chapter 3, presentists have good reason to reject. So endorsing presentism is one way of solving the problem of temporary intrinsics. Since we have already discussed presentism in some detail in Chapter 3, I shall not say anything further about it here. Instead, I shall focus on three of the most promising four-dimensionalist strategies for solving the problem.

Solution 1: Time-indexed Properties. In raising the problem, we assumed that change involves having properties like *bentness* and *straightness* only *temporarily*. One way to solve the problem is to deny this assumption and to say instead that change involves *permanently* having properties like *bentness-at-t1* and *straightness-at-t2*. These latter two properties are time-indexed properties. What does the time-indexing *mean*? It signals that the property is had *only in relation to the time*. The difference between saying that Homer is (untensed) *bent-at-t1* and Homer is (untensed) *bent* is like the difference between saying that jogging is pleasant-for-me and saying that it is just plain pleasant. The former says only that its pleasantness applies to me; the latter suggests that it is pleasant for absolutely everyone. (Usually, if one says "Jogging is pleasant," the index to the speaker is understood as implied. So, to appreciate the force of the example, imagine someone who says "Jogging is pleasant—no, I don't just mean that it is pleasant *for me*; I mean that it is absolutely, objectively pleasant!")

So, according to the proponent of this solution, in our initial setup of the problem we were not as clear as we could have been. Instead of saying simply that Homer is bent at *t1* and straight at *t2*, we should have said the following:

4.2 Homer is *bent-at-t1*.
4.3 Homer is *straight-at-t2*.

Furthermore, 4.1 is not as clear as it could be either. It should be recast as follows:

4.1★ For any x and t, if x is Φ-at-t, then x is Φ.

But once we have done all of this, we can see two things. Firstly, there is no contradiction in affirming both 4.2 and 4.3. Secondly, given how we are understanding the time indexing, 4.1★ is false. (4.1★ is analogous to the claim that, for any x and p, if x is pleasant-for-p, then x is absolutely pleasant.) One cost to this solution is the apparent loss of properties like *bentness* and *straightness*. Another potential cost is the fact that change no longer appears to be a "dynamic" phenomenon. Objects change, oddly enough, without ever gaining or losing any of their actual properties.

Solution 2: Time-indexed Property-Having. Just as we might index the properties that objects have, so too we might index the *having*, or *exemplifying*, itself. Suppose that Homer *is* bent. Typically, the italicized term is taken to express the link—property exemplification—between Homer and the property *bentness*; and, typically, this link is understood to involve no reference or relationship to particular times. But one might suppose that this typical understanding is mistaken. Perhaps, for example, there are a great many links between objects and their properties—one for every time. On this way of thinking, it is again never the case that Homer simply *exemplifies* bentness (unless by that we mean that he is now bent or is always bent). Rather, he *exemplifies-at-t1* bentness, or *exemplifies-at-t2* bentness, or . . . and so on. There are other ways in which one might try to "index the having"; but we shall focus only on this one.

Indexing property exemplification in this way solves our problem in a way similar to that in which property indexing solved it. It implies that neither the initial setup nor 4.1 was sufficiently clear and suggests revisions as follows:

4.4 Homer is-*at-t1* bent.
4.5 Homer is-*at-t2* straight.

4.1★★ For any *x* and *t*, if *x* is-at-*t* Φ, then *x* is Φ.

As before, once we have made our revisions, we can see both that 4.4 and 4.5 are consistent with one another and that 4.1★★ is false. The costs to this solution, however, are somewhat different. It is less clear that the dynamic nature of change is lost; nor do we lose properties like *bentness* and *straightness*. However, we do end up believing in a great multiplicity of different links between objects and properties where initially we thought that there was only one. Objects do not simply *have* their properties; rather, they are connected with their properties in a more complicated way that involves times. This is puzzling to say the least and so might well lead one to look for a better solution.

Solution 3: Temporal Parts. Consider the statement, "x is Φ." So far we have tried solving our problem by indexing the property (Φ) and by indexing the copula ("is"). There is one strategy left to try: indexing the subject ("*x*"). This solution is probably the most popular of the four. It comes in at least two versions, but for simplicity we will focus on the more widely discussed of the two: the doctrine of temporal parts.

Suppose you have a road that is bumpy for a stretch and then becomes smooth. The road is bumpy; the road is smooth; but nothing is both bumpy and smooth. Contradiction? Hardly. We dissolve this pseudo-problem by noting that the road is bumpy by virtue of having a *part* that is bumpy, and it is smooth by virtue of having a *different part* that is smooth. So likewise, we might say, in the case of change over time. Just as a road "changes" across space by having different parts in different locations with different properties, so too Homer changes over time by having different parts at different times with different properties.

At first this might sound puzzling. Homer is seated at *t1*, standing at *t2*. In what sense does this change involve *different parts*? Here we must distinguish between an object's *spatial parts* and its *temporal parts*. A spatial part of an object at a time is something that exists just at that time and completely occupies only *some* of the region that the object itself occupies. So, for example, your hand right now is a spatial part of you right now: It completely occupies some but not all of the region occupied by you right now. By contrast, a temporal part of an object *x* is something that completely occupies *all* of the spatial regions occupied by *x* during just *some* of the time that *x* exists. So, for example, there is a temporal part of you that includes all of the years between your birth and age five, another part that covers ages five to ten, another that covers the time you have spent today reading this book, and so on. So too with Homer. He has a seated temporal part at *t1* and a standing temporal part at *t2*. That is the sense in which Homer's change from sitting to standing involves different parts.

As with the other indexing solutions, the doctrine of temporal parts (DTP) suggests revisions both to the initial setup of our problem and to 4.1. The advocate of DTP will recast the crucial claims as follows:

4.6 Homer-*at-t1* is bent.
4.7 Homer-*at-t2* is straight.
4.1★★★ For any *x* and *t*, if *x*-at-*t* is Φ, then *x* is Φ.

Homer-*at-t1* and Homer-*at-t1* are both temporal parts of Homer: his *t1* temporal part and his *t2* temporal part, respectively. Since different temporal parts of a thing are different objects, there is no problem with them having different properties. So there is no contradiction in affirming both 4.6 and 4.7. And 4.1★★★ is clearly false. Given DTP, it does not follow from the fact that one of a thing's temporal parts is Φ that the thing itself is (untensed) Φ.

DTP is a view that many philosophers accept for a variety of reasons, not just because it provides a response to the problem of temporary intrinsics. It is, indeed, one of the two main theories about what it means for an object to last over time. The core idea is that objects persist by being *extended* in time in much the same way as they are extended in space. This mode of persistence has been dubbed "perdurance," and so DTP is sometimes referred to in the literature by the label "perdurantism." The contrasting view, *endurantism*, maintains that objects persist by being *wholly present* at every moment at which they exist.

Perdurantism helps to solve a variety of puzzles. We have already seen how it solves the problem of temporary intrinsics. As we shall see in the next section, it also affords a solution to some of the so-called **material constitution** puzzles. More importantly, it is the theory of persistence that seems to fit most naturally with the ever-popular eternalist theory of time.

As we have seen, eternalism implies that time is "extended" in a way that blurs the alleged differences between time and space. Moreover, relativity theory suggests that space and time themselves might be mere appearances of a more fundamental reality—namely, *spacetime*. (Spatial distances and temporal durations vary among different observers depending on how fast they are moving in relation to one another, whereas *spacetime intervals* do not vary in this way.) In light of all this, it is natural for eternalists to think of a persisting material object as nothing more or less than the material content of an extended region of spacetime. Thus, it is likewise natural to view the object itself as extended in spacetime, divided, like a loaf of bread, into numerically distinct slices at each moment along its career (as well as a wide variety of thicker slices that are themselves composed of thinner ones). In other words, it is natural to suppose that persisting objects perdure. Indeed, to suppose that such objects *endure* might seem downright bizarre. For on the endurantist–eternalist picture, a persisting thing is akin to a loaf of bread that has been divided into *numerically identical* slices along its length, so that there is just one slice existing in many different places and stuck together to form the whole extended loaf. As it happens, I still prefer the endurantist–eternalist combination. But it is easy to see the attraction, under eternalist assumptions, of the perdurantist view.

Why would anyone accept the combination of endurantism and eternalism? I have already given reasons for accepting eternalism in Chapter 3. So here I will focus on reasons for accepting endurantism. There are three worth highlighting.

The first is simply that endurantism seems to be the commonsense view. It's what we tend to believe before we are corrupted by the study of metaphysics. I remember being too small to go on some of the exciting rides at Disneyland, and it seems to me that the boy-shaped object that was too small to go on those rides is *identical* to the man-shaped object that is plenty tall enough to go on them now. I have no temptation to think that the boy-shaped object and the man-shaped object are mere (temporal) parts of some larger, temporally extended object. Perhaps you will have similar thoughts about yourself. If so, then you have at least one reason—even if only a weak and defeasible reason—to accept endurantism.

Second: Consider Frank Abagnale, Jr., a security consultant famous for his early exploits as a grifter, check-forger, and impostor. (His life provided inspiration for the 2002 film *Catch Me if You Can*.) Most of Abagnale's crimes were committed before he was thirty, and most were never prosecuted. Suppose we try to rectify this. We bring him to trial, but he offers the following defense:

> Perdurantism is true—just consider the problem of temporary intrinsics if you need to be convinced. But if perdurantism is true, then—in a deep twist of irony—the individual sitting before you now is yet another impostor! The crimes you wish to try were committed by another man (or *men*)—a motley composite of individuals comprising the "first-thirty-years" temporal part of the man named Frank Abagnale, Jr. But *I am not that man*. More carefully: I am certainly not the "first-thirty-years" temporal part; for I exist now, and he existed only then. (Nor am I any part of that man, for the same reason.) Perhaps you will say that I am the four-dimensionally extended Mr. Abagnale. I am not so sure about that. He and I occupy the same space right now. How do you know that it is him talking rather than his temporal part (me)? But even *if* I am Mr. Abagnale, I committed those crimes only by virtue of having that other man—the "first thirty years" man—as a part. But it is not up to *me* what temporal parts I have! I came into this world with him as a part as surely as I came into the world with hands and feet among my parts. My hands and my feet I can cut off, but I can't even cut off my "first thirty years" temporal part. Will you condemn and punish me, then, for something so utterly beyond my control? In the name of justice, then, you must release me.

No court would accept such a speech, but its availability in principle does point to a problem for DTP. The temporal parts of a person—especially the extended ones, as opposed to the instantaneous ones—have all that it takes to *be* persons; so it is hard to see why it would make sense to blame and punish (as we do, if DTP is true) the later temporal parts of a person for the actions of earlier ones. One can insist that in blaming and punishing the parts we thereby blame and punish the person, but that in no way mitigates the fact that in doing so we *also* blame and punish the innocent temporal parts.

The third objection is related to the second. Suppose you reflect on your childhood. You remember your sixteenth birthday, for example. You remember where you were, what you were doing, what the cake tasted like, and so on. Getting a bit more specific, suppose you think at *t1*, "I really enjoyed that cake," and then you think at *t2* "I'm glad that my sister was there." Obviously the transition from the one thought to another involves a change. Thus, DTP implies that you have different temporal parts at *t1* and *t2*, one of whom thinks "I really enjoyed that cake" and the other of whom thinks "I'm glad that my sister was there." Moreover, it is by virtue of having these two different temporal parts that you think those things at the relevant times. But now it looks as if we have *three different thinkers*—you, your *t1* part, and your *t2* part— where in fact we should have only one. This is bizarre. The doctrine of temporal parts implies that for every temporary thought you have, there is some *other thing*—a temporal part of you—that *also* has that thought. Worse, it implies that you have your thoughts derivatively: It is only *because* that temporal part of you has the thought he or she has that you have the thought that you have. Furthermore, the doctrine implies that some of the things thinking your thoughts have true beliefs and others don't. Your *t1* and *t2* parts never ate your sixteenth-birthday cake (they didn't exist at that time); and your sister is not their sister (they don't have sisters). Thus, they are mistaken when they think that they enjoyed your cake, and they are confused when they think of your sister as theirs. All of this, I submit, is very odd.

So DTP comes with some costs. I have not listed them all, but these three are among the most salient. However, DTP also comes in different varieties, which avoid some of the costs listed here while taking on other, different ones. For my part, the costs associated with DTP are too high. Endurantism seems a better way to go.

MATERIAL CONSTITUTION

You loan money to a friend, a substantial sum. Months later, weeks past the deadline for repayment, you contact your friend and ask for your money. Your friend offers instead a philosophical argument:

> Look at me: I'm just a collection of particles. You don't think there's
> something here *in addition* to the collection of particles, do you? I mean,

it's not as if, in addition to the 135-pound collection of particles there is *also* a 135-pound woman, right? So there is a collection here, and I am that collection. But, now think about it for a moment. I am obviously a *different* collection of particles from the one who borrowed money from you. For example, *this* collection of particles includes some of the stuff that composed my breakfast this morning; *that other* collection didn't include that stuff. So I am a different collection of particles from the one who borrowed the money. A human person *just is* a collection of particles. So I am a different person from the one who borrowed that money. So I don't owe you any money.

Obviously something has gone wrong. But what? How is the debtor's argument flawed?

The debtor has raised a puzzle about material constitution. Material constitution occurs whenever an object *a* and an object *b* (in this case, the debtor and the collection of particles that constitutes her) share all of the same parts at the same time. The phenomenon is puzzling because it is not at all clear what the relationship is between the relevant *a* and *b*. In particular, it is not clear whether *a* = *b*. The debtor assumes that she is identical with the collection of particles that now constitutes her and concludes that she is therefore not the same person as the one who earlier borrowed some money (because that person was identical to a different set of particles). No doubt we want to deny this. But what will we say instead? If we say that she is *not* identical to the collection of particles that constitutes her, do we say that there is a 135-pound person and a distinct 135-pound collection of particles occupying *exactly the same place at the same time*? If not, then what else can we say? We seem to have no good alternatives.

There are many different kinds of puzzles about material constitution in the philosophical literature, but all of them present us with scenarios in which it appears that an object *a* and an object *b* share all of the same parts but have different **modal properties**. (Modal properties are properties like *being able to survive being squashed* or *being possibly made of wood*.) In what follows, I will sometimes also speak of **persistence conditions**. Since persistence conditions are facts about what changes an object *can* or *cannot* survive, they too are modal properties. The fundamental problem that they all raise is known as "the problem of material constitution."

We will talk about solutions shortly, but first we should get several of the different puzzles out onto the table. The Debtor's Paradox, presented above, is one of them. In what follows, I will discuss three others: the Ship of Theseus, Body-Minus, and Lumpl/ Goliath. Familiarity with these three puzzles and their possible solutions is a gateway into a wide variety of core topics in contemporary metaphysics.

The Ship of Theseus. Consider a ship: the Ship of Theseus. At the beginning of its career, the ship is made entirely of wooden planks. The ship sails the same route for many decades and is "preserved" in the following way: Whenever one of the wooden planks wears out, it is discarded and replaced by an aluminum one. Eventually the time comes when all of the wooden planks have been replaced by aluminum ones. One day, however, an historian decides to gather all of the discarded planks and rebuild them in their original form. As a result of her work, each plank has the same position that it did in the original ship. She sells her ship to the local museum, and the curator then boasts that he has on display the Ship of Theseus. The crew of the aluminum ship, however, is outraged: "*We* are sailing the Ship of Theseus and have been for many years. The Ship of Theseus is here on the water, not there in your museum!" Who is right? Which ship is the Ship of Theseus?

Body-minus. Suppose that Tibbles is, at a certain time, a well-formed, properly functioning cat. At some later time, however, an unfortunate accident befalls her, resulting in the annihilation of her tail. Tibbles is understandably distressed. But we should be also. To see why, let us use "Body-minus" to name that part of Tibbles that includes all of her except for her tail—call it her torso. Before the accident, Tibbles is distinct from her torso. It is a **proper part** of Tibbles (i.e., the torso does not completely coincide with Tibbles). After the accident, Tibbles survives. Annihilating a tail doesn't normally destroy a cat. But Body-minus also survives. Annihilating a tail doesn't destroy a torso. But now we have a problem. On the one hand, we want to say that, after the accident, Tibbles is identical to Body-minus. Otherwise we would have two things in the same place at once. But Body-minus and Tibbles have different modal properties. Body-minus can exist as a mere torso; Tibbles cannot. Tibbles can be a cat with a tail; Body-minus cannot. So it seems that Tibbles cannot be identical to Body-minus after all.

Lumpl/Goliath. This puzzle was introduced by Allan Gibbard. A sculptor sets out to create a statue of Goliath, but he does so in the following way: He sculpts Goliath's upper body from one piece of clay, his lower body from another, and then finishes the statue by sticking the two pieces of clay together. In joining the two pieces of clay he simultaneously brings into existence a *new* piece of clay (call it "Lumpl") and a completed statue (call it "Goliath"). He allows the clay to harden, but then a day later, dissatisfied with his work, he smashes the statue, thereby obliterating both Lumpl and Goliath. The question is whether Goliath = Lumpl. There seems to be no good answer to this question. An affirmative answer is implausible, since Lumpl and Goliath seem to have different modal properties. For example (supposing the clay is still wet), Lumpl would survive if the piece of clay were reshaped in the form of a vase, whereas Goliath would not. And Goliath would survive if its left finger were annihilated, whereas Lumpl would not. But a negative answer is also implausible, at least initially, since such an answer appears to commit us to the conclusion that two distinct objects (a lump and a statue) can fully occupy the same region of spacetime.

All of these puzzles have roots in antiquity; and there are endless variations on each. But why think that they are all puzzles about material constitution? What are the relevant objects *a* and *b* in each puzzle that (allegedly) share all of the same parts and yet have different modal properties? The answer is straightforward in the first three puzzles. In the Debtor's Paradox, the relevant objects are the debtor and the collection of particles that constitutes her. Intuitively, the persistence conditions of persons and mere collections of particles are different: Removing particles from a collection leaves one with a *new* collection, whereas removing a few particles from a person doesn't seem to leave one with a new person (nor does it seem to destroy a person). Hence the difference in modal properties. In the Lumpl/Goliath puzzle, the objects are Lumpl and Goliath. Intuitively, lumps of clay and statues have different persistence conditions: The former, but not the latter, can survive being squashed. Hence they too have different modal properties. In the Body-minus puzzle, the objects are Tibbles and Body-minus; and I have already explained how it is that they have different modal properties.

The Ship of Theseus Puzzle is more complicated. Initially, it seems that the puzzle presents us not with two objects but at least *three*: the original ship, the aluminum ship, and the historian's ship (that is, the ship that has been rebuilt from the original planks). Moreover, at the end of the story it is not at all clear which (if any) of these objects constitute one another. Obviously the historian's ship and the aluminum one do not constitute one another. But does either constitute the original ship? That question seems equivalent to the one already under dispute. For if either of the two ships constitutes the original, it will do so only because it is *identical* with the original. Thus, it is hard to see how this puzzle presents us with an object *a* and an object *b* that share all of the same parts but appear for some reason to be *distinct* from one another.

But suppose we focus our attention not on the end of the story but on the beginning. At the beginning of the story, what kind of thing do the original planks compose? A ship, obviously. But what kind of ship? We start with the intuition that they compose a ship that can survive complete part-replacement, and this is what tempts us to identify the aluminum ship with the original. But during the story, another of our intuitions is uncovered. It turns out that we are also inclined to think that, at the beginning of the story, the planks compose a ship that *cannot* survive complete part-replacement. This intuition is what tempts us to identify the historian's ship with the Ship of Theseus. So, in other words, the puzzle arises because we have some reason to think that two ships coincide at the beginning: one which can survive complete part-replacement and one which cannot. By the end of the story, those two ships have split apart; one is made of aluminum, and the other sits in a museum. As with any puzzle about material constitution, we can just accept the conclusion that there were two ships at the beginning where we thought there was only one. Or we can insist that, at the beginning of the story, either the aluminum ship or the historian's ship did not exist, thus identifying the remaining one with the Ship of Theseus. Or we can look for some other solution to the puzzle.

What, then, are our options? How do we solve these puzzles? Speaking quite generally, each puzzle presents us with a choice among four solutions.

Option 1: Deny the assumption that if x and y share all of the same parts, then x = y. This option, of course, has been on the table from the very beginning of our discussion. None of the puzzles would be very puzzling if we did not have the strong intuition that two distinct material objects can never occupy exactly the same region of spacetime at the same time or share all of the same material parts. But one might think that precisely what the puzzles show us is that this deeply held intuition is false.

Option 2: Deny the existence of objects belonging to the kinds that are central to the puzzle. Each of the puzzles assumes the existence of at least two objects, each belonging to a different kind. The way these puzzles normally go, we start with a familiar kind of composite object (e.g., ship, statue, cat). We are then invited to believe in the existence of another kind of object (e.g., mere torso, mere collection of particles, etc.). Associated with each kind are different modal properties (e.g., statues can't survive squashing, but lumps can; cats can have tails, but torsos can't, etc.). This is what generates the puzzle. Thus, each of the puzzles can be solved by denying its existence assumptions. If there are no statues, or no mere lumps, then the Lumpl/Goliath puzzle is solved. If there are no torsos, the Body-minus puzzle is solved. If there are no composite objects at all, then all of the puzzles are solved.

Denying the existence of ships is not the same as denying that the world contains matter arranged in a general ship-like way. Nobody seriously denies the latter claim. Instead, they deny that arranging matter ship-wise suffices to bring a ship into existence. Likewise for those who deny the existence of torsos, cats, statues, and so on. If you find this puzzling, consider the fact that you yourself probably do not believe that arranging matter in any way whatsoever suffices to bring a new object into existence. For example, you probably don't believe that arranging matter in the form of a football team (i.e., putting uniforms on men and sending them out to a football field) brings a composite object of the kind *football team* into existence. Football teams, many of us think, are **mere pluralities**. That is, the term "football team" is not a name for an object but a device for referring collectively to several objects that do not together compose anything. But if we can say this about football teams, why *not* say something similar about ships, statues, cats, or—more radically—all (apparent) composite objects?

Good question. Answering it requires one to say something about the conditions under which composition occurs. This is a topic that has received a great deal of attention in contemporary metaphysics, and we shall discuss it briefly in Chapter 5. For now, I will simply note that few philosophers want to go so far as to deny the existence of composite objects generally but many do still want to deny the existence of quite a lot of composite objects that populate the ontology of common sense. Ships and statues are among the first to go. Cats and other living organisms, however, are more often allowed to remain.

Option 3: Deny the problematic modal properties. In discussing Option 2, I noted that, in every constitution puzzle, different modal properties are associated with each of the kinds mentioned in the puzzle. So, for concreteness, consider again the Lumpl/Goliath puzzle. In raising the puzzle, we assume that lumps have one set of modal properties, and statues another. But we can contest this assumption. So, for example, we might insist that at least some lumps—namely those that are also statues—cannot survive being squashed. We might insist that at least some collections of particles—namely, those that are human beings—have the modal properties of persons rather than the modal properties of mere collections. And so on.

We can put this solution more generally as follows. Suppose you are confronted with an object *a* and an object *b* that share all of the same parts but belong to two different kinds (K1 and K2); and suppose that the modal properties associated with K1 (e.g., *being able to survive squashing*) are incompatible with those associated with K2 (e.g., *being unable to survive squashing*). What you should say is the following: *a* = *b*, and that object belongs to both kinds. But not every object can have all of the modal properties associated with all of the kinds to which it belongs. Rather, every object has a *dominant kind*. An object's dominant kind is the one you'd refer to if you were in a position to give, for the object, the correct answer to the question, "What is the nature of that object?" So, in the case at hand, perhaps K1 is the dominant kind; perhaps K2 is the dominant kind; or perhaps neither is. Regardless, however, it won't be true that the object in question has the (incompatible) modal properties associated with *both* kinds.

This is an attractive solution, but it carries at least one unattractive cost. Suppose you shape a piece of clay into a statue. The piece you start with is a mere lump. The statue is also a lump, but (we might suppose) its dominant kind is statue. Since the initial lump was *by nature* a mere lump and the statue is not, it follows that the statue is not identical to the lump you started with. Shaping the lump destroyed it and replaced it with a statue. Similar results arise in the other constitution puzzles. This, then, is our cost: The present solution implies that what appear not to be destructive changes *are* destructive changes. Some philosophers find this to be highly counterintuitive.

Option 4: Deny that identity is necessary. Each of the puzzles tacitly assumes that identity is necessary. That is, each puzzle assumes that, for any objects *x* and *y*, if *x is* identical to *y*, then *x has to be* identical to *y*. (It follows from this assumption that if *x* is distinct from *y*, then *x* has to be distinct from *y*.) Denying this assumption—saying that identity is **contingent**—therefore suffices to solve all of the puzzles at once. The Debtor's Paradox would go away if only we could say that, although she is *now* identical to the collection of particles arguing about her debt, she *was* identical to the collection that contracted the debt. The Body-minus puzzle would go away if only we could say that Body-minus *is now* (after the tail removal) identical to Tibbles but *was not* identical to Tibbles when it was a mere torso. The Lumpl/Goliath puzzle would go away if only we could say that Lumpl *is* identical to Goliath but might not have been. The Ship of Theseus puzzle would go away if only we could say that Ship A *was* identical to Ship B but is no longer. Similarly for any other puzzle about material constitution.

The cost of this solution is just the fact that it is extremely counterintuitive. How could a thing possibly be distinct from itself? That said, this solution is not universally rejected. But its defenders tend to be few. Those who do defend it typically do so by adopting a somewhat unusual view about what it would mean to affirm the sentence, "Lumpl could have been distinct from Goliath," given that, in fact, Lumpl = Goliath. The most well-known version of this unusual view is called counterpart theory. We shall discuss counterpart theory in Chapter 6.

I said in the previous section that some constitution puzzles can be solved by embracing the doctrine of temporal parts; however, I have not listed the doctrine of temporal parts explicitly as one of the options one might take for solving the problem. Why not? Earlier, I said that material constitution occurs whenever an object *a* and an object *b* share all of the same parts at the same time. If objects have temporal parts in addition to their spatial parts, however, the idea of sharing all of the same parts (spatial or temporal) at a *single* time doesn't make much sense. Under the assumption that DTP is true, then, we should say that material constitution occurs whenever an object *a* and an object *b* share all of the same spatiotemporal parts, period. Once that is clear, however, it turns out that DTP "solves" the constitution puzzles that it solves simply by implying that what we *thought* was a case of material constitution is not *in fact* a case of material constitution. Furthermore, if we restrict our attention to puzzles in which an object *a* and an object *b* share all of the same spatiotemporal parts— puzzles, in other words, that even the temporal-parts theorist will agree are cases of material constitution—DTP as such has no solution to offer. Thus, I think it is misleading to consider it any kind of genuine solution to puzzles about material constitution.

To illustrate, consider Tibbles and Body-minus. According to DTP, Tibbles and Body-minus are both four-dimensional objects, spread out in time just as they are spread out in space. Tibbles is the object that fills the region of spacetime occupied by her body over the course of her entire life; Body-minus is the object that fills the region occupied by Tibbles' torso throughout its entire life. During the time that Tibbles is torso-shaped—that is, after the accident—Tibbles and Body-minus share all of their temporal parts in common. But before the accident the temporal parts of Body-minus are distinct from (though overlapping) the temporal parts of Tibbles. Thus, Tibbles and Body-minus do not share all of their temporal parts in common. Thus, they do not share all of their spatiotemporal parts. This solves the puzzle, because it removes any pressure we initially faced to say that there are two distinct objects sharing all of their parts in common. But it does so precisely by implying that Tibbles and Body-minus do not present us with a case of material constitution.

DTP would count as a solution to puzzles about material constitution if it implied that material constitution *never* occurs. But, as we have noted above, it does not imply this. Consider, for example, the Lumpl/Goliath puzzle. This one was crafted specifically to pose a problem for temporal-parts theorists. Lumpl and Goliath coincide for their entire careers. Thus, they share all of their spatial parts at every time at which either exists, and so they share all of the same temporal parts in common. DTP cannot solve this puzzle;

thus, in the face of this puzzle, DTP theorists are forced to accept one of the other four options listed earlier.

PERSONAL IDENTITY

We turn, finally, to the topic of personal identity. This is a topic on which almost everyone already has at least a few opinions, some grounded in common sense and experience and others perhaps grounded in religious convictions. As I've already suggested, virtually all of us will think that we are able to survive radical, nonfatal changes in our bodies and minds. We survive growth and development from infancy to adulthood; people survive the loss of limbs and all manner of surgical alterations; our beliefs, emotions, and personalities change over time; and so on. The topic of personal identity comprises a variety of philosophical questions about how such changes are possible and about the conditions under which a person can be said to *survive* from one time to the next.

Some of the questions one might ask on this topic look like nothing more than special instances of the more general questions about change and identity that we have already been discussing. How can one and the same person have different properties at different times? What is the relationship between a person and the mass of particles that constitutes her at any given time? Are persons composed of temporal parts or not? The puzzles discussed in the earlier sections of this chapter provide a natural starting place for reflection on these sorts of questions. But they provide only a starting place. For persons are not *ordinary* material objects (if they are material objects at all), and questions about the *survival of persons* from one moment to the next are in some ways more complicated than questions about the *identity of material objects* across time.

The questions become most vivid, and most relevant to our ordinary lives, when we consider the way in which human persons are affected by severe brain damage. Those suffering from Alzheimer's disease, for example, commonly experience massive memory loss which is sometimes also accompanied by radical changes in personality. Familiar faces and entire relationships are forgotten; core desires, values, and ambitions may change or be lost altogether; religious beliefs vanish. We find many of these same phenomena present in greater or lesser degrees when people suffer from mental illness, or when they suffer certain kinds of brain trauma. In such cases we find ourselves tempted to say that we are no longer dealing with the same person. We sometimes say that the original person is no longer there. We say these things, too, when a person enters a persistent vegetative state, wherein bodily functions continue to operate (sometimes with assistance) but cognitive activity has ceased. There is no question that there is *some* truth to these claims. But how much truth? Might a person's body survive longer than the person herself? Can a person survive apart from her body? These are among the questions raised by the literature on personal identity.

Let us define our topic a bit more clearly. The literature on personal identity has focused primarily on two issues: (1) the nature of persons and (2) the necessary and sufficient conditions for *survival* or *sameness of person* over time. The two issues are obviously related. If what it is to be a person is simply to be an immaterial soul, for example, then a necessary and sufficient condition for the survival of a person from one moment to the next will be the survival of her soul. Similarly if what it is to be a person is to be an organism, or a brain, or something else. If being a person is just being *an object* of a certain kind, *F*, then the necessary and sufficient conditions for *survival* or *sameness of person* over time will just be the necessary and sufficient conditions for the survival of *F*s.

The vast majority of thinkers who say that it is in the nature of a person to an object of a certain kind will go on to say that a person x and a person y are the same person if, and only if, $x = y$. In a slogan: Survival is identity. Not every theory of persons, however, identifies persons with objects. According to some philosophers, persons are more like software running on the brain, or logical constructs of a certain kind. Others wish to remain non-committal on the nature of persons but nevertheless have views about the necessary and sufficient conditions for survival. As a general rule, philosophers who do not identify persons with objects tend to think that two individual objects can be the same person even though they are not identical. In a slogan: Survival is not identity. Thus, within the literature on personal identity there are two camps: those who think that survival is identity and those who think that it is not. We shall discuss each view in turn.

We begin with a thought experiment which will help to lend concreteness to our discussion. Daryl Gregory's well-known science-fiction story, "Second Person, Present Tense" tells the story of Therese, a teenage girl who suffered complete memory loss as a result of a drug overdose. In rehabilitative therapy, Terry—whose body, at any rate, is the same as Therese's—has recovered some of Therese's memories, but she does not experience them as genuine memories. Rather, Terry experiences them as implanted pseudo-memories of events in Therese's life. Moreover, Terry's values, core desires, goals, and ambitions are not continuous with Therese's. Accordingly, Terry insists that she is *not the same person* as Therese. Terry believes this: Therese died with the overdose and Terry was born immediately afterward, sharing only a body with Therese. Therese's parents, however, disagree. Terry is *their child*, and they are hurt by Terry's refusal to recognize herself as Therese and them as her parents. Reflecting on the difference between Terry's and Therese's parents' views about personal identity will help us to sort out some of the most important considerations in deciding between competing answers to the problem of personal identity.

Consider first the perspective of Therese's parents. Why think that Terry is the same person as their daughter? One reason is the simple fact that Terry is the *same (identical) organism* as their daughter. In the story, it is clear that this fact is indeed what moves the parents most in the direction of affirming that Terry is Therese. To take this consideration as decisive is to endorse what is known as the *animalist* criterion of personal identity: To be a human person is to be a human animal; and x is the same human person as y if, and only if, x is the same human animal as y.

The animalist criterion has much going for it. Most importantly, as Eric Olson's "thinking animal" argument suggests, it seems to have the weight of common sense on its side. Look at yourself in the mirror. What do you see? A human animal. Not only that, but you see a thinking human animal. Do you see any other thinking thing there in the mirror? Surely not. But *you* are thinking. So you are that thinking animal.

This is a persuasive argument, but it is hardly decisive. Some philosophers, for example, believe that it is in the nature or essence of a human person to be or to have a particular *soul*. Some say that persons *are* souls and that a person's body is just an inessential appendage or tool used by the soul. This sort of view is commonly associated with a variety of ancient Greek philosophers, Pythagoras and Plato among them, and with the seventeenth-century French philosopher René Descartes. Others say that the relation between body and soul is more intimate, so that even though the soul can exist apart from the body, its natural state is to be embodied and the person whose soul it is cannot exist in a fully functioning state unless her soul is embodied. This latter view is commonly associated with St. Thomas Aquinas. On both views, personal identity is tied to the soul. More exactly: x is the same human person as y if, and only if, x is or has the same soul as y. Since a soul can exist apart from any particular human animal, proponents of this same soul criterion will deny the animalist claim that what one sees in the mirror is, strictly speaking, a thinking human animal. To be sure, it is true in a rather loose way of speaking that human animals think. But *properly* speaking, what thinks is the person, that is, the soul.

There are other reasons to reject animalism, even apart from belief in immaterial souls. Some do so on the basis of thought experiments like the following: Imagine a procedure whereby your cerebrum (the part that supports thought, not bodily function) is transplanted into a new body, and someone else's cerebrum is then transplanted into your original body. Let's call the organism that has your cerebrum "A," and let's call the other organism "B." Now suppose that, in advance of the procedure, you are told that one of the two resulting organisms will receive your heart's greatest desire and the other of the two will also receive something nice, but nothing like your heart's greatest desire. You are then asked to decide which organism receives which prize. Isn't it *obvious* that you should arrange for A to receive your heart's greatest desire? Clearly so; but it seems likewise clear that A is not the same animal that you were at the beginning of the procedure. (B seems to have the better claim to being the same animal.) Indeed, if one is willing to venture a bit further into science fiction, the case can be strengthened. Just imagine a procedure whereby your entire brain is removed and rigged up so as to control a wholly synthetic body. It seems possible that you survive such a procedure; but at the end of it you would not be an animal. Thus, the animalist criterion again seems false.

The criterion suggested by this thought experiment is a *same-cerebrum* criterion: x is the same person as y if, and only if, x is the same (identical) cerebrum as y. Moreover, one might motivate this criterion not just with thought experiments but with what Hud Hudson calls the "elimination principle":

> If x and y are both human person candidates and at most one of x and y is a human person, but y has superfluous parts whereas x doesn't, then x is the better candidate for the office.

Wherever we find an organism, we are faced with a situation wherein we must recognize *a single human person* from (at least) two candidates: the organism and the cerebrum. Both have what it takes to be conscious, but the organism has "superfluous parts," like hands and toes, none of which it needs in order to be conscious. The cerebrum, on the other hand, is just big enough to do the job. Thus, by the Elimination Principle, we should recognize the cerebrum and not the organism as the human person.

Each of the views just discussed falls into the "survival is identity" camp. Each identifies a human person with some specific object—an organism, a soul, a cerebrum—and each maintains that x is the same person as y only if $x = y$. Moreover, endorsing any one of these views would provide Terry's parents with an argument for the conclusion that Terry is the same person as their daughter. For Terry has the same brain as Therese, she is the same organism as Therese, and (assuming souls are substances that can survive the loss of any and all of their memories) there is no reason to doubt that Terry has the same soul as Therese.

What about Terry's perspective? Taking her perspective does not *require* that she deny that survival is identity. For example, she *could* maintain that given the psychological changes she's undergone, a new soul must have taken up residence in her body. That is an unlikely view, however. Terry's perspective is much more likely to be endorsed by someone who maintains what is known as a *psychological continuity* criterion of personal identity. This sort of criterion is typically endorsed by those who do not identify persons with material or immaterial objects and who deny that survival is identity.

The psychological continuity criterion is most widely associated with the seventeenth-century British empiricist John Locke, and also with the contemporary philosopher Derek Parfit. One version of the psychological continuity criterion is as follows:

P1 x is the same person as y if, and only if, x's psychological states display the right sort of continuity with y's psychological states.

Parfit, however, takes sameness of person to come in degrees, which suggests a different formulation:

P2 x is the same person as y just to the degree that x's psychological states display the right sort of continuity with y's psychological states.

What counts as "the right sort of continuity"? It is hard to say precisely, but any decent answer to that question will have to be consistent with basic intuitions like these: (1) I am the same person as the five-year-old boy whose first day of kindergarten I remember, and (2) no matter how much the mental lives of my contemporaries happen to resemble my own mental life, I am not the same person as any of them.

Parfit himself makes a helpful distinction between psychological *continuity* and psychological *connectedness*. A person x is psychologically connected to a person y if x seems to remember events that y actually experienced, or x sees her actions as carrying out intentions that were in fact y's intentions for her future self, or other mental states of x stand in other relevantly similar relations to mental states of y or events in y's life. And a person x stands in the relation of *psychological continuity* with y if, and only if, x and y are both links in a chain of psychologically connected persons (i.e., x is psychologically connected to a, who is psychologically connected to b...who is psychologically connected to y). In the normal case, x and y will be the same person only if x's psychological makeup is related to y's by a series of psychologically connected stages that looks like the development of a single mind over time.

Perhaps the most widely discussed contemporary motivation for the psychological continuity criterion is Parfit's famous double-brain-transplant scenario. According to Parfit, there is no question that a human person can survive the removal of one hemisphere of her brain. Moreover, he says, technology presents the only obstacle to surviving a hemispherectomy followed by a transplant of the resulting half-brain. So now imagine a case where half of one's brain is removed and transplanted and the other half is *also* removed and transplanted. Let Scarecrow be the person undergoing the procedure; let S1 be the person who results from the transplant of the left half of Scarecrow's brain, and let S2 be the person who results from the transplant of the right half. Given that a person can survive the removal and subsequent transplant of either half of her brain alone, it seems that we must admit that Scarecrow survives this procedure. After all, she would have survived if the right half had been destroyed rather than transplanted, and she would have survived if the left half had been destroyed rather than transplanted. Why, then, should the fact that *neither* is destroyed make it the case that she doesn't survive? But if she *does survive*, then she must survive as S1, as S2, or as both S1 and S2. According to Parfit, it would be wholly arbitrary to suppose that Scarecrow survives as just one of the two. Thus, she must survive as both. But *she cannot be identical to both*. Thus, survival is not identity; and the best way to make sense of our intuitions about survival under the supposition that survival is not identity is to adopt a psychological continuity criterion.

According to Parfit, then, psychological continuity and connectedness, not identity, are what matters in survival. Moreover, Parfit thinks that whether x is the same person as y is a matter of degree; and, indeed, the facts about sameness of person are sensitive to context and interest. So, for example, suppose that Scarecrow undergoes the double-transplant procedure, and then S1 and S2 are genetically modified so as to enable them each to regrow their missing hemisphere over the course of a year. At the end of the year, S1 and S2 each undergo the double transplant, generating S3—S6, each of whom also regrow missing hemispheres over the course of a year and subsequently undergo double transplants, generating S7—S14. Does Scarecrow survive as S14? Let us stipulate that S14 is psychologically continuous with Scarecrow. Still, she will surely be less so than S2 was. Thus, *if* she is the same person as Scarecrow, she will be so to a lesser degree than S2 was. Moreover, according to Parfit, whether she bears enough continuity with Scarecrow to count as the same person *at all* will depend in large part on our interests and on the context in which we are asking whether she is the same person. If, for example, we are trying to adjudicate a dispute about property ownership between S7—S14, we might well say that *none* of them counts as Scarecrow. On the other hand, if S14 is the sole survivor among her transplant siblings and we are wondering whether we can award Scarecrow a Nobel prize *by awarding it to her*... well, maybe in that case we would say that S14 is the same person as Scarecrow.

The psychological continuity criterion has enjoyed a fair degree of popularity, but there are serious problems with it. Suppose you are the one to undergo the double transplant, and suppose you are told that just one of the resultant persons will receive your heart's greatest desire, whereas the other will not. What would you hope for in that sort of scenario? What would you fear? For my part, I would *fear* that I would be identical to no one after the transplant and that the two resulting persons would be people other than me. I would *hope* that my fears are mistaken and that I would be identical to at least one of the resulting persons, preferably the one who receives my heart's greatest desire. These hopes and fears make no sense if our ordinary concept of survival is one according to which survival is not identity. But these hopes and fears *do* make sense. So, our ordinary concept of survival *is* one according to which survival is identity. Contra Parfit, identity *is* what matters in survival.

Might one embrace a psychological continuity criterion of survival while also maintaining (against Parfit) that survival is identity? Such a combination is possible, but implausible. The reason is simple; we can present it in the form of a dilemma. Either mental states have bearers or they don't. That is, either there is a *thinker* for every thought, or there isn't. If there is, and if survival is identity, then a psychological continuity criterion of survival is implausible; if there isn't, then survival cannot be identity.

Suppose that there is a thinker for every thought. Then *persons* are best identified with thinkers. (Persons have thoughts. So, if there is a thinker for every thought, what else would we identify the thinkers with if not the persons who have the thoughts?) But it is hard to see how the *identity* of a thinking thing could depend on what it happens to be thinking. But if survival is identity, a psychological continuity criterion of survival implies that the identity of a person *does* depend to some degree on what the person is thinking. (If she has all the wrong thoughts, after all, she will fail to be continuous in the right way with her earlier self.) So if survival is identity, then a psychological continuity criterion is implausible.

On the other hand, suppose that there isn't a thinker for every thought. Then, at any given moment, there is nothing more to a particular "person" than the various thoughts, sensations, and so on, that figure in that person's mental life at that moment. This view was famously endorsed by David Hume. Hume asked what evidence we have for believing in a self, and he concluded that we have none at all. When we introspect, we observe our thoughts and sensations, but we do not observe a self that has the thoughts and sensations. Thus, he concluded, "the identity which we ascribe to the mind of man is only a fictitious one." Indeed, on this picture, survival *cannot* be identity. For it is a truism that persons survive changes in their mental lives; and if survival is identity, this means that one and the same person can exist at multiple times with a different mental life at each time. But on this picture, either there are no persons at all (there are just thoughts and sensations, and we pretend that they are persons) or else persons are mere bundles of thoughts and sensations. Either way, persons do not, strictly speaking, exist at multiple times with a different mental life at each time. If there are no persons at all, then obviously no person exists at multiple times. Likewise, if there is nothing more to a person than a bundle of thoughts and sensations, then every time a thought or sensation is added to or subtracted from the bundle, we have a new bundle and therefore a new person. So if persons are bundles of thoughts and sensations, they might exist at multiple times, but not with different mental lives at those times. Persons therefore do not persist through psychological change.

The dilemma just offered also provides the makings of an argument against Parfit's views. Start with the second horn of the dilemma: the view that either there is no self, or the self is a mere bundle of thoughts and sensations. Hume accepted this view because of his empiricist scruples: He wanted to avoid believing in anything for which he did not have empirical evidence. But for those of us who do not share such scruples, this theory about the self has one major drawback: It conflicts with the deeply held intuition that *thought requires a subject*. Indeed, it is unclear that Hume himself managed to escape the grip of this intuition. Consider again the quotation above: "the identity which *we* ascribe to the mind of man." *We who?* Who does the ascribing? On the no-self view, or the mere-bundle view, there is *ascribing* taking place, but nothing doing the ascribing. What sense does that make?

So, if Parfit accepts that second horn of the dilemma, then his view faces a serious problem (even apart from its conflict with the intuition that survival is identity). As it happens, Parfit does not go so far as to say that there is *no* self, or that persons are mere bundles of thoughts and sensations, so he is not explicitly committed to the no-self or mere-bundle view. But it is hard to see how he can avoid accepting one or the other. For he does say that the self is not a substance: it is not to be identified with a soul, a brain, a body, or any other material or immaterial substance in the world. But if the self is not a substance, then what options are left besides the no-self and mere-bundle views? All of the most viable alternatives would seem to have been wiped off the table.

FURTHER READING

Selections from the writings of Parmenides on the topic of change, along with David Lewis's classic statement of the problem of temporary intrinsics are reprinted in *Arguing about Metaphysics*. On Zeno's paradoxes, see Wesley C. Salmon, *Zeno's Paradoxes* (Indianapolis, IN: Hackett Publishing, 2001). On the topic of supertasks, see Jon Pérez Laraudogoitia, "Supertasks," in *The Stanford Encyclopedia of Philosophy*, ed. Edward N. Zalta, spring 2011, available online at http://plato.stanford.edu/archives/spr2011/entries/spacetime-supertasks.

On change and temporal parts, see Roderick Chisholm, "Identity and Temporal Parts," and Mark Heller, "Temporal Parts of Four Dimensional Objects," both reprinted in *Arguing about Metaphysics*. My own "Temporal Parts Unmotivated," *Philosophical Review*, vol. 107 (1998), pp. 225–260, surveys several of the most important arguments for belief in temporal parts and provides replies. For book-length treatments (including discussion of the "stage theory" variant on perdurantism), see Theodore Sider's *Four-Dimensionalism* (Oxford: Oxford University Press, 2001); and Katherine Hawley's *How Things Persist* (Oxford: Clarendon Press, 2001).

Jeffrey Brower offers a novel *endurantist* solution to the problem of temporary intrinsics in his "Aristotelian Endurantism: A New Solution to the Problem of Temporary Intrinsics," *Mind*, vol. 119

(2011), pp. 883–905. This is the second version of the "indexing the subject" solution discussed in the text in connection with "Solution 3". Among the more important defenses of presentist replies to the problem of temporary intrinsics are Trenton Merricks, "Endurance and Indiscernibility," *Journal of Philosophy*, vol. 91 (1994), pp. 165–84; and Dean Zimmerman, "Temporary Intrinsics and Presentism," in Dean Zimmerman and Peter van Inwagen, eds., *Metaphysics: The Big Questions* (Cambridge, MA: Blackwell, 1998), pp. 206–220. The time- and copula-indexing responses are discussed in Peter van Inwagen, "Four Dimensional Objects," *Noûs* vol. 24 (1990), pp. 245–56; Sally Haslanger, "Endurance and Temporary Intrinsics," *Analysis* vol. 49 (1989), pp. 119–25; and David Lewis, "Tensing the Copula," *Mind* vol. 111 (2002), pp. 1–14.

On the subject of material constitution, a good place to start is Michael Rea (ed.), *Material Constitution: A Reader* (Lanham, MD: Rowman & Littlefield, 1997). Allan Gibbard's paper, "Contingent Identity," is among the articles reprinted there. The topic of material constitution is also discussed at some length in the books by Katherine Hawley, Mark Heller, and Theodore Sider mentioned above.

On personal identity, the articles by Derek Parfit and Eric Olson that were cited here—"Personal Identity" and "An Argument for Animalism," respectively—are both reprinted in *Arguing about Metaphysics*. So too is Daryl Gregory's "Second Person, Present Tense." In reply to Olson's view, see Hud Hudson's "I Am Not an Animal," in Peter van Inwagen and Dean W. Zimmerman, eds., *Persons: Human and Divine* (Oxford: Oxford University Press, 2007), pp. 216–234. Two classic, and highly accessible, books on the topic are John Perry's *A Dialogue on Personal Identity and Immortality* (Indianapolis, IN: Hackett Publishing Company, 1978) and Sydney Shoemaker and Richard Swinburne, *Personal Identity* (Oxford: Basil Blackwell, 1984).

All of these issues intersect with issues about composition. Peter van Inwagen's *Material Beings* (Ithaca, NY: Cornell University Press, 1990) is a very important resource on this topic.

SUBSTANCE

What is the difference between a vivid dream and the world outside? For mere mortals, even the most vivid dream is still a pale imitation of reality. But we can imagine that difference being removed. What further difference would there be? Our dreams are typically short and display precious little continuity with one another, especially by comparison with our waking lives. Few of our dreams are governed by natural laws in the way that the real world is. One could hardly do good science even within the longest of dreams. Indeed, one can hardly make *any* plans or predictions in one dream that will carry over reliably to the next dream, or even to the next moment. Our agency is diminished in our dreams, too. If we deliberate or act with intention, here again we find only a pale imitation of what transpires in waking life. But we can imagine all of these differences removed as well. We can imagine, that is, a genuine dream that is no less vivid than waking life, just as law-governed, extraordinarily long, and something within which we can plan and predict in just the ways in which we do in waking life.

So imagine it.

What differences remain now between dream and reality?

The difference is substance.

In ordinary life, when we talk about substances, we are usually talking not about objects but about undifferentiated masses of matter. Ask your friend to identify the substance on your desk and she will come looking for something more like a smear of peanut butter or a powder of unknown origin; she won't look for any particular kind of object. As we saw in Chapter 2, however, philosophers have something different in mind when they talk about substance. What they have in mind is an object that has at least the following two features: *independence* and *unity*. Dream-objects (and dreams themselves) lack the first feature. They depend for their existence and character entirely upon our minds. Arbitrary combinations of objects lack the second feature: They have no real unity, which is why many people do not think of such things as genuine composites.

Imagine placing a toy van in your *Radio-Flyer* wagon. Have you created a new object, a van-in-wagon? Most of us will say no. There are no van-in-wagons; just *vans* and *wagons*. Why? Because simply putting a van in a wagon isn't a genuine way of *unifying* two objects. It is not a way of making *one* object out of *two*. Contrast this with a process that manages to arrange *n* particles human-wise. This sort of process *does* seem to be unifying. Arranging particles human-wise creates a genuine unity: It creates one (additional) thing where previously we just had *n* particles.

Needless to say, however, not everyone believes in substances as I have just characterized them. More exactly, not everyone believes that there is a distinction to be made between *genuine* ways of unifying objects and merely apparent ways; and not everyone believes that there is a privileged class of independent things that is somehow set apart from all other things, the dependent objects. Those who do believe in a category of substance, furthermore, differ widely as to what things count as substances and what their specific character is like.

In the first two sections of this chapter, we shall examine three of the most important theories about substance: *bundle theory*, according to which nothing satisfies the traditional definition of substance; *substratum* theory, according to which the substances are bare particulars that somehow underlie all of a thing's properties; and *hylomorphism*, according to which a wide variety of familiar material objects count as substances. Next, we shall turn to the topic of composition, connecting questions about the conditions under which composition occurs with questions about the distinction between genuine and merely apparent unity. In the final section, we turn our attention toward God, who is identified in the Aristotelian hylomorphic tradition as a substance *par excellence*, the ground of all being.

BUNDLES VS. SUBSTRATA

Objects have attributes; nothing could be more mundane. Suppose we are realists about attributes: We think that attributes themselves are abstract objects of a certain kind—perhaps universals, perhaps tropes. One might now ask what *having* an attribute will involve.

Before addressing this question, let us first say something about the term "attribute." Attributes are just properties. Sometimes philosophers use the term "attribute" to signal their adherence to a particular conception of properties—for example, that properties modify the things that have them rather than belonging to them as constituents (as they would if properties are tropes) or having them as members (as they would if properties are sets). Sometimes, too, it seems that philosophers talk about attributes rather than properties because they are trying to focus on intrinsic properties, or just those properties that would exist if a sparse theory of properties is true. As I have mentioned earlier, in this book the term "attribute" is being used as if it is synonymous with the term "property." But for the remainder of this chapter I shall presuppose realism rather than nominalism about attributes. More specifically, I shall presuppose that attributes are either universals or tropes.

Given this assumption, there are, broadly speaking, two main answers that one might give to the question of what it means to have an attribute. One might say that attributes are constituents of the objects that have them; or one might say that attributes are in some sense external to the objects that have them. (Reminder: I have been using the term "constituent" throughout this book as if it is synonymous with the term "part.")

The difference between these two answers marks the difference between what are sometimes called *constituent ontologies* and *relational ontologies*. The labels are not entirely apt. For one thing, constituency itself seems like a relation; so there is really nothing any less "relational" about constituent ontologies than about their rivals. For another thing, treating exemplification as a relation is known to generate problems, since relations themselves are exemplified. So, for example, suppose that *exemplifying* something always involves standing in a relation to it. Now suppose object *a* exemplifies attribute F. This will mean that *a* and F together exemplify the *exemplification relation* (call that "E"). So *a* and F exemplify E. But this too will involve standing in a relation—again, E. So now *a* and F and E together must exemplify E. And this *too* will involve standing in a relation... and so on.

Let us set these worries aside for now. Despite the labels, the main difference between constituent and relational ontologies does not so much have to do with one involving relations and the other not. Rather, it has to do with the family of metaphors that proponents of each kind of ontology tend to use to talk about property-having (whatever exactly it amounts to). People who accept a constituent ontology tend to say that properties are somehow *in* their bearers, or that they *inhere* in the things that have them. They say that properties are *constituents* of the things that have them. Proponents of a relational ontology tend to talk about objects *participating in* properties, or they talk about properties being *transcendent* rather than *immanent*, or *external* to their bearers rather than *in* them as constituents.

Those who endorse relational ontologies typically maintain that attributes are just as independent as—maybe even more independent than—objects in the material world. On that sort of theory, attributes *are* substances. Although they are attributes, they also *have* attributes. (Plato, for example, thought that properties at least exemplify themselves.) They are also basic, or independent, things on which other things depend. Having no parts, they are also unified in the deepest sense of the term. Within Plato's relational ontology, properties are the only substances. But other relational ontologies might either hold them to be on a par with material substances or reject the substance–attribute distinction altogether.

Turning to constituent ontologies, we find two further options. First, to borrow a familiar classroom metaphor, we might think that attributes relate to substances as pins relate to a pincushion: Like pins, the attributes are somehow "stuck" to the substance, and the substance (i.e., the pincushion) is, in and of itself, a thing with no attributes. On this view, then, a substance is the sort of thing from which—conceptually speaking, anyway—all attributes could, in principle, be removed. For this reason, this first view is commonly referred to as the *bare particular*, or *bare substratum*, theory of substance. One might endorse a bare-particular theory and treat substrata and their properties as on a par in terms of their independence and unity. More commonly, bare particulars are seen as enjoying a kind of independence that attributes do not. Attributes are instead seen to depend for their existence on their attachment to bare particulars, but not vice versa. Thus, on this sort of view, there are no unexemplified attributes, and bare particulars are the only substances.

Secondly, we might think that the relation between objects and their attributes is like the relation between a bundle of sticks and the sticks themselves: that is, there is nothing more to the thing than the sticks. Notice that one might think of a bundle of sticks as an object that has the sticks as parts; or one might think of the bundle as a mere plurality—just some sticks which do not compose any further thing. If we take the first way of thinking, bundle theory is the view that everything is either an attribute or a bundle of attributes. If we take the second way of thinking, bundle theory is the view that, strictly speaking, everything is an attribute (since mere pluralities are not objects), and that what we *take* to be familiar objects are really nothing but mere pluralities of attributes. Either way, this is not an ontology according to which there are independent, unified things which *have* attributes. Bundles have attributes, but, being built up out of their attributes, they depend on their attributes rather than the other way around. Attributes, on this view, are independent, but they do not have attributes, for otherwise they too would be mere bundles. Thus, it is not really a theory about the relation between substance and attribute; it is, rather, a denial of substance altogether.

Both the bare-particular theory and the bundle theory have their fair share of problems. Consider first the bare-particular theory. The first and most obvious objection concerns the characterization of bare particulars themselves. It seems to be central to the view that bare particulars are *bare* (i.e., they have no attributes) and *particular*. But now we face a dilemma. Either we must say that bare particulars have the *attributes* of being bare and particular in such a way that, unlike every other attribute stuck to the cushion, those two could not possibly be stripped away; or we must say that the predicates "is bare" and "is particular" apply to and characterize bare particulars despite the fact that there are no attributes corresponding to the predicates. The first horn of the dilemma is problematic because the very concept of a bare particular is the concept of something from which *all attributes* can, in principle, be stripped away. Thus, it looks as if the very idea of an attribute like *being bare* is incoherent: Anything that has the attribute could not possibly have the attribute. But the second horn of the dilemma is also problematic. Bare-particular theory is, by its very nature, committed to realism about attributes. But if we really thought that it was possible for predicates like *being bare* and *being particular* to characterize objects in the absence of corresponding attributes, the motivation for believing in attributes would seem to be lost.

Another problem is that bare-particular theory seems to result in an unreasonable multiplication of subjects of predication. Suppose that Socrates is seated and is thinking about his wife, Xanthippe. According to the bare-particular theorist, this fact obtains because Socrates' bare particular has at least two attributes stuck to it: *being seated* and *thinking about Xanthippe*. But now we face another dilemma. Either Socrates is identical to his bare particular or not. Suppose Socrates *is* identical to his bare particular. Socrates himself is not bare; he has lots of attributes, and some of those attributes—like being capable of thought—are such that, were they stripped away from him, Socrates would cease to exist. So that option is not viable. Suppose then that Socrates *is not* identical to his bare particular. Now we have a different sort of problem. Socrates, as we have said, is seated and is thinking of Xanthippe. But it seems that his bare particular is as well; for, after all, those attributes are stuck to the bare particular—the bare particular *has* them. But if that is right, then there are two things seated in the same place at the same time, both thinking of Xanthippe and both, indeed, thinking that Xanthippe is their wife!

One might try to respond to this problem by arguing that Socrates has the attributes just mentioned in one way, whereas the bare particular has these attributes in a rather different way. If we say this, we will identify one way of having attributes as primary and another way as derivative. There is some precedent for this. For example, an apple is red. Strictly speaking, just the surface is red; but we talk as if the whole thing is red. So we might say that the surface has redness in the primary way, whereas the whole apple has redness derivatively—it counts as red simply *because* the surface is red. Likewise, one might think, with Socrates and his bare particular: One has *thinking of Xanthippe* in the primary way; the other has that attribute only derivatively.

Whatever its merits, however, this solution does not do much to mitigate our problem. For, on this view, Socrates and his bare particular still *have* the attributes in question. There are still two things seated in Socrates' chair and still two things thinking of Xanthippe and thinking that she is their wife. That one of the things is only derivatively thinking of Xanthippe does not seem to make this consequence any more palatable. But set that problem aside for now. The more significant problem looming here is one developed at some length by Andrew Bailey. It looks as if the bare particular has the attributes in the primary way, whereas Socrates has the attributes only because they are stuck to the bare particular. (It seems this way because it is the fact that the bare particular has the property in the way that it does that is supposed to explain Socrates' having the property—just as the redness of the surface of an apple explains the apple's being red. If we didn't think about it this way, we would have no reason even to believe in the bare particular.) But it seems wrong to say that Socrates manages to think about Xanthippe only because some other thing has the attribute of thinking about Xanthippe. One wants to say instead that Socrates has his own mental states in the primary way, not by virtue of what is going on with something else. But that is precisely what the bare-particular theorist cannot say.

Bare-particular theory has problems. Unfortunately, so too does the bundle theory. First, we might ask what exactly *bundling* amounts to. Even if bundles are mere pluralities, not every plurality of attributes comprises a bundle. (Half of my attributes and half of yours, for example, do not together comprise a bundle.) Suppose that attributes are universals. They are, in other words, necessarily existing abstract objects that can be instantiated in multiple places at once. What could it possibly mean to "bundle" some of those sorts of things together?

We might say that n universals are bundled together when they are instantiated in exactly the same place at the same time. But that won't quite work. Consider, for example, a bowl of spaghetti. According to the bundle theory, the bowl of spaghetti is a bundle of universals. But the colors and flavors of the bowl of spaghetti and the various textures are not all instantiated in exactly the same places. The tomato flavor of the sauce isn't instantiated in the same place as the hardness of the bowl, for example; and the mass of the entire composite isn't instantiated in exactly the same region as the color of the pasta (or even the same region as the composite color of the bowl of spaghetti taken a whole). And, of course, similar problems arise if we take attributes to be tropes rather than universals. The color tropes for the bowl of spaghetti wouldn't be in exactly the same place as the flavor tropes, or the hardness trope, or the mass trope. The typical response to this problem is to introduce a new relation—for example, "compresence"—and to say that bundling occurs whenever tropes or universals stand in that relation to one another. But, of course, that doesn't explain anything; giving that sort of answer really does little more than ask us to rest content with the mystery of bundling.

Secondly, we might ask how bundling—whatever exactly it is— manages to generate *concrete* objects. Suppose that attributes can be located in spacetime. It doesn't really matter now whether we think of attributes as tropes or universals; either way, they are going to be abstract objects, which is all that we need to generate the problem. Now you might wonder why we would suppose that attributes can be located in spacetime. After all, they aren't concrete objects; and it certainly seems odd to say, for example, that the tomato flavor of your spaghetti is sitting right there on the table in front of you. (Then again, if it isn't there on the table, where else might it be? And if the flavor were literally nowhere, then how could you ever get it into your mouth?) But the reason we should feel comfortable here assuming that attributes can be located is that bundle theory seems to require it. For, again, whatever exactly bundling attributes amounts to, it seems obviously to require that attributes can be put together in some locations without being put together in others. So, suppose we have an attribute A1 located in a particular region, R. If just one attribute is there, we obviously do not have a concrete object; we just have the attribute, which is abstract. So add an attribute, A2. Does that give us a concrete object in R? I do not see how it could. Where would the *concreteness* come from? So, add a third attribute, A3. Does that now give us a concrete object in R? Again, it is hard to see how it could. And so on.

One might say that concreteness is itself an attribute; so the concreteness comes only when we add *that* attribute to the bundle. But this will solve the problem only if concreteness is itself concrete. Initially, one would not think that it is. Concreteness is an attribute like any other, and attributes are supposed to be abstract on this view. If we do say that concreteness is concrete, there is some pressure to say that *all* attributes exemplify themselves. The reason is that it would be hard to find any principled reason for saying that some attributes exemplify themselves but others do not. If we do say that all attributes exemplify themselves, however, then we confront further oddities: Humanity is human (thus, we have an abstract human being); redness is red (so an abstract object has a color); beauty is beautiful (so an abstract object with *no other features* somehow counts as beautiful); and so on. None of these claims is obviously incoherent, but neither do they seem to be the sorts of commitments one should be happy to take on. But if we do not say that concreteness is concrete, then it is very hard to see how we could ever get a concrete object out of a process of "stacking" abstract objects together in a region of spacetime.

Thirdly, if the bundle theory is true, it is hard to see how objects could ever have different properties than they do at any given time. To take an analogy: Suppose you have a bouquet of roses. Now, suppose I replace a rose with a carnation. Do you have the same bouquet? Obviously not. Suppose instead I replace one rose with another rose. Now do you have the same bouquet? Again, it seems not. A bouquet of roses, which is just a bundle of flowers, seems to have its constituent roses *essentially*. That is to say, it is a necessary truth that that particular bouquet exists only if those particular roses are parts of it. Likewise with bundles of attributes. Replace one attribute with another and you have a different bundle. But if an object is nothing more than a bundle of attributes, then adding or removing an attribute to or from the bundle will leave you with a different object. For example, suppose that Socrates is seated. The bundle theory implies that Socrates is identical to a bundle (call it "B1") that has among its constituents the attribute *being a seated man*. If Socrates were to stand up, however, Socrates would be identical to a bundle (call it "B2") that has among its constituents the attribute *being a standing man*. B1 is not identical to B2; thus,

Socrates cannot be identical to both of them. Thus, either Socrates cannot stand up or the bundle theory is false.

One might try to resist this line of reasoning by rejecting the premise that says that replacing an attribute in a bundle leaves us with a new bundle. Saying this, however, seems to be at odds with the core idea of bundle theory. Paradigmatic substances have a kind of unity to their parts that goes some distance toward explaining why they can survive the replacement of their parts. A living organism, for example, has parts that are functionally organized in such a way that the *same life* can continue even as parts are gained or lost. It is at the heart of bundle theory, however, to deny that bundles have any such unity. There is nothing more to a bundle— no functional unity for example—besides its constituent attributes. (There is comprescence, but, as noted earlier, we do not really know what that is. Nor do we have reason to think that it is any more unifying than relations like *being in the same room*.) If we tried to develop our idea of a bundle into the idea of a more robust, genuinely unified sort of thing that could survive the gain or loss of some of its constituents, we would turn bundles into more than *mere* bundles: We would make them substances in their own right.

Fourthly, if the bundle theory is true and if attributes are universals, it looks as if objects cannot be duplicated, which seems implausible. Suppose we did try to duplicate something—say, a paperclip. If attributes are universals, a *perfect* duplicate of the paperclip would have exactly the same attributes as the paperclip. But if it had exactly the same attributes, it would be the same bundle, and thus the very same object (rather than a duplicate). The problem does not arise if attributes are tropes, however. For in that case, a perfect duplicate of the paperclip would not have exactly the same attributes as the original but rather attributes that perfectly resemble those of the original. So it seems that this particular objection implies that bundle theorists who want to allow for the possibility of perfect duplication ought to endorse trope theory.

Unsurprisingly, plenty of philosophers have tried to defend bundle theory from these and other objections. Each of these philosophers, Laurie Paul most notably, moves the bundle theory in the direction of saying that, ultimately, *everything is a property*. I think that it would be premature to say that this striking thesis, too, is a consequence of bundle theory; for perhaps there are yet ways of defending the theory that do not move in that direction. But for those who would rather not find themselves believing that everything is a property, bundle theory should be approached only with caution.

HYLOMORPHISM

The bundle theory and the bare-particular theory might be seen as agreeing on one basic principle. *All attributes are alike* in the following way: Either they all have to "stick" in the same way to an underlying individual subject, or none of them has to stick to an underlying subject at all. The bundle theorist takes the second option, denying substance altogether. The bare-particular theorist takes the first, positing intrinsically bare individuals as the underlying subjects. The bare-particular theory foundered, as we saw, in part because it is hard to see how anything can be intrinsically bare. But perhaps that problem is just an outgrowth of the idea that all attributes have to stick *in the same way* to an underlying *individual* subject. The theory of substance known as "hylomorphism" is not committed to this basic assumption (or, at any rate, not *every* proponent of hylomorphism commits to it), and so perhaps it offers a way forward.

The term "hylomorphism" derives from two Greek roots: *hylē* which means "matter," and *morphē*, which means "form." The core idea is that every material substance is a structured entity with two constituents, matter and form. Form is a special kind of attribute; it relates to its underlying subject in a way somewhat different from the way in which other attributes relate to their underlying subjects. Matter, likewise, is a special kind of subject; it is neither a bare particular nor a substance, which are the only other kinds of subject with which we are thus far acquainted.

The hylomorphic theory of substance has its origins in Aristotle. But it was also the dominant theory of substance in the Middle Ages and underwent a great deal of modification and development in the work of the great medieval philosopher-theologians, most notably St. Thomas Aquinas. A variety of early modern philosophers— Descartes and Leibniz, for example—also had their fair share to say about matter, form, and substance; and what *they* had to say about those concepts was influenced in part by developments in the natural sciences. If we skip ahead to the twentieth and twenty-first centuries, hylomorphism is undergoing something of a revival in contemporary metaphysics. Among the most important figures in that revival are Jeffrey Brower, Kit Fine, and Kathrin Koslicki, but their own versions of hylomorphism are informed by still other influences, including the formal logics developed in the early and middle twentieth century and various aspects of contemporary scientific theory. It is thus hard to say anything very uncontroversial about the *general* nature of hylomorphism; each proponent seems to have his or her own particular take on the theory. In fact, what we have at this point is not so much a single theory as a philosophical tradition that has given rise to a family of related theories.

As I see it, the central elements of hylomorphism are the following three theses:

H1   Objects are compounds of matter and form.
H2   An object's form is its *nature* or *essence*.
H3   Natures are principles of unity and development.

I will discuss each thesis in turn.

As I said earlier, matter is a special kind of subject: neither a bare particular nor a substance. What, then, is it? Perhaps the simplest characterization is that matter is whatever it is that a substance is made of. Consider, for example, a clay pot, created on a potter's wheel. Few in the Aristotelian tradition would actually regard clay pots as substances; as we shall see shortly, they don't have the right kind of "form." But never mind that for now; even Aristotle used examples like this to illuminate his concepts. When a potter forms a clay pot, the pot is made from an amorphous lump of clay. Before being shaped into a pot, the lump exists and is *potentially* a pot. The activity of the potter takes this preexisting stuff and makes it *actually* a pot by imposing a certain shape upon it. Thus, there are at least two things that we can say about the clay. Firstly, the clay is the underlying subject that receives the form *being a pot*, thereby bringing the pot into existence. Secondly, the clay is that aspect of the pot that, apart from the form, is *merely potentially* a pot. For this reason, in Aristotle's metaphysics, matter is associated with potentiality. It possesses the potentiality that is actualized by form, and it is sometimes said to be something that exists in potentiality. Form, by contrast, is associated with actuality. It actualizes the potentiality inherent in matter, and it exists in actuality.

We can now give a more general and accurate account of matter. Let "K" be a term that refers to a substance kind, like *human being* or *cat*. (In the Aristotelian tradition, living organisms are paradigm substances.) So, for example, saying that x is a K will be grammatically just like saying that *x* is a human being, or that *x* is a cat, or whatever; and talk about K-ness will be grammatically like talk about *humanity* or *felinity* or whatever. Given this terminology, we can characterize matter as follows: The matter for a K is whatever (1) is the underlying subject of the form K-ness and (2) is, apart from its K-ness, merely potentially a K. In a human being, the matter is the mass of tissue and bone and other stuff that is arranged human-wise. In a tree, the matter is the mass of wood and sap and other stuff that is arranged tree-wise. And so on.

But now we face a further question. Do these masses I have just mentioned themselves have further matter? Is the mass of tissue and bone that plays the role of matter in a particular human being itself a compound of matter and form? Here is one of the places where different hylomorphic theories diverge. There are three main options. One option is to say that, for example, the matter for a human being is itself an individual substance whose form is something like *being a mass of tissue and bone, and so on*. Few in the tradition would take this option. A second option is to say that the matter for a human being is a mere plurality of smaller substances (cells, fundamental particles, etc.), not itself an individual thing at all. A third option is to say that the matter for a human being is an individual pseudo-substance. According to this third option, there is a hierarchy of material objects: Some are substances in the primary sense of the term; others are substances only in a secondary or perhaps analogical sense of the term (which is why I call them "pseudo-substances"). Living organisms, for example, would likely count as primary substances; artifacts and mere lumps and so on would count as substances in the secondary or extended sense of the term. The primary substances, then, would have matter and form in the primary senses of those terms; the other objects would have matter and form in secondary or extended senses of those terms. Finally, a fourth option is to say that, in fact, the matter for a human being or tree or whatever is not a mass of tissue, bone, and so on, but rather a mass or portion of what has typically been called *prime matter*—stuff that, in and of itself, has no qualities whatsoever. (Those who believe in prime matter usually say that some, but not all, objects have prime matter as their matter. They then take one of the other three options in accounting for the matter of objects that are not compounds of prime matter and form.)

The idea of prime matter is about as puzzling as the idea of a bare particular, but it is better off in at least one respect. A bare particular is supposed to be a substance—a genuinely unified and individual thing, a basic entity on which other things depend for their existence. As a substance, the bare particular seems to be the sort of thing which ought to have an intrinsic nature. That is, we ought to be able to say *what it is* to be a bare particular. And there is precisely our problem: To be a bare particular is, if anything, to be an individual thing that has no intrinsic nature. The idea seems contradictory. Prime matter, on the other hand, is not supposed to be the sort of thing that has an intrinsic nature. Indeed, in and of itself, "it" is not a *particular* thing, nor is it any *sort* of thing at all. It has no independent existence whatsoever, and it has no intrinsic features. This is a hard doctrine, but it is not manifestly incoherent in the way that the idea of an intrinsically bare particular seems to be.

Still, prime matter is baffling. The problem with trying to explain the idea is that it seems that we can only do so under the assumption that prime matter is some particular kind of thing that has certain kinds of features. That, after all, is how we describe *anything*. So if we say that prime matter isn't a particular, it belongs to no kind (not even the kind "prime matter"!), and has no intrinsic features, we are stuck—we have no idea what we are talking about. For this reason, quite a lot of people have been reluctant to believe in prime matter.

That said, I think that we can at least take a few steps toward trying to make sense of the idea of prime matter, even if we can't come close to addressing all of the objections against it. Suppose you have a simple substance (a fundamental particle, say). Now suppose you take away its form—the complex property that makes it what it is—and suppose you don't replace the form with any other form. (You can't really do that, of course; but play along.) What would you have left? It seems that you wouldn't have a bare particular—that is, you wouldn't have a substance that has no features. You wouldn't have a particular at all. It's also not right to say that you would have literally nothing. For a thing isn't identical to its form. Whatever it is that would be left, whatever it is that would be *shared in common* between the original thing and whatever thing would come into existence once the form was replaced, is the prime matter. You can't say what that stuff is since, apart from the form, there is no substance there, and, indeed, there is nothing at all with an intrinsic nature. But (one might think) "it" is there nonetheless.

Enough about matter for now; what about form? We have already had a glimpse of what forms are supposed to be. They are more than mere shapes; they are complex organizational properties. Furthermore, as we have already said, forms are associated with actuality; among other things, they actualize the potentiality in matter. Accordingly, forms are typically also said to be the things that make something *what it most fundamentally is*. They are principles of unity, and they are the essences or the natures of the things that have them. The essence of a thing, in the Aristotelian tradition, is, very roughly, a complex property that (1) explains a large number of scientifically interesting features of the object—that is, features of its outward appearance, behavior, natural development, and so on—and (2) is shared in common by other objects and provides a basis for sorting those objects into a kind that is definable in terms of necessary and sufficient conditions. As natures, they are also principles of development. It is by virtue of having the particular nature that it has that a thing changes and develops in the ways that are characteristic of things of its kind.

Return again to the example of a human being. Apart from his or her form, there is nothing really to a human being besides some tissue, bone, and other materials. Those materials on their own, obviously, do not make a human being; they have to be *arranged* in the way that is characteristic of human beings. And by "arranged" I do not just mean that they have to be laid out in the shape of a human being; for arranging tissue, bone, and other materials in a human *shape* does not suffice for having a (living, functioning) human being. The arrangement, thus, has to include complex causal connections between the bits of tissue, bone, and so on. This is why I said earlier that form isn't mere shape.

Once the form is imposed on the tissue, bone, and so on, we have *a single human being*; before that, we don't have much by way of genuine unity at all. There is, for example, no system relative to which the bits of tissue, bone, and other materials have functions (or, at any rate, there does not seem to be). Those things are not playing any particular functional role in a larger whole. So this is one indication that, absent the form, there is no real unity to the matter. It is in this sense, then, that the form is a principle of unity: It takes us from having a mere plurality of substances, or a pseudo-substance, or just some stuff that is not yet a particular thing, to having a single unified substance; and, again, *functional arrangement* is at least an indicator of, if not a necessary condition for, the presence of genuine unity.

Note that it is plausibly the functional arrangement of the parts of a substance that determine how the substance is supposed to change and develop over time. A human zygote has its parts functionally arranged in a particular way. Again, it is not just that they have a certain shape; rather, they have been put in certain causal relations to one another. Those causal relations, furthermore, together determine how the zygote will develop into an adult human being. It is in this way that natures play the role of principles of change and development.

I said earlier that forms are special kinds of attributes. We can now be more specific about the ways in which they are special. First, forms join with matter to generate substances. Furthermore, they *inhere in* matter without *characterizing it*. Humanity, for example, inheres in Socrates' matter. But it doesn't characterize Socrates' matter; his matter isn't human. Rather, humanity characterizes Socrates. Other attributes, on the other hand, do not join with matter to generate substances, and they characterize that in which they inhere. If Socrates is seated, seatedness inheres in him. It also characterizes him. And the inherence of seatedness in Socrates does not generate a substance.

Here we must pause to attend to a complication. Throughout this discussion I have been using the term "form" as if all forms are substantial forms—that is, all forms are the forms of substances; all forms correspond to substance-kinds, like *humanity* or *felinity*. That is certainly the primary sense of the term "form." However, some Aristotelians think that just about any attribute can *play the role* of form. Thus, for example, some will say that when Socrates sits down, a new compound—Seated Socrates—comes into existence.

In Seated Socrates, *Socrates* plays the role of matter and the attribute *seatedness* plays the role form, generating a new object (though not a new substance), Seated Socrates, that exists for just as long as Socrates is seated. Aristotle himself used examples like this. Some people recoil at the thought of objects like Seated Socrates. But I think that in fact most of us believe in such things. You probably believe that *Socrates' being seated* names an event. Why not say instead that it names an object, Seated Socrates? You probably believe you can make a fist. Your fist is perhaps not a substance. But it seems to be a matter–form compound whose matter is your hand and whose form is a particular fist-like shape. In any case, what this means is that what I have said about the way in which forms are special applies *only* to substantial forms and not to whatever other attributes might happen to be playing the role of form. To avoid confusion, however, I will continue the practice of using the unqualified term "form" to refer only to *substantial forms*. When I want to talk about the constituents of things like fists, or Seated Socrates, I shall be careful to speak either of "non-substantial forms" or of attributes *playing the role* of form. End of complication.

Secondly, forms are kind properties: They are properties the having of which determines what kind of thing an object is. Or, if objects can somehow belong to more than one kind, they determine an object's dominant kind. (A single object cannot have two forms. But if the dominant-kinds theory is correct, a thing can belong to a kind without possessing the form associated with that kind.) Insofar as they determine an object's kind, they also determine its persistence conditions.

We have now characterized matter and form; we have seen, too, the basic rationale behind the three theses that I identified as the core of hylomorphism. I want to close this section by briefly considering one further issue that naturally arises in connection with this discussion—namely, the question of how hylomorphists can address the problem of material constitution that arose in the last chapter.

The problem of material constitution, recall, arises whenever it appears that an object *a* and an object *b* share all of the same parts but have different modal properties. We considered various solutions to this problem in Chapter 4, but one that I ignored there is what I have elsewhere called the "Aristotelian Solution."

Consider again the Lumpl/Goliath puzzle (and let us suppose for now that *statue* is a substance kind and *lump* is not). In the region occupied by Goliath there appear to be two distinct material objects: a lump and a statue. Note, however, that within a hylomorphic framework the lump and the statue can be seen as standing in an interesting kind of relationship with one another: Either one is the matter for the other (i.e., perhaps the statue is just a compound of the lump and the form *being a statue*) or they share the same matter (i.e., the same underlying plurality, or the same prime matter, bears a substantial form—*being a statue*—and one of those secondary, non-substantial forms mentioned in connection with "the third option" discussed earlier—*being a lump*). We can run these two options together by saying that two things share all of the same matter in common if, and only if, either one is matter for the other or the matter for one is also the matter for the other.

The question, then, is what we shall say about objects like this that share all of the same matter in common. Notice, first of all, that only one of the objects is a substance: the statue. So, right away, we preserve the intuition that there is just *one* primary subject of predication in the region. However, we also preserve the intuition that the lump is a real thing and is something different from the statue. Still, we face the question of how many *material objects* there are in the region. Here, Aristotle has something interesting to say. In cases like this one, it seems that what Aristotle wants to say is that the statue and the lump are *one in number* but not *one in being*. That is, they are different things but are to be counted as one material object. The idea, then, seems to be that the statue and the lump are *numerically the same* material object. Goliath *is* Lumpl, and there is just one material object in the region occupied by it. But they are nevertheless distinct *hylomorphic compounds*.

Initially this seems completely baffling. How can *two hylomorphic compounds* be *one and the same material object*? The answer comes in two parts. First, we note that this solution presupposes the following (controversial) principle of relative sameness:

RS   States of affairs of the following sort are possible: x is an F, y is an F, x is a G, y is a G, x is the same F as y, but x is not the same G as y.

In the case at hand, Lumpl and Goliath provide an instance of RS. Each is a material object, and each is a hylomorphic compound; and Lumpl is the same material object as Goliath but not the same hylomorphic compound. How can this be? Here we come to the second part: What it *is* for one thing to be the same material object as another is just for the one thing and the other to share the same matter in common. That is just part of the concept of being a material object: We count one material object wherever we have some matter with one or more forms imposed upon it.

That last claim should be completely intuitive. It is, I think, commitment to that last claim about the conditions under which we count one material object that makes us recoil at the thought of saying that Lumpl and Goliath are *two* material objects. But notice that we do not recoil at the thought of saying that two *things* occupy the same place at the same time. Two events can easily occupy the same place at the same time—for example, the event of your sitting and the event of your thinking about philosophy. Hylomorphism gives us the resources to respect these basic intuitions. The fact that substances are compounds of matter and form, together with the fact that the same matter can bear multiple forms (even if some of the forms are not *substantial* forms) gives rise to cases where we want to count *two* things (two hylomorphic compounds) but just *one* material object (since, again, we count one material object wherever we have some matter bearing one or more forms).

We have now finished discussing the theories of substance on which I wanted to focus in this chapter. I want to end the chapter by considering two topics that naturally arise in connection with discussions of substance. The first is composition; the second is God. The first arises because theories of substance are in part theories about what things in the world are genuine unities. They therefore imply at least partial answers to the question of what the conditions are under which a plurality of objects composes an individual thing. The second arises because substances are supposed to be basic entities, which naturally leads into the question whether there is a single *most basic* entity (God?) on which everything else depends, or a plurality of such entities, or an infinite chain of dependent things.

COMPOSITION

In his widely influential book *Material Beings*, Peter van Inwagen raised the following question: What, in general, does one have to do, and what would suffice, to get some objects to compose some other object? He called this question the "special composition question" (SCQ). Some answers can be dismissed right away: Gluing things together, for example, is not sufficient for getting objects to compose something. Glue two people together and, it seems, we do not thereby create a new object. In fact no particular kind of *bonding* seems to be sufficient. Bond two human beings together in whatever way you like; that by itself will not create a new object. Thus, much of the focus in the vast literature that has been spawned by the SCQ has been on two "extreme" answers: universalism, according to which any objects whatsoever compose something; and nihilism, according to which there are no composite objects at all. Van Inwagen's own answer—composition occurs whenever you arrange things so that their activity constitutes a life—has, of course, also received a fair bit of attention, since it implies that the only genuine composites are living organisms.

Given the commonsense assumption that vans, wagons, fish, moons, and so on, all count as genuine composite objects, universalism implies that, for example, there are also objects like the van-in-wagon mentioned at the outset of this chapter, as well as an object composed of your nose and the moon, or of all the fish in the sea, etc. Many philosophers find this view counterintuitive. Just as it doesn't seem that two human beings glued together compose something, so too it doesn't seem that all the fish in the sea compose something. All the fish in the sea seem more like a mere plurality. Both nihilism and van Inwagen's answer, however, seem to rule out too many objects, for both imply that, strictly speaking, there are no computers, cars, tables, chairs, etc. There are, of course, things arranged table-wise, computer-wise, and so on. But the point here is that, on these views, arranging objects table-wise or computer-wise does not get those objects actually to *compose* a table or a computer.

A hylomorphic theory of substance can offer some help. The theory does not specify fully informative conditions under which composition occurs, of course. To do that, one would have to identify the conditions under which a mode of arrangement rises to the level of being a (substantial or non-substantial) form; and hylomorphism as such does not help us to identify such conditions. However, hylomorphism can at least provide a framework for thinking about the SCQ that reveals what some of the salient issues might be.

Hylomorphism alone among the theories of substances we have discussed in this chapter allows that the primary substances in the world are composite objects that undergo change and development. Furthermore, the hylomorphist separates the substances from the non-substances precisely on the basis of differences in the mode of arrangement displayed by the (alleged) parts of a thing. Those modes of arrangement that impose *genuine unity* upon things join with matter to generate substances; those that do not, do not. Thus, hylomorphism implies that wherever we find a mode of arrangement that imposes genuine unity upon things, we find a composite object. Thus, we have a sufficient condition, even if not a maximally informative one, for when composition occurs.

For the hylomorphist, then, the first decision point in addressing the SCQ is to ask whether there are substantial forms. It would be strange, though not impossible, to be a hylomorphist and to believe that no modes of arrangement whatsoever count as substantial forms. Thus, the likely answer to the question whether there are substantial forms is "yes." Nihilism is ruled out.

Another decision point is to ask whether all forms are substantial forms. Suppose we say, "Yes." It is clear that not *every* way of arranging objects is going to count as a substantial form. My children arrange their toys in my living room every day in ways that display no functional unity or any other obvious form of unity. If the toys together did compose something, what they compose would have no internal principle of change and development. In short, it would have no substantial form. Indeed, if we said that even the toys in my living room *do* compose an object with a substantial form, we would likely lose all basis for saying that there is a distinction to be drawn between genuine unity and merely apparent unity. The substance/non-substance distinction would become meaningless, and so there would be no point in characterizing *any* forms as substantial forms. So if we say that *all* forms are substantial forms, we should also say that the toys in my living room do not compose something. Universalism is therefore ruled out.

Universalism is *not* ruled out, however, if we allow that there are non-substantial forms. In that case, we might say that some attribute collectively exemplified by the toys is playing the role of form, albeit rather poorly, or only in an extended sense. That might suffice for the toys to compose an object, even if not a substance. And we might say the same for *any* attribute collectively exemplified by *any* objects whatsoever. If we do say this, then we have opted for universalism after all. In saying this, however, we will still want to draw distinctions between modes of arranging objects, identifying some as sufficiently rich and unifying to count as substantial forms and identifying others as falling short of that threshold, even if they do nevertheless impose some relatively weaker sort of unity upon things. (We will want to say that non-substantial forms genuinely unify their parts. The difference between substantial and non-substantial forms will just be in the degree and kind of unity imposed.) In saying all of this, then, we can, even if we endorse universalism, do justice to the intuitions of those who prefer moderate answers to the SCQ. We can say that those who endorse moderate answers—like van Inwagen's answer, according to which only living organisms count as composites—have incorrectly identified the substance/non-substance distinction with the object/mere plurality distinction. This doesn't resolve the dispute, but it clarifies a significant issue on which the dispute depends.

A final decision point, of course, concerns the criteria for genuine unity. What must a mode of arranging objects be like in order to impose genuine unity upon objects? (If we believe in both substantial and non-substantial forms, we might further ask what a mode of arranging objects must be like in order to impose *enough* unity upon objects to generate a substance.) Must it be a mode of *functional* arrangement? Must it be a mode of arrangement that, given the laws of nature, guarantees that the object whose form it is will change and develop in predictable ways all of its own accord in something like the way that living organisms do? Must it be a mode of arrangement that guarantees that the object whose form it is will be self-maintaining in some sense? These are difficult questions—no less difficult, really, than the SCQ itself.

The fact that we still face such difficult questions, however, does not mean that hylomorphism makes no progress with the SCQ. As we have seen, endorsing hylomorphism gives us at least two clear decision points that will help us to decide between extreme answers to the SCQ. Moreover, reframing the SCQ, as hylomorphism encourages us to do, as a question about what it takes to unify some objects opens up avenues of exploration that might otherwise not have occurred to us. There is, for example, a sizeable philosophical literature on functions that can be brought to bear on the question of what it takes to functionally organize objects. Doing so might shed light on the question whether functional organization is really any more unifying than other modes of arrangement. It might also shed light on the question whether sharp lines can be drawn between things that are functionally organized and things that are not. All of this can help the hylomorphist to flesh out her understanding of form and, in so doing, to craft a more fully informative answer to the SCQ.

GOD

For much of our discussion in this chapter we have focused on the idea of substances as things whose parts are genuinely unified. Now it is time to focus more on the idea of substances as things on which other things depend. In the Aristotelian tradition, as we have seen, living organisms and perhaps other composites are counted as substances. Forms join with matter to produce hylomorphic compounds, which are, then, the subjects in which all other attributes inhere. Furthermore, it is typical within the Aristotelian tradition to say that attributes depend on substances for their very existence. There are no uninstantiated attributes; indeed, attributes do not even *exist* in the primary sense of the term.

One might notice, however, a couple of problems with this framework. First of all, doesn't it seem that material substances are dependent things after all? True, their attributes might depend on them in the sense that, had there been no such things, then the attributes distinctive of material substances would not have existed. But, as hylomorphic compounds, these things seem, in turn, to depend on their constituents—on their matter and form. Secondly, material substances are the sorts of things that *come into existence* and *pass out of existence*. But if *they* are the things on which everything else depends, that would seem to imply that (1) everything is destructible; and (2) the universe contains an infinitely long sequence of generated and destructible objects.

These claims together, however, seem puzzling. For if everything is destructible, one would not expect there to be an infinite sequence of anything; one would rather expect that, after a suitably long time, any sequence of objects would end with the ultimate destruction of everything. It would be sheer coincidence, it seems, if a sequence of destructible beings lasted forever, and it seems we should not believe that such remarkable coincidences occur. So, for this reason, it seems that we shouldn't think that the universe contains an infinitely long sequence of destructible things. A sequence of destructible things that extends infinitely backward in time would surely have come to an end long before now; so our very existence seems to be evidence that there is no such sequence.

It seems, then, that the sequence of material substances must be finite; it must have a beginning and (short of some miracle) an end. Let us ask, now, about the beginning. Is that the culmination of some other sequence of changes extending infinitely backward in time? Or is it the result of the activity of some cause that is not a material substance? Or did the finite sequence of material substances pop into existence by chance?

Let us rule out the chance hypothesis. I do not know how to show that hypothesis to be absurd, but it is hard to imagine how *anything* could simply pop into existence by chance.

Suppose we say that the *beginning* of the sequence of material substances is the culminating result of some other sequence of changes extending infinitely backward in time. On this picture, there is a point in time when material substance comes into existence, but before that time and, indeed, extending infinitely backward in time, there is still change of some sort and, indeed, one or more of these changes ultimately resulted in the generation of material substance. For convenience, let us refer to the changes that are taking place before the generation of material substance as the "primordial changes." We may now ask what are the subjects of these primordial changes. Change occurs only if something changes; so what are the things that are undergoing the primordial changes? They cannot be material substances, for the primordial changes predate the existence of material substance. But what else is there? That is our first question. Our second question is whether each primordial change has a cause, so that there is an infinite sequence of causes, or whether there is some first cause.

Answering the first question provides a response to an earlier question that we have thus far left hanging. Toward the beginning of this section, I asked whether it seems that material substances themselves depend upon their constituents. For rather complicated reasons that are best ignored in this discussion, those writing in the hylomorphic tradition have been reluctant to elevate *matter* to the level of substance. But form—which, as we have seen, is traditionally associated with *actuality*, which constitutes the very *nature* of a substance, and which is also traditionally regarded as a principle of change and development—does have some claim to the status of substance. One can be human apart from any particular "portion" of matter, but one cannot possibly be human apart from humanity itself. Furthermore, as a principle of development, the form plays an important causal role in bringing a substance to, and maintaining it in, its mature and properly functioning state. Thus, it seems that material substances depend on their form in a way in which they don't depend on their matter. Furthermore, forms have a kind of independence that prime matter, at any rate, does not. Like familiar substances, and unlike prime matter, forms admit of intrinsic characterization; they are things in their own right (universals or tropes). Finally, there is no reason to doubt that forms have their own internal unity. Thus, there seems to be good reason to accord them the status of substance. If we do, we have an answer to the question of what *besides* material substances there might be. There might be something like a pure form.

Note, however, that I say only "something like" a pure form. If forms are truly attributes, and *if* attributes truly depend on their instances, then there cannot be an unexemplified form. Thus, if immaterial substances preexist material substances, they might well be form-like. Following Aristotle, for example, we might characterize such a thing as *pure actuality* and regard it as a primordial cause, a principle of change and development that explains other changes in the universe. But we could not say they are pure attributes (or anything like attributes) without giving up the principle that forms, like other attributes, depend upon their instances.

As to the second question, the answer depends upon whether one thinks that it is sensible to believe in an infinite sequence of causes. Aristotle did not, and many in his wake—theists and atheists alike— have not. Atheists who follow Aristotle on this point typically say that the "first cause" is just the initial singularity from which emerged the Big Bang. This is a hard doctrine, however, within an Aristotelian substance ontology. For if the initial singularity is a material substance, then it will be the sort of thing that is generated and destructible (which then means that we can sensibly ask where it came from). If it is not a material substance, then, whatever it is, it is neither a genuine unity nor an independent thing. It is thus the sort of thing whose existence demands an explanation.

Aristotle, as I have said, thought that there was a first cause; and, on his view, the first cause *had* to be not a material substance but rather *pure actuality*. This, as we have just noted, would make the first cause something like a form. Aristotle went on to argue that the first cause had to be eternal, immovable, and, indeed, good (since goodness is a principle of motion, and the first cause is the ultimate explanation of all motion). Ultimately he identified the first cause with God.

The argument I have just presented is a fleshed-out reconstruction of a line of argument that can be found in Book XII of Aristotle's *Metaphysics*. The basic ideas in this argument have, as many readers will know, been developed in various different ways (and typically with greater reliance on claims about causation, explanation, and dependence) throughout the history of philosophy—most notably in the Middle Ages by the Islamic philosophers Al-Kindi (801–873) and Al-Ghazali (1058–1111), and by St. Thomas Aquinas. The versions developed in the Middle Ages have come to be known as versions of "the Cosmological Argument."

Although the conclusion of the Cosmological Argument is that God exists, we should note that the conception of God that emerges from that argument is a relatively thin one. It is what Martin Heidegger called the "god of metaphysics," the "ground of all being." Heidegger himself complained that the god of metaphysics is not one before whom we can sing and dance, the idea being that if our concept of God is *simply* the concept of something that is posited to explain the existence of all other beings, the God we have thus conceived is not one that inspires passionate devotion. But, of course, virtually nobody wielding the Cosmological Argument for the existence of God would think that the concept of God is exhausted by the concept of a first cause; nor would they think that the Cosmological Argument is our only source of insight into what God might be like. To flesh out the concept of God, however, would take us well into the realm of theology and thus far beyond the proper scope of a book primarily devoted to the basics of metaphysics.

FURTHER READING

On the topic of substance generally, two important works are Michael J. Loux, *Substance and Attribute: A Study in Ontology* (Dordrecht: D. Reidel, 1978); and Joshua Hoffman and Gary S. Rosenkrantz, *Substance: Its Nature and Existence* (London and New York: Routledge, 1997). Robert Pasnau's *Metaphysical Themes, 1274–1671* (Oxford: Oxford University Press, 2011) is another excellent resource. (It is particularly useful on the topic of substance, but it provides a very helpful historical perspective on other topics treated in this book as well.)

On the bundle theory, Max Black's paper, "The Identity of Indiscernibles," *Mind*, vol. 61 (1952), pp. 153–164, is famous for pushing the objection that bundle theorists cannot admit the possibility of duplication. Two of the more important recent discussions of Black's article are John O'Leary Hawthorne and Jan A. Cover, "A World of Universals," *Philosophical Studies*, vol. 91 (1998), pp. 205–219; and Dean Zimmerman, "Distinct Indiscernibles and the Bundle Theory," *Mind*, vol. 106 (1997), pp. 305–309. For several different versions of the bundle theory, as well as the main objections discussed in this chapter, see James van Cleve, "Three Versions of the Bundle Theory," *Philosophical Studies*, vol. 47 (1985), pp. 95–107. I said that L. A. Paul was among those pushing the bundle theory in the direction of saying that everything is a property. For her own developments of that theory, see L. A. Paul, "Logical Parts," *Noûs*, vol. 36 (2002), pp. 578–596; and L. A. Paul, "Building the World from its Fundamental Constituents," *Philosophical Studies* vol. 158 (2012), pp. 221–256.

On bare-particular theory, Edwin Allaire's, "Bare Particulars," *Philosophical Studies*, vol. 14 (1963), pp. 1–7, is a classic article. See also Theodore Sider's more recent "Bare Particulars," *Philosophical Perspectives*, vol. 20 (2006), pp. 387–397, and Andrew M. Bailey, "No Bare Particulars," *Philosophical Studies*, vol. 158 (2012), pp. 31–41. Although Bailey opposes the bare particular theory, his paper is an excellent resource for those looking for references to others who defend the view.

My own understanding of the views of Aristotle and Aquinas, and of hylomorphism in general, is heavily influenced by Michael Loux and Jeffrey Brower. In particular, see Michael Loux, *Primary Ousia* (Ithaca, NY: Cornell University Press, 1991) and Jeffrey Brower, *Aquinas on Material Objects* (Oxford: Oxford University Press, 2013). For contemporary defenses of hylomorphism, see (in addition to Brower's book) Kit Fine, "Things and Their Parts," *Midwest Studies in Philosophy*, vol. 23 (1999), pp. 61–74; Kathrin Koslicki, *The Structure of Objects* (Oxford: Oxford University Press, 2008); Kathrin Koslicki, "Substance, Independence and Unity," in Edward Feser, ed., *Aristotle on Method and Metaphysics* (Basingstoke: Palgrave Macmillan, forthcoming); Michael Rea, "Sameness without Identity: An Aristotelian Solution to the Problem of Material Constitution," *Ratio*, vol. 11 (1998), pp. 316–328; and Michael Rea, "Hylomorphism Reconditioned," *Philosophical Perspectives*, vol. 25 (2011): pp. 341–358.

On the topic of composition, Peter van Inwagen's *Material Beings* (Ithaca, NY: Cornell University Press, 1990) is a must-read. Beyond that, working through the articles and books on temporal parts and material constitution that were listed at the end of Chapter 4, as well as the *Metametaphysics* volume cited at the end of Chapter 1, will provide anyone interested in this topic with a reasonably good guide to the relevant literature and the various positions within it.

On the cosmological argument mentioned at the end of this chapter, I recommend, for starters, the set of readings on that topic in Michael Rea and Louis Pojman, eds., *Philosophy of Religion: An Anthology*, 7th edn. (Boston, MA: Cengage, 2013).

6

FREEDOM

Whatever will be, will be. Most often, these famous words simply express a carefree attitude toward the future: "Let things unfold as they will; whatever will be, will be!" Sometimes, however, they express an attitude of wistful resignation to whatever fate has ordained: "Nothing I do can make any difference to what happens; the future is set, and there is nothing I can do about it; I can't do anything except sit and wait to see what happens; whatever will be, will be." It is this latter sense of those words that is of interest for purposes of this chapter. Is the future inevitable and unchangeable? Is it true that there is nothing we can do about the future? If so, doesn't this mean that we are not free? These questions point us toward one of two philosophical problems concerning freedom of action that we shall discuss in this chapter: the problem of fatalism.

We rarely *act* as if we believe that we are fated to act in a particular way. We deliberate, sometimes long and hard, about what we ought to do in various circumstances. In doing so, we manifest our belief that we actually have a choice about what we do, that how things will turn out depends on what we now choose, and that the future is not already settled. Likewise, we take ourselves to be responsible for our actions, as if it is genuinely up to us whether we do the things we in fact do. If we sincerely believed that our lives are subject to fate, how could we sensibly take ourselves to be responsible for what we do?

Yet we often talk about the future as if there are now facts (i.e., true propositions) about what we and others will be doing. We routinely say things like, "I will be home for another hour; feel free stop by anytime," or "Kristina will babysit Gretchen and Matthias this afternoon, so let's go get coffee at one o'clock," or "Tim will leave for the airport in a minute, so you had better quickly say your goodbyes." Moreover, it seems that we can look back on the past and make retrospective inferences about what future-tense claims were true before certain dates. Buzz Aldrin took his famous moon walk on July 21, 1969; therefore it seems that the following must have been true at every time prior to that date: "Buzz Aldrin will walk on the moon on July 21, 1969." But if there are future-tense facts like this, then it seems that the future *is* already settled, our current deliberations can make no difference in what will come to pass, and we have always been fated or destined to act exactly as we do.

So there seems to be a tension in the beliefs that many of us have about the "openness" of the future. We think and act as if we have many available alternatives, but we also seem to think that there are facts about what we will do and about how things will go. It is unclear how these two otherwise commonsensical beliefs can both be correct. This apparent tension gives rise to the fatalism problem.

The second problem with freedom is related to the first in that it, too, arises out of beliefs many people have that conflict with the commonsense belief that freedom involves having some kind of *control* over our actions. This is the *determination problem*. It arises because many have thought that our acts are determined in various ways, and these forms of determination all seem to preclude our having genuine control over our actions.

Some people believe that the laws of nature are deterministic, that the universe is like a machine that *has to* unfold in one very specific way. Others reject this view about the laws of nature but think that human action is subject to various other kinds of determination. For example, we seem to have no direct control over our beliefs and desires at any given moment. (If you think otherwise, then I have a terrific diet plan for you: Just stop desiring unhealthy foods. I also have a terrific plan for quitting smoking: Just stop desiring to smoke. This plan also works for low self-esteem: Just start believing that you are a wonderful person and that everyone likes you.) But our beliefs and desires together seem to determine all of our actions. Likewise, we have no control over the laws of physics and chemistry that govern the behavior of our brains, which, in turn, determine the behavior of our minds and bodies. All of these determination theses threaten the idea that we have genuine control over our actions. What is worse, rejecting them doesn't seem to help with the problem. For if neither our beliefs and desires nor the laws of nature determine our behavior, what else besides sheer chance could explain why we do what we do? But chance events are no more up to us than the laws of nature. So it seems that the threat to our belief that we control our actions lingers even if we reject all of the above determination theses.

TERMS AND DISTINCTIONS

Let us begin with some of the central "isms" in the free-will literature. There are six of them: (1) **determinism**, (2) **indeterminism**, (3) **compatibilism**, (4) **incompatibilism**, (5) **libertarianism**, and (6) **hard determinism**.

Determinism is commonly defined as the thesis that there is, at any given moment, only one physically possible future. We might also put it this way: Let's say that a *world-statement* is a statement describing the complete state of the world at a particular time, that is, one that fully describes how everything *is* at that time but omits any truths about how things were or will be. (A world-statement is just like an abstract time, except that the time would include whatever facts there are about how things *were* and *will be*.) Let's say that a law-statement is a statement that describes *all* of the laws of nature that hold in the world. Then determinism is the thesis that the world-statement for a time *t* together with a law-statement logically entails *every* world-statement for every time later than *t*.

The other "isms" are easy to characterize. *Indeterminism* is the thesis that determinism is false. *Compatibilism* is the view that freedom is compatible with determinism—that is, it is possible for us to act freely even if determinism is true. *Incompatibilism* is the view that freedom is incompatible with determinism. *Libertarianism* is the view that incompatibilism is true and human beings are free. *Hard determinism* is the view that both incompatibilism and determinism are true. People sometimes talk about "libertarian freedom" or "compatibilist freedom," as if these are different kinds of freedom. But they aren't. One has libertarian freedom if, and only if, libertarianism is true. One has compatibilist freedom if, and only if, one is free and freedom is compatible with determinism.

What does it mean to be free, or to act freely? I have no informative definition to offer, but we can home in on our concept of freedom by looking at three other concepts with which it is closely connected. Firstly, the concept of freedom is connected with the idea of control: To be free is to have a certain kind of control over one's acts. Having control over one's acts, in turn, requires being (in some sense) their source. To the extent that we act under coercion, for example, our freedom is undermined. Secondly, the concept of freedom is connected with the notion of responsibility: Our free acts seem just to be those acts for which we can be held responsible. (This is not to say that every free act is morally significant, though. One can be responsible for one's coffee-sipping acts, even if taking a sip of coffee is wholly morally neutral.) Thirdly, the concept of freedom is connected with the idea of being able to choose among incompatible courses of action. Where we are unable to act otherwise, we seem not to act freely.

Together, these claims give us a pretty good idea of what we mean when we say that an agent acts freely. Each of them, however, is problematic. The claim that freedom requires control is imprecise, as is the claim that having control involves being the source of one's actions. Does having control require having alternative possibilities for action? If you could not have done otherwise than what you in fact did on some occasion, does it follow that you lacked the right sort of control over your action? Does being the source of your actions mean being subject to *no* outside influences, or just relatively few? If the latter, then which outside influences undermine freedom and which do not? These questions are hard to answer. The claim that our free acts are just those for which we are responsible is not quite so imprecise, but it is controversial. Some philosophers think that freedom and moral responsibility come apart: One can freely perform an act for which one is not morally responsible, or vice versa. Likewise with the claim that freedom requires the ability to do otherwise. There is, as one might guess, a vast literature exploring all of these issues.

Trying to conduct our discussion in a way that remains neutral on the issues just mentioned is unworkable. It would make things too complicated. Likewise, trying to settle the issues by way of argument is unworkable. It would take a long book rather than just a section of a chapter. So I will simply make some decisions. Following Alicia Finch (2013), I will say that, necessarily, a person S performs an act A freely only if each of the following claims is true:

- *S has or had a choice about whether S* performs A.
- It is or was *up to S* whether S performs A.
- S is or was *able to A and able to refrain from A-ing*.
- It is or was true that *S can A and S can refrain from A-ing*.

(I should note that my wording here isn't exactly Finch's. I am quite sure, however, that the modifications I have made are in the spirit of what she intended.) In the remainder of this chapter, I will use the italicized locutions interchangeably, taking them to be equivalent to one another. In doing so, I set aside talk about "control" or about being the "source" of one's actions as ways of understanding freedom, and I come down in favor of the claim that freedom requires alternative possibilities for action. I shall also assume that freedom goes hand in hand with responsibility, that the acts for which we are responsible are just those with respect to which we are free. Making these assumptions does not substantially affect the content of the discussion that follows; it just prevents the discussion from getting overly complicated. Readers interested in a fuller exploration of these issues, together with considerations for and against the various assumptions I am making here should see Meghan Griffith's *Free Will: The Basics*.

In addition to asking what freedom is, one might also ask what things are properly said to *be* free (or unfree). I have already indicated that I think *actions* are the sorts of things that can be free. But just as often one hears people talk about the *will* being free, or about *agents* being free, or about *decisions* or *choices* being free. Can all of these things be free? Or just some of them?

Decisions and choices seem to be types of action, so there is no obvious problem with treating them as potential bearers of freedom. We might say that an *agent* is free just when certain actions of hers are free. Which actions? The answer depends on context. Are prisoners free? Generally, that is, in most contexts, we will say no, because there are a great many actions that prisoners are unable to perform because of their confinement. But, of course, even prisoners still manage to act freely. In prison, one still has a choice about whether to obey the guards or resist them, about whether to participate actively in the riot at the end of the week or try to sit it out, about whether to pick up the telephone handset to talk to one's visitor or just to sit there and gesticulate silently, and so on. In contexts where it is clear that it is these sorts of actions we have most saliently in mind, we might well say that even prisoners are free. Still, though we can make sense of talk about agents being free, our discussion will be more rigorous if we avoid it.

What about the will? Not one's *willings*, which are acts just as decisions and choices are acts, but the *will itself*. Is the will free? John Locke famously argued that the question whether the will is free rests on a confusion. According to Locke, the will is nothing but a *power*: a power to choose. Furthermore, according to Locke, freedom is also a power: a power to act as one chooses. Thus, on his view, to say that a person's will is free is to say that her power to choose has a certain power to act. But this is nonsense. Mere powers to choose cannot themselves have powers to act. So Locke concludes that it is simply confused to ask whether the will is free. Is he right? That depends to some extent on whether he is correct in thinking that freedom and the will are both powers. Freedom does seem to be a power or capacity of some sort. But one might think of the will as something more like a decision-making module within one's mind or brain. Thought of in this way, a person's will would be a *part* of her, and it might make as much sense to talk of the powers of the will as it makes to talk of the powers of one's brain or heart or kidneys. So, in short, it is unclear whether we should follow Locke in saying that it is confused to talk about freedom of the will. Regardless of what we decide, however, it seems that an agent's will is free if, and only if, some of her acts are free. So, it is ultimately unnecessary to focus on freedom of the will itself, and we shall avoid doing so for the remainder of our discussion.

THE DETERMINATION PROBLEM

The determination problem arises because human freedom seems impossible regardless of whether determinism is true and regardless of whether our actions are subject to various kinds of local determination. In this section, I will explain the problem more fully, and then I will examine several of the most well-known strategies for resolving it.

Let us note, first, that throughout this chapter our focus shall be restricted to the actions and freedom of *natural* agents—that is, human beings and other creatures in the natural world, rather than, say, God or angels. So, unless it is otherwise indicated, talk about *agents* is to be construed as talk about natural agents. This focus makes sense, given that we have defined determinism by reference to the laws of nature, which means that it is a thesis about the natural world.

Now let's start with global determinism. The standard argument for incompatibilism is the Consequence Argument. There are various different versions of this argument, but the following is probably the simplest and most straightforward. Let us assume that, necessarily, if agents exist at all, then there are times before which any agent ever existed. (This assumption helps us to avoid some unnecessary complications.) Let us stipulate that times in the "remote past" are times before any agent ever existed. Given all of this, we may argue as follows (adapting Peter van Inwagen's *An Essay on Free Will*):

6.1 Determinism is true. (Assumption.)

6.2 If determinism is true, then no matter what act any agent performs, it is a necessary consequence of the law-statement and the world-statement for a time in the remote past that she performs that act. (From the definition of determinism.)

6.3 No agent has or ever had a choice about the truth of the world-statement for any time in the remote past. (Premise.)

6.4 No agent has or ever had a choice about the truth of the law-statement. (Premise.)

6.5 An agent has or had a choice about a necessary consequence of a proposition only if she has or had a choice about whether the proposition itself is true. (Premise.)

6.6 Therefore, no agent has or ever had a choice about whether she performs any of her own acts. (From 6.1–6.5.)

6.7 An agent acts freely on some occasion only if she has or had a choice about whether she performs the act on that occasion. (From our earlier stipulations about freedom.)

6.8 Therefore: No agent ever acts freely. (From 6.6, 6.7.)

If sound, this argument establishes incompatibilism. Determining whether the argument is sound is primarily a matter of determining whether premises 6.3–6.5 are true. Premise 6.1 is just an assumption to get the argument going. Premises 6.2 and 6.7 are obviously true, given the definitions and stipulations laid out in the first section of this chapter. Premise 6.6 has to be true if 6.1–6.5 are true. So all of those premises are immune to substantive criticism. If one wants to avoid the conclusion of this argument, one has to resist 6.3, 6.4, or 6.5.

Let us begin by examining 6.5. It is easy to find examples that conform to 6.5. Suppose you are a bachelor. It is a necessary consequence of your being a bachelor that you are both unmarried and male. Sure enough, then, you have a choice about whether you are unmarried and male only if you have a choice about whether you are a bachelor. But finding examples that conform to 6.5 isn't at all the same as *proving* 6.5, and it is hard to know how one might prove it. Given this, we should perhaps be a little suspicious of 6.5.

We find more reason to be suspicious when we realize that it is not at all clear what exactly "has a choice about" means in 6.5. We might raise this concern for 6.3 and 6.4 too, of course, but the problem is particularly pressing in the case of 6.5 because it is not at all clear that *both occurrences* of the phrase can mean the same thing. The first occurrence can easily be replaced by talk about freedom or ability. That is, the phrase "one has a choice about the necessary consequence of some event or proposition only if..." is easily paraphrased as follows: "Suppose A is the necessary consequence of some event *e* or proposition *p* or both; then nobody does A freely (or: nobody is able to refrain from doing A; or: it is not up to anybody whether A occurs) unless..." The problem, however, is that the second occurrence is not so easily explained. What would it mean to be *free with respect to* the truth of a proposition? How could we even begin to paraphrase that second occurrence in terms of *ability*?

Admittedly, it isn't so hard to see what it would be for the truth of a proposition to be *up to* an agent. The truth of a proposition is up to me if I can act so as to make it false. If it is now 2 P.M., and I am seated, and I am generally free with respect to whether I am seated, then I can act so as to make it false that I am seated at 2:05 P.M. The truth of the proposition that Michael Rea is seated at 2:05 P.M. is therefore up to me. But now we face another problem. Suppose we recast 6.5 as follows:

> 6.5★ Suppose the proposition that S does A is a necessary consequence of some other proposition *p*. Then A is not and has never been up to anybody unless the truth of *p* is or was up to somebody.

A compatibilist will insist that, even if determinism is true, an agent *can* act so as to falsify a proposition about one of her own acts. Suppose that my standing at 2:05 P.M. is, in fact, determined by the remote past and the laws of nature. Still, it is *possible* that I remain seated. If the past or the laws were different in just the right ways, I *would* remain seated. Thus, because the past and the laws could have been different in those ways, I can remain seated. I just *won't* do so. Given the present understanding of what it is to be up to an agent, then, compatibilists can be expected to think that many of our acts are up to us even though they are the necessary consequences of propositions (i.e., the law-statement and a world-statement about some time in the remote past) that are not up to us. Thus one cannot simply assert 6.5★ and expect to garner even tentative assent from a compatibilist.

So, despite being highly intuitive, 6.5 is suspicious. For when we try to say exactly what it means, we find that either we cannot assign uniform meaning to the phrase "have a choice about" or we end up equating 6.5 with something very controversial. Still, I do not think we should rest too much on this objection. For one might think that we understand 6.5 well enough even if we are not able to unpack it in a way that is wholly satisfying. That is, one way of responding to the objection is simply to admit one's inability to paraphrase 6.5 adequately, while insisting that most of us will understand it nonetheless. And, for those who think they do understand 6.5, it is certainly hard to find counter-examples.

Premises 6.3 and 6.4 together say that nobody has a choice about the laws of nature or about the occurrence of events in the remote past. Is this true? The answer depends partly on what one thinks the laws of nature are and partly upon what one thinks it means to *have a choice* about something.

Consider first the laws of nature. Laws of nature are regularities in nature; but not just any regularity will be a law. Nothing goes faster than light, and electrons repel one another. These are laws. No human being has set foot on Pluto. That is a regularity about human beings, but it is almost certainly not a law of nature. What is the difference?

Some philosophers say that the difference is some kind of necessity. Humans haven't set foot on Pluto, but they *can*. Nothing has gone faster than light, and, furthermore, things *cannot* go faster than light. All electrons (that get sufficiently close to one another) *do* repel one another; furthermore, they *have to*. It is hard to say what this necessity consists in, or what grounds it. It is probably not, for example, what we have been calling *metaphysical necessity*, for (according to most philosophers) the laws of nature themselves are not metaphysically necessary. So it must be some weaker kind of necessity. But never mind that complication for now. The main thing to notice is that people who think of laws this way will generally agree that the laws are inviolable, except perhaps by divine intervention. Laws, on this view, determine the boundaries of what is physically possible; and nobody has a choice about what is physically possible.

Other philosophers, however, think of the laws as nothing more than regularities that have a certain role to play in our theorizing. The laws are, roughly, regularities whose descriptions have the following property: They are simpler, provide better explanations, and have greater predictive power than descriptions of other regularities, and so they are more suitable than descriptions of other regularities for inclusion in a scientific theory. On this view, a regularity can be a law even if it has exceptions. If, in some far corner of the universe, two electrons attract one another, it might still turn out that the statement, *electrons repel one another*, is, by virtue of its simplicity and explanatory and predictive power, more suitable than any relevant rival for inclusion in scientific theory. So, on this way of thinking about laws, there is no obstacle to saying that one has a choice about the truth of a proposition fully describing the laws of nature. As David Lewis argues in his famous paper, "Are We Free to Break the Laws?," this does not mean that we can *cause* a law of nature to be broken. The laws are not optional in that sense. You can't set out to work miracles and expect to succeed. But, as we have just noted, the laws can have exceptions; and if they had had the right sorts of exceptions in the chain of events leading up to some action of yours, you might have acted differently. So you *could* have acted differently; and had you acted differently, a law would in fact have been broken. You would not have caused the law to be broken, but it would have been broken nonetheless.

One might say the same thing about propositions describing the remote past. The initial configuration of matter could have been different. Or perhaps divine intervention at some later point could have affected the course of events without *changing* the laws of nature. (The laws would have been violated, of course; but, on some views about laws of nature, the truth of a proposition fully describing the laws would remain unaffected.) Had either of those two things occurred, the laws would remain the same, but some of the world-statements about the remote past that are in fact true would have been false. Had this been the case, you might have acted differently. Thus, you could have acted differently. You would not have *caused* the past to be different, but it would have been different nonetheless.

But does any of this show that one might *have a choice* about the past or the laws of nature? This is where what it means to have a choice about something becomes really crucial. Here is one way of understanding what it means to have a choice about something:

CHOICE 1: S has or had a choice about whether *p* is true if, and only if, S has or had at least two options such that (1) it is possible that S choose either of the two options; (2) if S were to choose one of the options, *p* would be true; and (3) if S were to choose the other option, *p* would be false.

On this way of understanding "have a choice," it seems that the views just described do show how one might have a choice about the occurrence of events in the remote past or about the truth of a proposition describing the laws of nature. For example, suppose you ran a marathon yesterday, and suppose further that determinism is true. Let p be the conjunction of the law-statement and a (true) world-statement about a time in the remote past. Now, a compatibilist might say that, before running the marathon, you had two options: begin the race, or refrain from beginning the race. It was possible that you choose either of the two, so condition (1) is satisfied. Furthermore, we know that if you were to choose to begin the race, p would have been true. We know this because you *did* choose the first option, and p is true. So condition (2) is satisfied. Moreover, we know that if you were to choose to refrain from beginning the race, p would have been false. We know this because we are supposing that determinism is true, and determinism implies that had you acted differently, p would have been false. So condition (3) is satisfied. So, on this interpretation of what it means to have a choice about something, you had a choice about whether to begin the race.

Here is another way of understanding what it means to have a choice about something:

CHOICE 2: S has or had a choice about whether p is true if, and only if, S is or was able to cause p to be true and S is able to cause p to be false.

On this account of having a choice about something, it seems that the views described above do *not* show how one might have a choice about the remote past or the laws. For I have not described *any* view in the preceding paragraph that tries to explain how we might *cause* either the law-statement or a true world-statement about the remote past to be false. I do not myself think that either Choice 1 or Choice 2 provides an adequate account of what it means to say that someone has a choice about the truth of a proposition; so I do not think that our task right now is to pick one over the other. My point is simply that by moving in the direction of an account like Choice 1, one can open the door to compatibilism, whereas by moving in the direction of an account like Choice 2, one can hope to keep that door closed.

If you are persuaded by the Consequence Argument, it may be tempting to think that rejecting determinism is necessary *and sufficient* for preserving freedom. But this is not true. There are three further threats that need to be considered. One is a threat from indeterminism itself. Another is a threat from the fact that our acts of will seem to be subject to *local determination*. The third is a threat from the fact that the very idea of *control of the will* seems to be incoherent. I will discuss each in turn.

In "The Mystery of Metaphysical Freedom," Peter van Inwagen offers the following argument (known as the "Replay Argument") for the conclusion that indeterminism is inconsistent with freedom (and, hence, that it is impossible for libertarianism to be true):

> If the laws are indeterministic, then more than one future is indeed consistent with those laws and the actual past and present—but how can anyone have any choice about which of these futures becomes actual? Isn't it just a matter of chance which becomes actual? If God were to "return" an indeterministic world to precisely its state at some time in the past, and then let the world go forward again, things might indeed happen differently the "second" time. But then, if the world is indeterministic, isn't it just a matter of chance how things *did* happen in the one, actual course of events? And if what we do is just a matter of chance—well, who would want to call that freedom?" (p. 370)

The basic argument here is as follows. If our acts are not fully determined by the causal past and the laws, then they occur partly by chance. If they occur partly by chance, then they are not under our control. If they are not under our control, then they are not free. So, if our acts are not fully determined by the causal past and the laws, then they are not free.

Van Inwagen is perhaps the best known defender of libertarianism. But the Replay Argument, which gives expression to an intuition that many compatibilists before him have cited in favor of their position, moves him in the direction of saying that free will is a mystery. His position seems to be that (1) freedom is *clearly* inconsistent with determinism, but (2) it is also very hard to see how freedom could be consistent with indeterminism. If this is correct, it looks as if we should conclude that freedom is impossible. So the threat posed by the Replay Argument in conjunction with the Consequence Argument looks rather serious. But van

Inwagen has the conviction that we are morally responsible and that moral responsibility requires freedom. Thus, he continues to affirm that we are free but declares freedom to be a mystery. So at the very least the Replay Argument threatens the claim that freedom is intelligible and at worst it contributes to an overall case for the conclusion that freedom is impossible.

One way of responding to the Replay Argument is to attempt to give an account of free action that makes it clear why free acts are not merely chance events, even though indeterminism is true. This is quite a challenge, but one popular approach has been to try to offer a theory of **agent causation**. Since belief in agent causation also provides a response to the next two problems, I shall defer consideration of that until the end of the section.

I turn, then, to the second threat: the local determination problem. (Local determination contrasts with *global* determination. Determinism is a global determination thesis, saying that *everything in the universe* is subject to a certain kind of determination. When we talk about *local* determination, we are talking about the determination of specific phenomena within the universe by relevantly nearby causal factors.) We can deal with this problem relatively quickly because the issues are similar to those at work in the Consequence Argument, and so the relevant responses will be very similar to the responses we considered in connection with that argument. For the sake of brevity and simplicity, I shall only present an informal version of the local determination argument.

Consider an arbitrary agent, S. Even if determinism is false, S's mental life, at least, is wholly determined at any given time by the physical events that are occurring in her brain. That is, *given* what is taking place in her brain at any given time, she *has* to have the various thoughts, sensations, acts of will, and so on, that she has at that time. Moreover, nobody has or ever had a choice about the occurrence of the particular physical events in her brain that determine her own acts of will. We can, of course, influence the events in our brain by, say, looking around, turning on music, drinking caffeine or alcohol, and so on. But we have no idea which specific events correlate with our specific acts of will. So we cannot bring about or prevent particular acts of will by bringing about or preventing particular physical events in our brains. For this reason, then, we have no choice about the occurrence of the physical events that determine our acts of will. But an agent has or had a choice about the necessary consequences of an event only if she has or had a choice about the occurrence of the event itself. So S neither has nor ever had a choice about the particular acts of will that she performs. But if an agent neither has nor ever had a choice about her own acts of will, then she neither has nor ever had a choice about *any* of her acts and therefore does not act freely. Thus, S does not act freely.

I shall consider two responses to this argument. First, some people say that the physical events in a person's brain do not determine her thoughts and mental acts but rather her thoughts and mental acts somehow determine what physical events are occurring in her brain. This sort of view is most promising under the assumption that human minds are immaterial substances—souls— and that our brain activity is merely correlated with our mental activity instead of determining it. But the view is also accepted by philosophers who do not believe in souls. These philosophers say that, although physical events (the movement of particles and so on) underlie all of our mental acts in just the same way as they underlie all other macro-phenomena in the world, the *determination* relation between mental and physical events is "top-down" (i.e., going from the macro-level to the micro-level) rather than "bottom-up." In other words, in the special case of the relationship between the mental and the physical, the macro-phenomena determine the micro-phenomena rather than the other way around.

So believing in souls or believing in "top-down" causation offers a solution to this particular problem. However, I think that it is only a temporary solution; for there are other reasons for thinking that our acts of will are not up to us. One reason is that our acts of will seem to be consequences of our beliefs and desires, over which we have no immediate control. (We can control them indirectly— say, by going to school, or repeatedly exposing ourselves to certain stimuli. But we cannot simply will to have different beliefs or desires.) The more important reason, however, is that there is reason to think that it is simply incoherent to suppose that our acts of will are up to us. I shall defer consideration of this argument until the end of the section, however.

Secondly, one might object to the claim that, if an agent neither has nor ever had a choice about her own acts of will, then she neither has nor ever had a choice about *any* of her acts. This is the reply that I find most promising, but I shall defer consideration of it until we have discussed the next, and final argument that I wish to focus on in this section: the regress argument for the conclusion that it is incoherent to think that one has a choice about one's acts of will.

What would it mean to have a choice about your acts of will? So far as I can see, it can only mean one thing: Your acts of will are themselves the products of your own free acts of will. In fact, if one of your acts of will is not the product of your own free acts of will, there seem to be only two other options for how it might have come into being. It might have occurred spontaneously, that is, as a matter of sheer chance. In that case it was clearly not under your control. Or it might have been caused by some prior event that is neither identical to nor the product of one of your acts of will. In that case too it is clearly not under your control. So, again, your acts of will are under your control only if they are the products of your own free acts of will.

But now we must confront the notorious Regress Argument. Again, let S be an arbitrary agent. The following argument reduces to absurdity the assumption that S has a choice about at least one of her own acts of will:

6.9   S has or had a choice about at least one of her acts of will, A. (Assume for *reductio*.)

6.10 If S has or had a choice about an act of will, then that act of will is preceded by a distinct free act of will. (Condition on having a choice about one's free act of will.)

6.11 Therefore: A is preceded by a free act of will, B ($\neq$ A). (From 6.9, 6.10.)

6.12 An act of the will is free only if one has or had a choice about whether it occurs. (Earlier stipulations about freedom.)

6.13 S has or had a choice about whether B occurs. (From 6.11, 6.12.)

6.14 B is preceded by a free act of will, C. (Condition on having a choice about one's free act of will.)

6.15 If premises 6.9–6.14 are true and are justified in the ways described, then S has or had a choice about A only if A is preceded by infinitely many acts of will. (Premise.)

6.16 No human agent performs infinitely many acts. (Premise.)

6.17 Therefore: S neither has nor had a choice about A.

**Contradiction

If the argument is sound, then S neither has nor had a choice about any of her own acts of will. If that is right, then it is easy to derive the conclusion that S does not act freely.

6.18 S neither has nor had a choice about any of her acts of will. (From 6.17.)

6.19 If S neither has nor had a choice about any of her acts of will, then S neither has nor had a choice about any of her acts. (Premise.)

6.20 Therefore: S neither has nor had a choice about any of her acts. (From 6.18, 6.19.)

6.21 Therefore: S does not act freely. (From 6.19 and our earlier stipulations about freedom.)

One might try to reject 6.15 or 6.16, but I cannot imagine either strategy being at all successful. As I see it, there are only two promising replies. One is to reject 6.19, a reply that would also address the local determination problem. The other is to reject the argument for the conclusion that an agent has a choice about her acts of will only if they are the products of her own free choices. Doing so would leave us with no reason to accept 6.10. As it happens, the two responses are connected: Both seem to require belief in something like agent causation.

According to the agent-causation theorist, it is a mistake to think that our acts are explained either by chance or by causal relations to prior events. Instead, says the friend of agent causation, our acts are explained simply by *us*: Agents cause their most basic acts in a direct, immediate way, not by way of choices, beliefs, or desires, and not as a matter of pure chance. If this view is true, the Replay Argument is defanged: The supposition that indeterminism is true does not at all imply that our acts are the product of pure chance. Likewise, the local determination problem and the Regress Argument are both defanged. For premise 6.19 is important to both arguments, but the agent-causation theorist has no reason to accept it. She might just say that *willing* isn't an act; rather, willing is simply *agent causation.* In that case, there won't be any acts of will, and so one will not have a choice about any acts of will, but it will not follow from this that one has no choice about any of one's acts. Believers in agent causation will also reject premise 6.10 in the Regress Argument. For, according to the agent-causation theorist, there is no reason to think that acts of will—if there are such things at all—are produced by preceding acts of will. Rather, they would be produced directly by the agent.

Agent causation is a fascinating idea, but critics say that it is ultimately unintelligible. Suppose S agent-causes her decision to stand up. What, exactly, is the difference between her causing that decision and the decision's just happening? We cannot say that S *does* something to cause it. For that "something" would be a prior event. What one wants to say is that the decision is caused simply by S's *agent-causal activity*. But the trouble is that there is not—and, indeed, cannot be—any object or event in the world with which to identify her agent-causal activity. In short, her agent-causal activity seems to be *nothing at all.*

THE FATALISM PROBLEM

I turn now to the fatalism problem. The fatalism problem arises out of the apparent fact that, if it was ever true that S will do A, then from that point forward S has been unable to refrain from doing A. So if it was true long before S was born that S will do A at t, then it looks as if S never had nor ever will have a choice about whether she does A at t—in which case, given our earlier stipulations about what it means to be free, it follows that S does not do A freely. Since it seems that *every* act of ours is such that it was true long before we were born that we will do just that act at just the time when we in fact do it, we have here a general threat to freedom.

Let us put the argument a little more rigorously. Suppose the present time is t, and let $t^\star$ be some time 1,000 years prior to now. Let S again be an arbitrary agent. Now suppose that S stands up at t. We'll take that as our first premise and will proceed from there:

6.22 S stands up at t. (Premise.)
6.23 If an event e happens at t, then it was true at every time prior to t that e will happen at t. (Premise.)

6.24   Therefore: It was true at $t^\star$ that S will stand up at t. (From 6.22, 6.23.)

6.25   It is a necessary consequence of 6.24 that S stands up at t.

6.26   S never had and never will have a choice about whether 6.24 is true. (Premise.)

6.27   An agent has or had a choice about a necessary consequence of a proposition only if she has or had a choice about whether the proposition itself is true. (Premise.)

6.28   Therefore: S never had and never will have a choice about whether she stands at t. (From 6.24–6.27.)

6.29   Therefore: S does not stand at t freely. (From 6.28 and our stipulations about freedom.)

Obviously "stand up" could be replaced by a name for *any* act that an agent might perform and the argument would reach the same conclusion. So the conclusion generalizes: If the argument is sound, then nobody ever does anything freely.

Is the argument sound? Let's briefly examine each of the premises.

Premise 6.22 is not the sort of proposition anyone would object to; it is just an assumption to get our argument going. Premise 6.23 is supposed to be a datum of common sense; but, as we have seen throughout this book, common sense is often one of the casualties of philosophical reasoning. So let us flag this premise for further consideration later. Premise 6.24 *has to be* true if 6.22 and 6.23 are true. So if we want to object to that, we would have to reject either 6.22 or 6.23. Premise 6.25 is uncontroversial so long as we assume that changing the past is impossible. Let us assume that for now, just to simplify our discussion. Rejecting 6.25, then, won't be an option for us. Premise 6.26 is supposed to be true because facts about the past and facts about logical entailment aren't up to us. This, too, is plausible if we assume that changing the past is impossible. But there are some interesting questions to be raised about 6.26, so let us flag this premise for further consideration later on as well. Premise 6.27 is a principle that we have already discussed. As we have seen, principles like this are suspicious, but it is hard to find counter-examples to them. As I indicated in the previous section, I do not think that rejecting principles like 6.27 is ultimately promising, so we'll leave this principle alone. But now we are at the end of the argument. Given the truth of all of the premises up to 6.28, 6.28 has to be true as well—as with 6.24, one can object to it only by rejecting one of the premises that justifies it. Given what we have said earlier about what it means to be free, 6.29 has to be true if 6.28 is true. What then shall we say?

In our brief examination of the premises, we flagged two for further consideration: 6.23 and 6.26. Let us look more closely at these now.

If we reject 6.23, then we can say that, although the event of S's standing up occurs at t, the proposition that *S will stand up at t* was never true at any earlier time. Saying this defuses the argument. Those who wish to defend this sort of response generally take one of two routes. Either they say that (with a few exceptions) propositions about what creatures will freely do *have no truth value*, or they say that such propositions have a truth value, but all of them are false. The difficulty with the first option is that it seems to require the rejection of standard logic. One principle of standard logic is the law of excluded middle, which says that, for any proposition p, the following is true: *p or not-p*. Where p is the proposition that *S will stand up at t*, excluded middle implies that the following proposition is *always* true: *Either S will stand up at t or it is not the case that S will stand up at t.* Furthermore, in standard logic, if this disjunction has always been true, then at least one of the disjuncts has always been true too—which is just what proponents of the first response want to deny. Thus, the first response requires rejection of some feature of standard logic. It is, by the way, because of its reliance on these features of standard logic that the fatalist argument we have so far been discussing is commonly called an argument for *logical fatalism*.

Can one sensibly reject standard logic? That is a thorny question. On the one hand, the correct principles of logic are not like principles of etiquette, varying from culture to culture. They are, instead, necessary truths about what follows from what. On the other hand, one *can* question the logical principles that we take to be true; and standard logic is not the only logical system from which one can choose. In the end, the question whether one can sensibly reject it comes down to the question whether alternative systems of logic provide a better overall fit with our intuitions. My own view is that they do not, but there is no way to defend that view in the space available here.

The other way in which one might reject 6.23 is, as I have noted above, to say that propositions about what creatures will freely do are all false. This view was discussed in the 1960s by A. N. Prior, who attributed it to the early twentieth-century pragmatist, C. S. Peirce; but it seems to have been largely ignored until very recently. It is now undergoing something of a revival, having been defended briefly by Christopher Hughes and at greater length by Amy Seymour. The view depends, in part, on making a sharp distinction between the claim that *e will not occur* and the claim that *it is not the case that e will occur*. To say the former is to say that it is now fixed or settled that *e* won't happen, whereas saying the latter is consistent with its not now being fixed or settled one way or the other whether *e* will happen. Thus, with respect to S and her standing, the proponent of this view maintains that, before *t*, both of the following claims are true: It is not the case that S *will* stand up at *t*; and it is not the case that S *will not* stand up at *t*. In other words, at every time prior to *t*, the future includes *neither* S standing nor S refraining from standing at *t*. Obviously this view preserves the law of excluded middle, so that is an advantage; and it fits well with more general intuitions about the openness of the future.

Are there disadvantages to this second strategy? The view is inconsistent with eternalism. But presentists—like Seymour, for example—will not be at all concerned by this. More troublingly for some, this view is inconsistent with the view that there exists a divine being who knows what every free creature will freely do at every time in the future. For, after all, knowing what every free creature *will* do at every future time requires that, for every future time *t* and every free creature S, there are truths of the form S will do A at *t*. Also troubling is the fact that this view seems to be inconsistent with the possibility of time travel. If a time traveler from the future shows up on your driveway today, it seems that you can deduce from this that it is true now that someday in the future, she will make a time-travel journey. Moreover, if you ask that person what people around her were doing right before she stepped into the time machine, it seems that you can deduce from this all manner of additional future-tense truths: that, for example, the time traveler's little brother will be playing video games at just about the time she steps into the time machine, and so on. But wouldn't it be strange if these were the *only* fixed truths about the future? It seems much more sensible to suppose that, if time travel is possible, 6.23 is true. There are other, more technical difficulties with this proposal as well, but, as with the problems besetting the strategy that involves rejecting excluded middle, exploring those difficulties in detail would take us too far afield.

What about 6.26, the premise that S never had, nor will have, a choice about the prior truth of *S will stand up at t*? Those who reject this premise typically start by making a distinction between propositions that *depend on the future* and propositions that do not. Propositions like *S will stand up at t* fall into the category of propositions that *do* depend on the future; propositions like *S is standing now* do not fall into that category. They then make a distinction between "hard facts" and "soft facts" about the past. The soft facts about the past are ones that depend to some extent upon what is taking place now or in the future. So, for example, between the times t^* and t the fact that *it was true at t^* that S will stand up at t* would count as a soft fact, because it would depend on what takes place at t. Hard facts, on the other hand, are ones that do not display this sort of dependence. The fact that Brutus stabbed Caesar is, plausibly, a hard fact about the past, since it displays the right sort of independence from things taking place now. (I say "plausibly," though, because it is notoriously difficult to nail down the hard-fact/soft-fact distinction precisely enough to prevent counter-examples.)

But how can the truth of a proposition depend on the future? How could an agent have a choice about *any* fact about the past? The easiest way to answer these questions is to assume eternalism and then observe that the predicate "true at t" is (given eternalism) much like the predicate "true in Indiana." One might *say* things like:

1 "An earthquake is happening out west" is true in Indiana.

But what one would mean by saying such a thing is that it is just plain true that an earthquake is happening, and that, from the point of view of Indiana, the occurrence of the earthquake is to the west. Likewise, then, with a claim like *it was true at t^* that S will stand up at t*: To say this is just to say that, when t^* was present, "S stands at *t*" was just plain true, and the occurrence of that event was in the future from the point of view of *t*★. Once this is clear, the fatalist argument is defanged. For now there is very good reason for thinking that S has a choice about the truth of 6.24—namely, the fact that, at *t*, she seemingly has a choice about the truth of 6.22. In fact, to assume at the beginning of the argument that she doesn't have a choice about the truth of F1 is simply to beg the question in favor of the fatalist's conclusion.

In making this response, I assumed eternalism. Is the response also available to a presentist? I do not think that it is. The problem is simply that there is no way of explaining how S *will stand up at t* could possibly depend on the future at *t*★ when (as the presentist believes) future objects and events do not exist. In other words: A proposition cannot depend on the future if there is no future. Thus, despite the problems associated with these strategies, I think that the most promising route for presentists to take in responding to the logical fatalist is to try to reject 6.23.

In closing this section, I should like to note that, although we have focused here on what is commonly referred to as *logical fatalism*, there is a related problem that goes by the label *theological fatalism*. According to the theological fatalist, it is not merely the past *truth* of claims like S *will stand at t* that threatens our freedom, but rather God's foreknowledge of such truths. The strategies for responding to the logical fatalist carry over as strategies for responding to the theological fatalist. One might argue, for example, that there simply aren't truths like S *will stand at t*, since propositions like that either are false or have no truth value. One might also argue that the fact that God infallibly believed at *t*★ that S will stand at *t* is as much a soft fact about the past as the fact that it was true at *t*★ that S will stand at *t*. Each of these strategies, however, poses new problems in the theological context. For example, the first strategy forces revisions in our concept of omniscience; the second has been seen as requiring some revision in our understanding of the hard-fact/soft-fact distinction (since facts about what God *believed* in the past seem, intuitively, as if they should be hard facts). Moreover, there are other strategies for responding to theological fatalism that don't solve the logical fatalist argument. For example, denying the existence of God solves the former problem, but not the latter.

FURTHER READING

In the text, I cited or quoted from two important works by Peter van Inwagen: *An Essay on Free Will* (Oxford: Oxford University Press, 1983) and "The Mystery of Metaphysical Freedom," reprinted in *Arguing about Metaphysics*. In my discussion of the consequence argument, the reasons I gave for being suspicious of principle 6.5 were derived from Thomas P. Flint, "Compatibilism and the Argument from Unavoidability," *Journal of Philosophy*, vol. 84 (1987), pp. 423–440. I also discussed David Lewis's "Are We Free to Break the Laws?," *Theoria*, vol. 47 (1981), pp. 113–121.

The local determination argument I adapted from the chapter on free will in John Searle's *Minds, Brains, and Science* (Cambridge, MA: Harvard University Press, 1984). In connection with that argument, I mentioned the idea of "top-down causation." For a defense of that view, see Trenton Merricks, *Objects and Persons* (Oxford: Clarendon Press, 2001).

In connection with fatalism, I cited A. N. Prior, *Past, Present, and Future* (Oxford: Clarendon Press, 1967); Christopher Hughes, "Openness, Privilege, and Omniscience," *European Journal for Philosophy of Religion*, vol. 4 (2012), pp. 35–64; and Amy Seymour, *Presentism, Propositions, and Persons: A Systematic Case for All-Falsism* (unpublished). I also recommend Richard Taylor's "The Story of Osmo," and the second chapter of Peter van Inwagen's *An Essay on Free Will*, both reprinted in *Arguing about Metaphysics*.

Beyond these texts, I think that the best places to start for readers interested in the topics discussed in this chapter are Meghan Griffith's *Free Will: The Basics* (London and New York: Routledge, 2013); and Robert Kane, *The Oxford Handbook of Free Will* (Oxford: Oxford University Press, 2002).

7

WORLDS AND WORLDMAKING

It is commonplace to talk about "the world" as if there is just *one* world—namely, the one four-dimensional universe in which, as it were, we live and move and have our being. But many philosophers and scientists believe that, in fact, there are many things that deserve to be called worlds. Some believe in parallel *universes*. Some believe that even within our universe there are, at any given time, many branching "paths" along which the future might unfold, and that these paths are no less concretely real than the events you are presently experiencing. Some believe in special kinds of abstract states of affairs that constitute complete, alternative ways in which our universe (or multiverse) might have turned out. All of these kinds of things and more have been characterized as *other worlds*; and, what's more, metaphysicians commonly identify some of these other worlds as *merely possible* worlds.

There are many different reasons for believing in other worlds of various kinds. Some do so because they think that the existence of such things is probable on the assumption that spacetime is infinite. Some posit other worlds to explain certain features of quantum mechanics. Some say that if we don't believe in other worlds, then it appears that certain features of our universe can only be explained by supposing that a cosmic designer exists. These motivations are commonly characterized as *scientific* reasons for believing in other worlds. I shall talk about them briefly in the first section of this chapter.

In metaphysics, talk about other worlds is usually talk about *possible worlds*. I have mentioned possible worlds before in this book. In the second section of this chapter I shall talk more systematically about them. Philosophers posit possible worlds primarily as a way of making sense of our talk about possibility and necessity, about how things *could have been* and how things *must be*. As I have mentioned earlier in this book, philosophers sometimes distinguish different kinds of possibility and necessity: physical, logical, metaphysical, and so on. I shall say a bit more about these distinctions later. For now, I'll simply note that when I talk unqualifiedly about possible worlds, or about what is simply possible or necessary, it is generally metaphysical possibility and necessity that I have in mind.

It is surely tempting to suppose that, whatever possible worlds might be, they are very different sorts of things from the worlds under discussion in the first section of this chapter. In fact, as we shall see, most philosophers think that possible worlds are abstract states of affairs. However, some philosophers do not believe in abstract possible worlds but instead think that certain kinds of parallel universes deserve to be called possible worlds. If they are right, then possible worlds are quite similar to some of the worlds that we shall be discussing in the first section. Part of our task, then, in the second section, will be to flesh out these two different conceptions of possible worlds more fully and to explore some of the reasons for and against endorsing each one.

The third and final section focuses on a different sort of world altogether. It is a mundane fact that different people sometimes conceive of the world in very different ways. They categorize things differently; they adopt different theories to explain roughly the same experiential data; and so on. According to some philosophers, however, there is a very real sense in which people who conceive of the world differently *live in different worlds*. The reason is that, on this view, the character and the contents of the world are at least partly constituted by our ways of thinking about it. Initially, such a view might sound crazy. We *make* the world have the features that it has? How could that be? Once the view has been explained and some of the main reasons for endorsing it have been clarified, however, we find that the view is a lot more seductive than it initially appears.

PARALLEL UNIVERSES

In his 2003 *Scientific American* article, "Parallel Universes," cosmologist Max Tegmark explains that many physicists believe our observable universe to be but one universe among many, that is, just one universe in a larger multiverse. By "our observable universe," he means simply a region of spacetime that includes everything from which light has been able to travel to us since the Big Bang. Given this way of understanding the notion of a universe, Tegmark identifies four different "levels" to the multiverse. At each different level, there is a different kind of multiverse. In this section, I shall very briefly explain these different levels and the reasons why physicists believe in them.

Before getting into the levels, however, let us pause to clarify some terminology. A *spacetime* is (roughly) a manifold of points, or regions, or locations that can be broken up into spatial and temporal dimensions. There are disputes among philosophers and physicists about whether the spacetime in which we live is made up of points and about whether there is anything at all to it beyond just the various relationships between the objects that are said to exist in spacetime. My characterization of spacetime here is intended to bypass these disputes. As I have noted in Chapter 3, according to the usual interpretation of relativity theory, the spacetime in which we live isn't *objectively* divided into spatial and temporal dimensions; rather, space and time are mere appearances of a more fundamental reality.

Let us say that *our spacetime* includes absolutely everything that is spatiotemporally related to us, that is, everything that is located at some spatial or temporal distance from us. If there are things that exist in spacetime but aren't spatiotemporally related to us, then they exist in *another* spacetime—one spatiotemporally unrelated to ours. What Tegmark is calling "our observable universe," then, is just a particular volume (called a "Hubble volume") within our spacetime. Specifically, it is the volume that includes everything from which light could have traveled to us since the Big Bang. But, of course, there might well be lots of things within our spacetime but outside our Hubble volume; and there might be still more things that exist outside of our spacetime altogether. Departing a bit from Tegmark's terminology, I am henceforth going to restrict my use of the term "universe" to refer to other spacetimes. Everything else that he calls a universe I will call a world. Worlds like what he calls our observable universe I'll call Hubble volumes (and our own "observable universe," of course, I'll refer to as "our Hubble volume").

We can now characterize Tegmark's first level. Those other things that exist in regions of our spacetime outside our Hubble volume belong to the worlds that exist at Tegmark's first level. Since they exist *within* our spacetime—indeed, since they are simply other Hubble volumes like ours in spacetime—these worlds are governed by the same laws of physics. Moreover, since our spacetime seems to be infinite, we should expect that there are infinitely many Hubble volumes and that every physically possible configuration of matter, no matter how improbable, is realized within some such volume. (Indeed, by this reasoning every Hubble volume should have a great many duplicate volumes, as well as a great many near-duplicates, not-so-near duplicates, and so on.)

Already we have reached a hypothesis that should boggle the mind. Let your fantasies run wild, and, so long as they do not involve violations of the laws of physics, there is a physical configuration of matter somewhere that realizes exactly those fantasies. Is this credible? It is, to say the least, a hard pill to swallow. But let us set our concerns aside and move on to the second and third levels.

Let us follow Tegmark in referring to the plurality of infinitely many Hubble volumes within spacetime as the "Level-1 multiverse." Now imagine that there are infinitely many Level-1 multiverses, each with the same laws of physics but with different spacetime geometry and different **physical constants**. (The laws we might think of as the mathematical equations that govern the behavior of things in the universe—things like the Schrödinger equation or the ideal gas law. Constants are apparently universal and unchanging physical quantities, like the speed of light in a vacuum or the gravitational constant.) These multiverses are spatiotemporally related to one another, but they exist at an *infinite* distance from one another. So imagine it like this: First we have our own Hubble volume, but elsewhere, all at finite distances from us, are infinitely many other Hubble volumes. Now take that plurality of Hubble volumes, travel an infinite distance from that ... and you will find another infinitely large plurality of Hubble volumes. And another. And so on *ad infinitum*. Each of these multiverses is a *world* at Tegmark's second level. Taken together, these Level-2 worlds comprise the Level-2 multiverse.

Why would anyone believe in the Level-2 multiverse? Tegmark presents belief in the Level-2 multiverse as a scientific hypothesis, but here, I think, the disciplinary boundaries are quite fuzzy. He reports that the Level-2 multiverse hypothesis "is an extension of the big bang theory and ties up many of the loose ends of that theory, like why the universe is so big, so uniform and so flat." He then goes on to say that, "[a]lthough we cannot interact with other Level 2 worlds, cosmologists can infer their presence indirectly because their existence can account for unexplained cosmic coincidences." In order to understand this rationale for believing the Level-2 multiverse hypothesis, however, we must first say a bit about the larger debate into which the hypothesis is supposed to fit. In doing so, we shall see more clearly why it makes sense to include discussion of the Level-2 multiverse (and higher-level multiverses) in a textbook about metaphysics.

There is a venerable argument for God's existence that reasons from *apparent intricacy and functionality* in nature to the existence of an intelligent designer. The reasoning is typically reinforced by an analogy. Suppose, in exploring a distant planet, you were to come across a complicated machine of some sort—one that controls floodgates on a river, say, or displays a hologram map of the surrounding region. You would automatically assume that the machine has a designer for the simple reason that it bears all of the standard marks of design: intricacy, complexity, functionality, etc. Hence the analogy. *Many* things in the cosmos, particularly biological organisms and their complex parts like eyes and hearts and so on, are like machines of alien origin. We do not see their designer, but they bear all of the marks of design; hence we should infer that, like any other machine, they too are the products of design.

Most philosophers agree that, in its traditional form, this argument from design for the existence of God is flawed. Evolutionary theory is generally thought to show how intricate, highly functional machine-like beings might come into existence wholly apart from the activity of any sort of cosmic designer. Thus, inferring the existence of a designer *merely* from the marks of design that we find in living organisms and other natural structures is generally regarded as highly suspect.

However, in more recent years, philosophers have breathed new life into the argument from design by resting it not on the appearance of design in natural objects but rather on the apparent "fine-tuning" of the physical constants and the observable features of spacetime. Proponents of the so-called fine-tuning argument for the existence of a designer commonly point out that life would have been impossible if (for example) the strong nuclear force had been slightly weaker, if the electromagnetic force had been slightly stronger or weaker, if the ratio of neutron mass to proton mass had been slightly different, if the force of gravity had been even *very* slightly stronger or weaker, or if spacetime had not been as flat as it is. In light of such facts, it looks as if the constants and the geometry of spacetime in our own Level-2 world have been "fine-tuned" for the existence of life. (Remember, a single world at Level 2 is a multiverse at Level 1. So our own Level-2 world is likewise our Level-1 multiverse.) On the assumption that our Level-2 world came into existence together with its particular laws of nature and physical constants wholly by chance, the odds of it turning out to be hospitable for life are vanishingly small. But on the assumption that it was produced by an intelligent and extremely powerful designer who *wanted* it to be hospitable for living organisms, the chances that the universe would be hospitable for life are much, much higher. On the chance hypothesis, our Level-2 world's ability to support life is extremely surprising; on the design hypothesis, it is exactly what we would expect. Thus (say the proponents of this argument), the apparent fine-tuning of the physical constants and the geometry of spacetime constitutes evidence for the existence of a designer.

There is much to say about this argument, but for present purposes just one particular sort of response is relevant. Suppose you flip twenty coins and they all land heads. The odds of this happening by chance with fair coins are worse than one in a million. So, on the assumption that this was just a one-off event, you should find the outcome very surprising. But suppose it wasn't just a one-off event. Suppose, in fact, you are part of a grand experiment wherein a *billion* people are flipping twenty coins. Now you shouldn't find it at all surprising to discover that someone flipped twenty coins and they all landed heads. Given the odds, you'd expect it to happen several times. It might be surprising that *you* were one of the ones who got to see it, but that it happened shouldn't be the least bit surprising. So, likewise, some say, with the fine-tuning of our world. If its existence is a one-off event, then yes, the fact that it is fine-tuned for the existence of life is very surprising indeed. But if there are infinitely many Level-2 worlds, then the fact that some of them are hospitable for life isn't the least bit surprising; it is exactly what we would expect. Moreover, on this latter scenario it is *also* unsurprising that we are among those who get to "witness" the occurrence of a universe hospitable for life. It isn't surprising because the universes hospitable for life are the only ones in which we can exist to witness anything at all!

We are now in a position to appreciate why Tegmark says that belief in the Level-2 multiverse provides an explanation for cosmic coincidences. The cosmic coincidences he has in mind are just the facts about fine-tuning that we have been talking about. The Level-2 multiverse hypothesis explains these coincidences by rendering them wholly unsurprising. Of course, it doesn't tell us *why* our Level-2 world in particular displays those coincidences. But sometimes a reason not to be surprised by a phenomenon counts as explanation enough for it. And the Level-2 multiverse hypothesis does give us a reason not to be surprised. Given the vast number of Level-2 worlds, some are bound to be hospitable for life in the way that ours is. Since it is only in such worlds that creatures like us are able to make observations, we should not be the least bit surprised to observe that ours is as it is.

One might ask why the Level-2 hypothesis, rather than simply the Level-1 multiverse hypothesis, is needed to accomplish this goal. After all, *every physically possible configuration of matter* is supposed to be realized within the Level-1 multiverse. Why isn't that enough to explain why our Hubble volume is hospitable for life? The answer is that what counts as physically possible depends in part upon the physical constants and the geometry of spacetime. By hypothesis, these do not vary within the Level-1 multiverse; and what is surprising is that these locally invariant features of our world are hospitable for life. Positing the Level-2 multiverse renders that fact unsurprising.

The trouble with the Level-2 hypothesis, however, is that it does not seem to give the opponent of the fine-tuning argument what she needs in order to avoid a design inference. As Tegmark himself acknowledges, the primary justification for believing the Level-2 multiverse hypothesis is the fact that it *ties up loose ends* in our cosmological theory and *explains cosmic coincidences*. But the Level-2 worlds all belong to the same spacetime, so we might just as well regard them simply as different domains within a single universe. And, as Stephen Barr points out, a multi-domained universe that permits life in some but not all of its domains is no less "coincidental" than a single-domained universe that is life-permitting. So, in other words, consider the following two hypotheses:

H1 Our universe has many domains with different spacetime geometries and physical constants in each domain; and some of these domains are life-permitting.

H2 The physical constants and geometry of spacetime are invariant throughout universe, so our universe has just a single domain; and that domain is life-permitting.

Barr's idea is that if H2 is surprising, then H1 is equally surprising. Positing a Level-2 multiverse, therefore, does *not* render the fact that our universe is hospitable for life unsurprising. If this is correct, then it is hard to see why Tegmark's proffered justification for belief in the Level-2 multiverse should be considered strong enough to command belief.

It is perhaps worth noting that claims about what is surprising are bound to be highly controversial. In the end, a big part of what is at stake in this debate is the question whether H1, if true, would demand further explanation. All parties to the debate seem to agree that H2, if true, would demand further explanation. Proponents of the fine-tuning argument say that H1 would as well, and that one needs to posit a designer in order to give the right sort of explanation. Believers in the Level-2 multiverse disagree.

Thus far, we have been focusing on reasons for believing in other worlds that arise out of cosmology. The reasons for believing in other worlds at Tegmark's next level, however, arise out of quantum mechanics. In particular, they are posited as part of what is commonly called the *many worlds* interpretation of quantum mechanics. Quantum theory implies that, before we use instruments to detect the states of, for example, photons or electrons, these objects are, in some sense, in *multiple incompatible states at the same time*. This phenomenon of being in multiple incompatible states at once is called a superposition; and, importantly, super-positions themselves are never observed. So, for example, as Jim Baggott explains in *The Meaning of Quantum Theory*, it is possible to set up an experimental situation such that, before observation, a single photon has two distinct polarities (vertical and horizontal) at once. Observation, however, invariably assigns just one polarity to any given photon. So it looks as if measurement somehow *does* something to the things we are measuring. But what, exactly, does measurement do? This question is not answered definitively within quantum theory itself; rather, it takes some interpretation to answer it. According to the many-worlds interpretation, Baggott says, "the act of measurement splits the *entire universe* into a number of bran-ches, with a different result being recorded in each." It is these branch worlds that comprise Tegmark's Level-3 multiverse.

The main thing I wish to note about the many worlds of quan-tum theory is that, like the worlds that comprise the Level-1 and Level-2 multiverses, the Level-3 worlds are spatiotemporally related to us and therefore qualify on every philosophical theory of actu-ality as part of the actual world. Whatever happens in the parallel worlds of quantum theory is (like whatever happens within the Level-1 or Level-2 multiverses) part of what *actually* happens. It is, of course, an interesting question whether the reasons favoring the many-worlds interpretation are, on balance, stronger or weaker than those favoring alternative interpretations of quantum theory, but pursuing that question is well beyond the scope of an intro-duction to the basics of metaphysics.

Finally, there is the Level-4 multiverse. This is a multiverse in which we find genuine parallel *universes*, i.e. spacetimes that are not spatiotemporally related to ours, unlike the spatiotemporal regions that comprise the worlds at Levels 1, 2, and 3. At Level 4 there are not only universes with different configurations of matter, different physical constants, and different spacetime geometries, but also universes with different laws of nature altogether. Belief in a vast number of universes not spatiotemporally related to ours avoids the "just one more coincidence" problem that I raised in connection with the Level-2 multiverse hypothesis, and it otherwise accom-plishes much the same goal as that hypothesis does.

The trouble, however, as Stephen Barr notes, is that there seems to be virtually no *scientific* evidence for the existence of the universes at this level. Tegmark himself talks as if the Level-4 hypothesis *is* a scientific hypothesis. But the only reason he offers for believing in the universes at Level 4 is this: By positing a distinct universe for every possible set of laws, we thereby explain the laws of nature that obtain in our universe. Is this a *scientific* reason? It seems that Tegmark would say, "Yes," whereas Barr would say, "No." My own view is that here is just another place where the boundaries between disciplines are rather fuzzy.

The real question, of course, is not whether Tegmark's rationale for believing in Level-4 worlds is scientific but whether it is a *good* reason. That depends on whether the hypothesis can do the explanatory work that he thinks it does. I myself find it hard to see the Level-4 hypothesis as very explanatory. In fact, although we cannot really claim that the existence of the Level-4 multiverse is "just one more coincidence" that needs to be explained, it does seem that we can say that the existence of the Level-4 multiverse is *no less* in need of explanation than the fundamental laws of nature that hold in our universe. Neither can be called surprising, exactly, but if one is in need of explanation, then surely the other is as well.

But there is another consideration that might be brought to bear on the Level-4 hypothesis. As I have hinted earlier, philosophers have supposed for a very different set of reasons that there might be multiple universes that are not spatiotemporally related to our own. In particular, they have supposed that belief in such things might help to give sense to our talk about necessity and possibility.

POSSIBLE WORLDS

The English language has a variety of **modal expressions**: "may," "might," "must," "can," "is possible," "is necessary," and so on. Philosophers posit possible worlds in order to explain what we mean by these expressions. But before discussing different concepts of possible worlds and the role possible worlds play in helping us to make sense of our modal expressions, we should first make some very basic distinctions and explain some of the terminology that will be central to our discussion.

We noted earlier that philosophers make distinctions between logical, physical, and metaphysical modality. But there are other forms of modality as well: deontic (pertaining to moral duties) and epistemic (pertaining to what we believe or know), for example. Roughly speaking, the various kinds of modality are distinguished from one another by the various kinds of "laws" relative to which they are supposed to hold: what is physically or **nomologically** possible is what is permitted by the laws of nature; what is logically possible is whatever is permitted by the laws of logic; what is epistemically possible is whatever might be true given what you believe (or know) about the world; and that which is *morally permitted* is the analog of "possibility" in the deontic realm. Accordingly, we might go on to say that what is metaphysically possible is whatever is consistent with the "laws of metaphysics" (whatever those might be). Alternatively, we might just say that what is metaphysically possible is just whatever is possible in the broadest, most all-inclusive sense of the term. As I said earlier, whenever I talk unqualifiedly about possibility or necessity, it is metaphysical possibility and necessity that I have in mind.

As we have seen already in this book, many philosophers think that physical, logical, and metaphysical possibility diverge from one another. (It is obvious that metaphysical possibility diverges from deontic and epistemic possibility. For example, plenty of things are possible but not morally permitted; and plenty of things that might be true for all we know are nonetheless metaphysically impossible.) If the laws of nature could have been different, as many philosophers think, then what is metaphysically possible is broader than what is physically possible. If some logically consistent proposition could not have been true, then the fact that something is logically possible doesn't imply that it is possible, period. For example, many agree that the proposition *that God has done something wicked* is not logically contradictory. But one might still think that it could not possibly be true. But I shall not try to argue that these modalities diverge. I shall continue to assume that they do, but readers should bear in mind that that is not a universally shared assumption.

Pretty much everyone agrees that modality attaches to propositions, as follows: Some propositions are necessarily true; some are necessarily false; some are contingently true; some are contingently false; some are possibly true; and some are possibly false. These modal expressions are interdefinable. A proposition is necessarily true if, and only if, its negation is not possibly true. A proposition is contingently true if, and only if, it is true but not necessarily true.

A proposition is contingently false if, and only if, it is false but not necessarily false. A proposition is possibly true if, and only if, its negation is not necessarily true. And so on. Many philosophers have hoped that modal expressions could be defined solely in terms of non-modal expressions; but so far that hope has not panned out. Thus, people often speak of "the modal circle" to convey the idea that, although modal expressions can all be defined in terms of one another, ultimately the definitions just go in a circle; there is no way to define the modal in terms of the non-modal.

Many philosophers also think that at least some of the properties of objects have modality built into them. In Chapter 4, we called these properties *modal properties*. Examples include properties like *being able to survive squashing*, or *being necessarily (or essentially) a cat*. But the idea that objects have modal properties is a lot more controversial than the idea that modality attaches to propositions. When philosophers wish to talk about modality construed as attaching to propositions, they speak of *de dicto* modality ("*de dicto*" meaning something like "pertaining to what is said"). When they wish to talk about modality construed as built into the properties of objects, they speak of *de re* modality ("*de re*" meaning something like "pertaining to the object").

Finally, it will be helpful to introduce some of the logical symbols that enter into discussions of possibility and necessity and which are, accordingly, scattered liberally throughout the literature in contemporary metaphysics. Following standard conventions, I shall use "$\Box$" to mean "necessarily" and "$\Diamond$" to mean "possibly." The box and diamond are called *logical operators*: we attach them to sentences (like "God exists" or "Sally stands up") to form new sentences (like "Necessarily, God exists," or "Possibly, Sally stands up"). We'll use the following symbol for strict implication, or entailment: "$\Rightarrow$". To say that p strictly implies, or entails, q is just to say that it is a necessary truth that if p is true, then q is true.

So much, then, for preliminaries. Now we can turn to our discussion of possible worlds. Possible worlds, as I have indicated, were introduced to help explain what the modal operators mean. Of course, in one sense we already know what they mean: The box means "necessarily"; the diamond means "possibly." But in another sense people had no real clue what they meant. To see why, just consider the fact that we can keep on adding operators to the beginnings of our sentences to form new (meaningful!) sentences. Thus, consider a sentence like, "□(God exists)." Suppose you know what this means. Still, we can form a new sentence by adding another operator out front, as follows: "◇□(God exists)." Is it clear what this means? If so, how about this: "◇◇□(God exists)"? Or this: "◇◇□◇□(God exists)"? If all you know about the box and the diamond is that they mean "necessarily" and "possibly," you will have a very hard time making sense of these sentences.

Now you might wonder, *who really cares about weird sentences like these?* Even if they are meaningful, their meaning will surely be something highly abstract and so not very useful for our lives (or even for serious philosophy). But the fact is, there are several different formal systems—the different logics—that logicians have developed to try to express the principles of sound reasoning about necessity and possibility; and you will sometimes reach very different conclusions in metaphysics depending upon which of these logics you accept. To take just one example, here is an argument for the existence of God that is valid in one modal logic (the one that most metaphysicians accept, as it happens) but not in many of its rivals:

6.1 ◇God exists)
6.2 ◇(God exists) ⟹ ◇□(God exists)
6.3 Therefore: ◇□(God exists)
6.4 Therefore: □(God exists)

Premise 6.1 looks like an innocent assertion of possibility. Of *course* it is possible that God exists. Premise 6.2 is supposed to be a conceptual truth about God. The concept of God is supposed to be the concept of a *necessary* being, a being who couldn't fail to exist. So, if it is possible that God exist, it is possible that God be a necessary being; hence, it is possible that God exist necessarily. So 6.3 follows from 6.1 and 6.2. But then comes another inference—the one from 6.3 to 6.4. Is *that one* valid? It is if the following principle is true:

6.5 ◇□p ⟹ □p

But how might one begin to assess this principle? Again, if all we know is that "◇" means "possibly" and "□" means "necessarily," it is very hard to tell. What one needs in order to facilitate understanding and to make proper evaluation of claims like 6.5 possible is a *semantics* for the modal operators, an account of what those operators mean.

In 1963, Saul Kripke proposed what was to become the standard semantics for the modal operators. According to Kripke's interpretation, sentences with modal operators in them are sentences about other possible worlds. Thus, "□p" is true if, and only if, p is true in *every* world that is possible relative to ours, and "◇p" is true if, and only if, p is true in *some* world that is possible relative to ours. Another way of putting this is to say that the box and the diamond are *quantifiers* over possible worlds. "◇p" is true if, and only if, *there exists a world* that is possible relative to ours in which p is true. "□p" is true if, and only if, *for any world w that is possible relative to ours*, w is a world in which p is true. This way of interpreting the symbols helped philosophers to get an intuitive grip on the differences among various rival systems of modal logic.

To appreciate this a little better, just imagine a space of possible worlds. Let's think of worlds as being like the universes that populate Tegmark's Level-4 multiverse. The one we live in is the actual world; the others represent other possibilities for how the universe might have gone. Intuitively, then, every one of those universes counts, from our perspective, as *a way things might have gone*. Furthermore, suppose that for *every* possible way things might be, there's a parallel universe in which things are just that way. Some of the universes have different laws of nature; thus, our universe might have had different laws of nature. None of them have spherical cubes; so there being a spherical cube is not possible—it is not included in any way things might have gone. And so on.

Now, ask yourself this question: From the perspective of one of those other universes, is *ours* a way things might have gone? And is every universe that is possible from the point of view of one of those other universes *also* possible relative to ours? If you say, "Yes," then you are probably thinking of the space of possible worlds as analogous to a classroom full of students and the "relative possibility" relation as being analogous to the *is in the same classroom as* relation. Everyone is in the same classroom as herself; furthermore, if x is in the same classroom as y, then y is in the same classroom as x. Also, if x is in the same classroom as y and y is in the same classroom as z, then x is in the same classroom as z. Once we have arrived at this way of thinking about the relative-possibility relation, we can now evaluate 6.5. Consider someone in the same classroom as me. Now suppose that, from her point of view, *everyone in the classroom* is wearing a red shirt. Well, then it has to be the case that from *my* point of view too, everyone in the classroom (including me) is wearing a red shirt. So likewise: Consider one of the worlds possible relative to ours. Now suppose that, from the point of view of that world, *every* possible world is one in which *p* is true. It follows, then, that from the point of view of our world too, every possible world (including ours) is one in which *p* is true. But this is just to say that 6.5 is true.

On the other hand, suppose you think differently about relative possibility. Suppose that when you considered the perspective of one of the worlds possible relative to ours, you thought like this: Maybe from the point of view of *that* world there are ways things could have gone that simply aren't, from our point of view, ways things could have gone. In that case, you are probably thinking of the relative-possibility relation as analogous to the *has a friend in common with* relation. Everyone has a friend in common with herself, and if *x* has a friend in common with *y*, then *y* has a friend in common with *x*. But it is not generally true that if *x* has a friend in common with *y*, and *y* has a friend in common with *z*, then *x* has a friend in common with *z*. So consider someone who has a friend in common with me. Now suppose that everyone who has a friend in common with her has read *The Lord of the Rings*. Does it follow that I have read *The Lord of the Rings*? Yes. But does it follow that *everyone who has a friend in common with me* has read *The Lord of the Rings*? No. So, likewise, if relative possibility behaves like the *has a friend in common with* relation, 6.5 will be false.

Understanding possibility in terms of possible worlds helps us in evaluating claims like 6.5. Thus, it helps us to determine which of the different modal logics we want to accept. Once I have adopted this framework for understanding the modal operators, however, we have to ask: What are these possible worlds that we are talking about? There are various answers to this question, but I want to single out two for consideration here: (1) concrete objects; and (2) abstract states of affairs.

David Lewis recommends thinking about possible worlds in roughly the same way that Tegmark thinks about the universes that populate the Level-4 multiverse. A bit more accurately, Lewis understands possible worlds as follows. Let us say that two things are *worldmates* if, and only if, they are spatiotemporally related to one another. According to Lewis, the *actual world* is a giant (universe-sized) concrete object whose parts are *us and all of our worldmates* and nothing else. Moreover, Lewis also thinks that there are other things that are not our worldmates. So now consider one of these things—call it *Fred*. According to Lewis, there is another world (distinct from ours) whose parts are just *Fred and Fred's worldmates*. This too will be a universe-sized concrete object; and (like Fred) it will not be spatiotemporally related to us. And so on. For every object that is not spatiotemporally related to us, there is a universe-sized object whose parts are it and all of its worldmates. Each of these universe-sized objects is a world; and, by definition, no two worlds are spatiotemporally related to one another. According to Lewis, there are infinitely many worlds, enough to represent absolutely every possible way things might have been.

Why believe in possible worlds? We have already seen a couple of reasons: Doing so gives us the resources to understand modal logic; and doing so in the particular way in which Lewis does, that is, believing in *concrete* worlds, helps to explain a certain kind of cosmic coincidence. David Lewis's famous answer in his book *Counterfactuals* was, surprisingly, an appeal to common sense:

> I believe, and so do you, that things could have been different in countless ways. But what does this mean? Ordinary language permits the paraphrase: there are many ways things could have been besides the way they actually are. I believe that things could have been different in countless ways; I believe permissible paraphrases of what I believe; taking the paraphrase at its face value, I therefore believe in the existence of entities that might be called "ways things could have been." I prefer to call them "possible worlds."

This is only a partial answer to the question, however. It gives us belief in possible worlds but not yet belief in the *concrete* possible worlds that Lewis believed in. His answer to the question of why we should believe that possible worlds are concrete is, quite simply, that abstract possible worlds cannot do all of the theoretical work that he thinks concrete worlds can do. Most importantly, abstract worlds either fail to represent all of the possibilities or else leave it a complete mystery as to how they represent any possibilities at all.

Before examining this objection to abstract worlds, let us briefly sketch the way in which Lewis thinks concrete worlds represent alternative possibilities. Remember that "$\Diamond p$" means *there is a possible world in which* p *is true*. Where *p* is a sentence like "light travels faster than 186,000 miles per second" or "donkeys fly," it is easy to see how another concrete world might "represent" such possibilities. The possibility of donkeys flying is represented in another world if, and only if, the world contains donkeys and, lo and behold, they fly. What is harder to see is how other concrete worlds might represent possibilities for particular objects—*de re* possibilities, that is. So, for example, let *p* be the sentence, "Michael Rea is an Olympic archer." It is indeed possible that I be an Olympic archer. But the problem is that there is no concrete world other than this one that has me as a part. Worlds, on Lewis's view, do not share parts in common. (He gives various reasons for this. One simple reason is that, if they did share parts in common, then overlapping worlds would be spatiotemporally related to one another, which would make them parts of the *same* world.) And if no possible world other than this one has me as a part, then it is hard to see how another possible world could represent *me* as being an Olympic archer.

Lewis's solution to this problem is called *counterpart theory*. According to Lewis, what it is for an object in this world to exist "according to" another possible world is for it to have a counterpart in that world. Which things in other worlds count as an object's counterparts is determined by similarity relations that hold between the object and things in other worlds. Our counterparts, then, are our representatives or stand-ins in other worlds; and worlds represent possibilities for us by including counterparts of us who do things differently than we did. Thus, to say that I could have been an Olympic archer is, on this view, to say that there is another possible world in which a counterpart of me, a man distinct from but relevantly similar to me (by virtue of his history, intrinsic features, and so on), *is* an Olympic archer.

More generally, counterpart theory affirms the following claims:

- x has a property p according to a world w if, and only if, x has a counterpart in w that has P.
- x has the property of *being possibly* P if, and only if, there is a world according to which x has P.
- x has the property *being necessarily (or essentially)* P if, and only if, x has P according to every world according to which it exists at all.

Note, however, that things in other worlds do not count as your counterparts simply by resembling you in some way or other. If they did do so, everything in every world would automatically be your counterpart, since everything in every world is similar to you in some way or other. You would have counterparts that are horses, rocks, atoms, electrons, and so on *ad infinitum*; and it would follow from this, on counterpart theory, that you have modal properties like *being possibly an electron* and *being possibly a rock*. So, counterpart theory includes two further theses: (1) not every similarity relation is a counterpart relation; and (2) *which* similarity relations are counterpart relations is determined by context.

These two further theses are best understood in light of an example. Consider again the Lumpl/Goliath puzzle from Chapter 4: In the region occupied by Goliath, we have a statue; we also have a lump of clay (Lumpl). Goliath could not have been shaped as a ball; Lumpl could have been shaped as a ball. So, do we have two things in the same place at the same time? Lewis says no, and he explains our different judgments about the modal properties of Lumpl/Goliath as follows. Suppose we just point at the object and ask, "Could that thing have been shaped as a ball?" There is, perhaps, not enough context to the question to enable us to make a judgment. But in a context where it is known that "Lumpl" is supposed to refer to a lump and "Goliath" is supposed to refer to a statue, the names "Lumpl" and "Goliath" evoke different counterpart relations. That is, they give us different cues as to what ought to count as "relevantly similar" to the thing here in front of us. When we say that Goliath could not have been shaped as a ball, what we mean is that *this object has no statue-counterparts in other worlds that are ball-shaped*. When we say that

Lumpl could have been shaped as a ball, what we mean is that *this object has a lump-counterpart in some other world that is ball-shaped.* Interestingly, counterpart theory also gives us a way of making sense of contingent-identity claims. Lumpl is identical to Goliath, but counterpart theory, if correct, allows us to say truthfully that Lumpl could have been distinct from Goliath. When we say this, what we mean is that *there is a possible world in which either the object (Lumpl/Goliath) has a lump-counterpart that is not identical to any statue-counterpart of the object, or it has a statue-counterpart that is not identical to any lump-counterpart.*

What should we think of Lewis's theory? Perhaps the most common "objection" against the view that possible worlds are concrete is what Lewis has famously referred to as "the incredulous stare." People think that it is very strange to believe in a wide variety of other universes for the sorts of philosophical reasons Lewis gives for believing in them. Lewis has replied to this objection, however, by noting that "oddity is not falsity" and then by showing that belief in concrete possible worlds has a great deal of theoretical usefulness. For example, in addition to the advantages we have highlighted in the present chapter, we have seen that belief in other concrete possible worlds enables Lewis to provide a theory of properties (as sets of their instances) and of propositions (as sets of worlds). Lewis has also invoked possible worlds to help build theories about counterfactuals (claims about what *would* or *might* have been the case had matters gone differently) and about mental content. Some of this work could be done by abstract worlds, but not all of it can be, and even the work that could be done by abstract worlds would have to be done differently.

Counterpart theory has also been a source of objection. One of the main worries is that our counterparts are just *other individuals* living in other universes, so it is hard to see what their activities have to do with possibilities for us. When I say that I could have been an Olympic archer (if I had a different set of skills and a different background and so on), I mean that *I* could have done this—the possibility in view is one that involves *me*, not some other guy who strongly resembles me. Lewis's response to this objection has been to insist that facts about our counterparts do represent possibilities that involve us. The *possibilities* involve us; the counterparts simply *represent* those possibilities. Still, many have found it hard to swallow the idea that what our counterparts in fact do is at all relevant to what we ourselves could have done.

Finally, opponents of Lewis's view have pressed the following more general objection as well. Not only do facts about our counterparts seem irrelevant to what is possible for us, but facts about Lewis's alternative possible worlds in general seem to have nothing to do with possibility and necessity. It seems that, had Lewis's concrete worlds not existed, it still would have been possible for things to be otherwise. I could have been an Olympic archer regardless of whether there is a concrete world in which some guy very much like me happens to be an Olympic archer. Indeed, the very fact that we can entertain the *possibility* in which no concrete worlds (except our own) exist ought to raise our suspicions. If all of the possibilities that exist are in fact represented by the concrete worlds, then it is *impossible* that there be no concrete worlds, since there is no concrete world that represents such a possibility. But it does seem possible that there be no concrete worlds; and it also seems possible that there not be enough concrete worlds to represent absolutely all of the possibilities.

Let us turn, then, to the alternative: abstract possible worlds. Whereas Lewis thinks of worlds as complete concrete universes, Alvin Plantinga takes worlds to be abstract states of affairs. We are well acquainted with simple states of affairs: *Sally's sitting on the park bench*, for example. But there are also complex states of affairs corresponding to long and complex events that may or may not actually have happened: for example, the French Revolution, or the coronation of the first king of the United States of America. Now imagine a state of affairs that comprises an entire possible history of the world, plus all of the metaphysical truths, plus all of the facts about mathematical objects and laws of nature and so on. Such a state of affairs would be a possible world.

We can express this idea more precisely as follows. Let us say that a state of affairs S is *maximal* if, and only if, it has the following feature: For *every* state of affairs $S^\star$, S either *includes* $S^\star$ or *precludes* $S^\star$. One state of affairs includes another if, and only if, the first can obtain only if the second also obtains. One state of affairs precludes another if, and only if, the two cannot both obtain. So a maximal state of affairs will either include or preclude *my being an Olympic archer*; it will either include or preclude *your reading this textbook*; and so on. A maximal state of affairs that is consistent (i.e., it does not include two states of affairs that preclude one another) is an abstract possible world.

According to Plantinga, a proposition p is true in a possible world w if, and only if, p would have been true, had w been actual. Moreover, an individual exists in a world w if, and only if, the individual would have existed, had w been actual. Likewise, an individual x has a property F in a world w if, and only if, x would have existed and would have been F, had w been actual. And, again, "$\Diamond p$" means that there is a possible world in which p is true, and "$\Box p$" means that p is true in every possible world.

Earlier I said that one concern about abstract worlds pertains to how they manage to represent alternative possibilities. As we have seen, concrete worlds represent either directly or by way of counterparts. According to Lewis, there are only three possibilities for how an abstract world might represent something: It could represent in the way that sentences do, or it could represent in the way that pictures do, or it could represent "magically" (i.e., in some other way that we can't really explain). Lewis has interesting objections against the idea that abstract worlds might be like pictures, but I'll set that whole discussion aside, because I don't know of anyone who has seriously endorsed the pictorial understanding of how worlds represent. So the two options I'll discuss are these: Worlds are like sentences, or worlds represent by magic.

What would it mean for worlds to be like sentences? Sentences are made up of words, and the words pick out various bits of reality. So, for example, names pick out individuals; predicates pick out properties; and when you put them together, the sentence represents the individual as having the property. Different combinations of words, furthermore, generate different sentences and, therefore, different representations of reality. Maybe states of affairs are like this too: maybe, like structured propositions, they have parts that "mean" or "refer" to various bits of reality, and maybe different states of affairs are generated by different recombinations of those parts. (This is a very natural view for those who identify propositions with states of affairs.) If that is right, then possible worlds, on this view, will represent reality in the way that sentences do.

Lewis's main objection against this way of understanding possible worlds is that it is insufficient to represent all of the possibilities that there are. Words of real languages like English and German can only refer to objects that actually exist. We can't name merely possible objects or merely possible properties because we haven't the means to connect our words to those things. We can describe them if they are constructed out of properties or objects with which we are acquainted. For example, we can describe the property of being a gold mountain because that property is built up out of *being a mountain* and *being gold*, both of which are properties with which we are acquainted. But merely possible *fundamental* properties, properties that are in no way built out of properties we are acquainted with, will not be describable in this way. So if states of affairs represent the world in just the way that real-language sentences do, then they will be subject to the same limitations: They won't—indeed can't—have any parts that represent fundamental properties or particular objects that don't exist here in the actual world. This is the problem of *aliens*. If worlds represent in the way that linguistic items do, they haven't the resources to represent certain kinds of alien properties or alien individuals.

Of course, one could insist that states of affairs aren't sentence-like and that some of their parts somehow do manage to represent alien properties and alien individuals. But to say this is simply to move to the other option: the "magical" view. According to the magical view, there is no story to be told about *how* particular states of affairs represent the things that they do. So, for example, consider the state of affairs *my being a philosopher*. That state of affairs represents the real-world fact that I am a philosopher. But, on this view, we cannot explain *how* it represents this by saying, for instance, that it has parts—one corresponding to the word "philosopher," another corresponding to the name "Michael Rea," etc.—that have been assembled in just the right way to correspond to the fact that I am a philosopher. Nor can we point to some particular intrinsic feature of the state of affairs that explains why it represents the fact that I am a philosopher rather than (say) the fact that Notre Dame is a university. On this view, the state of affairs in question just *does* represent the fact that I am a philosopher, and that is all there is to be said about it. Lewis's objection, in short, is that the magical view makes representation wholly mysterious.

So, in short, believers in abstract worlds, according to Lewis, must admit either that abstract worlds cannot represent all of the possibilities there are (the problem of aliens) or that they have no idea what the representation relation amounts to (the problem of mystery). The first horn of the dilemma seems clearly unacceptable. To admit that your theory of possible worlds lacks the resources to represent all of the possibilities is to admit that it is a failure as a theory of worlds. The second horn of the dilemma, however, is not so obviously problematic. Not everything can be explained; perhaps here is a place where we must rest content with mystery. At any rate, the problem of mystery doesn't point to any outright incoherence in the view that worlds are abstract. Nor does it show that the view lacks the resources to do what it claims to be able to do. Still, what Lewis will claim is that the problem of mystery counts as a theoretical disadvantage. It is a coin on the *concrete-worlds* side of the scale. The question, then, is whether the overall balance of coins tips the scale in the direction of Lewis's view or in the direction of Plantinga's.

There is one other issue to discuss in connection with the abstract-worlds theory. It is a problem that is in some ways connected with the problem of aliens. Consider a possible world in which Socrates does not exist. Surely from the point of view of that world it is *possible* that Socrates exist. Thus, from the point of view of that world, Socrates is an alien individual. As we have seen, there is, then, a question to be raised about how the world represents the possibility that Socrates exists. But there is another question as well. How does the world represent Socrates as *not existing*? This is, of course, just another form of the problem of nonexistent objects. We have already seen a few strategies for dealing with this sort of problem in Chapter 2, but it is worth revisiting the issue briefly so as to make it clear how the problem connects up with our discussion of possible worlds.

Another way of putting our question is: How it could be true in a world *w* that Socrates does not exist. The question poses a problem because, intuitively, a proposition *p* is true in a world *w* if, and only if, *p* would have been true, had *w* been actual; and it is initially hard to see how a proposition like *Socrates does not exist* could possibly be true. For it seems that the truth condition for the proposition that Socrates does not exist would have to be something like the following:

TC1   The proposition that Socrates does not exist is true if, and only if, Socrates exemplifies nonexistence.

TC1, in turn, suggests the following more general condition:

TC2   For any x, the proposition that x does not exist is true in a world w if, and only if, x would have exemplified nonexistence, had w been actual.

But TC1 and TC2 are highly implausible. As we saw in Chapter 2, there is something deeply puzzling about the idea of something exemplifying nonexistence. For a *thing* x can exemplify nonexistence only if there *is* such a thing as x, despite the fact that x does not exist. In other words, TC1 and TC2 presuppose that being and existence come apart, which seems impossible.

Significantly, Lewis's theory of worlds does not face this problem. A world w in which Socrates does not exist is one which neither has him as a part nor includes a counterpart of Socrates. Is it *true* in w that Socrates does not exist? Yes; but that truth is not problematic for Lewis. For what is true, strictly speaking, is just that Socrates does not exist *in w*; it is not true, strictly speaking, that Socrates does not exist. (From the point of view of w, Socrates exists, but in some other parallel universe.)

The problem arises, then, primarily for believers in abstract worlds. One solution, of course, is to embrace TC2. Those who take this solution maintain that, in addition to all of the things that actually exist, there are also *merely possible* things that do not actually exist. This is a theory known as "possibilism." Possibilism is different from views (mentioned in Chapter 2) that maintain that even *impossible* objects, like round squares, have being. This is because TC2 does not by itself imply that there are or could have been such things. But it is obviously related to those views. The opposing view, according to which everything that has being exists, is known as "actualism." I have nothing further to say about possibilism here except that I cannot imagine how it could be true.

How, then, might an actualist solve the problem?

One way is to insist that everything exists necessarily: so, in other words, to deny that there are possible worlds in which Socrates (or anything else) fails to exist. This solution sounds incredible, but it has been defended quite persuasively in recent years by Timothy Williamson. Part of Williamson's idea is that when a thing *x seems* to come into or pass out of existence, in fact what is happening is that *x* is becoming or ceasing to be a concrete thing. Thus, nothing *really* comes into or passes out of existence; it simply becomes or ceases to be concrete. So, likewise, a world in which there are no human beings whatsoever—the sort of world in which we would normally say that it is true that Socrates and the rest of us human beings do not exist—are in fact worlds in which Socrates and the rest of us exist but fail to be concrete objects. Of course, saying all of this does not necessarily make Williamson's view *easy* to accept, but it at least takes some of the sting out of the claim that everything exists necessarily.

Another, more common solution is to say that, in worlds where Socrates does not exist, the proposition that Socrates does not exist is true because properties like *socrateity* or *being identical to Socrates* are unexemplified. Properties like these are *individual essences* of Socrates. A property *P* is an individual essence of an object *x* if, and only if, (1) *x* cannot exist without having *P*; and (2) necessarily, nothing other than *x* has *P*. Unlike Socrates himself, essences of Socrates exist (according to proponents of this solution) in every possible world. Thus, there is no problem invoking them to account for the truth of propositions like *Socrates does not exist*. So in general, this solution maintains that a proposition of the form *x does not exist* is true in a world *w* if, and only if, every individual essence of *x* would have been unexemplified, had *w* been actual.

Does this last strategy work? It is certainly popular, but it is also a bit puzzling. We can get at the puzzle by asking this question: In a world in which Socrates does not exist, does *socrateity* bear any relationship to Socrates? Suppose it does not. So as to avoid the illusion that it bears some relationship to Socrates, let us rename the property *greebe*. Why think that the fact that *greebe* is not exemplified in a world would suffice for Socrates not existing in that world? *Greebe* has nothing at all to do with Socrates, so whether or not it is exemplified shouldn't be the least bit relevant to whether

Socrates exists. On the other hand, suppose that it does bear some relationship to Socrates. Then we can infer that *there is an* x *such that (1)* x *bears a relationship to Socrates and (2)* x = *socrateity*, from which we can also infer that *there is an* x *such that* x = *Socrates*. But this last claim is equivalent to the claim that Socrates exists! What then shall we say? Maybe only this: In every possible world, Socrateity exists and *represents* Socrates, but it does so by magic, not by way of any particular relationship to Socrates. This is a difficult claim to accept, but at least it assimilates this problem to a problem of magical representation in general, a problem that most believers in abstract worlds already face.

WORLDMAKING

I want to close now by considering a very different sort of "world" altogether: the world that some philosophers think that we make for ourselves by conceiving of reality in the ways that we do. The idea is that human mental activity somehow contributes to *making* things what they are, helps to determine their persistence conditions, and even helps to determine the boundaries of what is possible for things in the world. There are various names for this sort of view, and it comes in different varieties. Alvin Plantinga calls it "creative anti-realism"—*creative* because it attributes a strong kind of creative power to the human mind; *antirealism* because it denies a certain kind of objective reality to the world. Others call it "constructivism," since it is a view according to which human minds play an unexpectedly important role in constructing the world. The view has been associated (somewhat controversially) with philosophers like Immanuel Kant, Hilary Putnam, Richard Rorty, and Nelson Goodman. Nelson Goodman is responsible for the term "worldmaking," which I have adopted as the title for this section, and it is his version of constructivism that I shall take as my focus. My goal here is quite limited: I want just to briefly explain some of the core ideas and motivations behind this form of antirealism and to say a few words about how adopting it might affect the way in which one thinks about some of the other topics that have been discussed in this book. It makes for a fitting end to the book because, in a way, it circles us back around to some of the methodological worries that emerged in the very first chapter.

Realism is the view that everything either is a mind or is among the contents of a mind. Obviously that is a view according to which things in the world depend on minds. Constructivism is not idealism, but it is implied by idealism. It does not affirm that everything either is a mind or is among the contents of a mind; rather, it is the view that a certain logical consequence of idealism is true: Things in the world *somehow* depend on mental activity for being the way that they are. But what could this thesis possibly mean? How could minds and their activity be even partly responsible for how the world is?

Let us begin by setting aside some very obvious ways in which minds make a difference to how the world is. Firstly, there *are* minds, and there are ideas; so those facts about the world, that it contains minds and that it includes ideas, depend on minds for their existence. Set that aside; it is wholly uninteresting. Secondly, and only slightly more interestingly: Minds make a *causal* difference in the world by causing bodily movements, which, in turn, cause matter to be configured in ways that it would not otherwise have been. Your own mental activity, for example, moves your body in particular ways, which results in your body traveling various places throughout spacetime, pushing matter around in various ways, making sounds that affect the mental activity of other people and animals, and so on. All of this makes a difference—maybe a big difference—in how the world is. The world contains wars and weddings, airplanes and automobiles, televisions and toys, and a whole lot more, all because of the activities of minds. This is a very significant way in which how the world is depends on what minds are doing. But set that aside too; for, as I just said, it is not very philosophically interesting. Setting aside very general doubts about causation and about our commonsense views about how mind and body interact, nobody really doubts that minds make this sort of causal difference in the world. The sort of mind-dependence that is philosophically interesting and highly controversial is something wholly different from this.

The sort of mind-dependence we are interested in is best understood by way of example. Consider again the Ship of Theseus. At the end of the repair process, we have an aluminum ship sailing the ship's former route, and we have a pile of planks in somebody's yard. An art historian finds the planks, rebuilds them according to the ship's original blueprint and declares that *she* now has the original Ship of Theseus. A dispute ensues. The crew of the aluminum ship scoffingly points out that ships obviously can survive gradual replacement of their individual parts; and the ship that they are currently sailing is the product of just such a process. The art historian argues that restoration of artifacts—*restoration*, not *replication*—often involves rebuilding things from their partially or wholly disassembled parts. Indeed, transporting artifacts often involves this too. We take the artifact apart, put the pieces in a box, ship them off somewhere, and rebuild the artifact elsewhere. Her ship, of course, is the product of just such a process. Thus we have a disagreement. The disagreement is primarily one concerning the persistence conditions of ships (though perhaps it is also a disagreement concerning the persistence conditions of artifacts more generally, or of historically important objects).

One way to approach the disagreement is to try to figure out *who has the objectively correct answer*. What does it mean for there to be an objectively correct answer to the question, "Which ship is the Ship of Theseus"? Roughly this: (1) there is a correct answer, and (2) that answer's being the correct one does not entail that anyone has specific beliefs about which ship is the Ship of Theseus, or about which things (if any) count as ships, or about the conditions under which one ship is the same as another. Intuitively, the answer to the question is objectively correct if it would have been correct even if nobody thought that it was the correct answer, and even if nobody had opinions about the existence, persistence conditions, or other modal properties of ships. Commonsense realism, according to which familiar material objects have their existence and persistence conditions independently of human mental activity, is committed to the idea that there is an objectively correct answer.

According to commonsense realism, there is an objective fact about whether there are ships, and, if there are ships, whether ships have intrinsic natures; what a ship is does not depend in any way upon what human beings think that it is or upon whether human beings think that there are ships at all. Furthermore, either a ship's intrinsic nature allows it to survive the gradual replacement of its parts or not; either its nature allows it to survive being disassembled and rebuilt in a museum or not; and so on.

The constructivist view, however, which is somewhat tempting in the present example, is that this commonsense idea is simply wrong. There is no objective fact about what the Ship of Theseus can and cannot survive. If you're an art historian, you will regard the original parts as important and so, on your view, an artifact simply can't survive the loss of too many of its original parts. If you're a sailor, you won't much care about the original parts; on your view, perhaps, a ship can survive the loss of any of its original parts so long as the form is preserved. And, on the constructivist view, it is just these sorts of opinions that *make it the case* that the ship can survive certain sorts of changes but not other sorts of changes. It might be that the relevant facts are relativized to the opinions of a particular person or community, so that, for example, it is true-for-art-historians that ships cannot survive complete part replacement but true-for-sailors that they can. Or it might be that once a sufficiently large number of people agree on what ships can and cannot survive, their opinions on that score are true, period, and people who disagree are simply mistaken. Either way, however, the crucial thing to see is that, according to both views, there is a correct answer to the question, "Which ship is the Ship of Theseus?" only if people have specific beliefs about which answer is correct, or general beliefs about the existence and persistence conditions of ships. In other words, what people think about ships determines whatever facts there are about what the ship can and cannot survive.

The view just described is one according to which the persistence conditions of ships, or, at any rate, of *this* ship, are mind-dependent. But persistence conditions go hand in hand with kind properties: properties like *being a ship*, *being an electron*, *being a horse*, and so on. That is, what kind of thing something is (or what counts as a thing's dominant kind) is ultimately settled by the facts about what it can and cannot survive, and vice versa. So, on the constructivist view, the facts about *what the Ship of Theseus is* are also mind-dependent in the ways just described. Whether it even counts as a ship, as opposed to a mere collection of wood planks or something else, depends on how we think of the matter in the region occupied by the ship. Furthermore, according to the constructivist, what goes for ships goes also for trees and horses and human beings and literally everything else in the world as well. Whether we live in a world of ships and horses and human beings and trees and planets and so on, or just a world of simple atoms, or a world of very different kinds of things with different persistence conditions altogether depends quite literally on how we conceive of things. On this view, as Goodman says, we even "make the stars."

Here is an analogy. It is as if the world is a great cloud formation, and we human beings all get to look at it and simply decide what we see in it. When two people look at a cloud formation, it doesn't make sense for them to argue about whether there are "really" three trees, a car, and the face of a woman in the clouds. Nor does it make sense for them to argue about whether the gradual movement of the clouds has objectively created or destroyed any of the objects they see there. For, independently of their thought processes, there is *nothing* objectively there apart from a grand configuration of grey and white stuff. They see what they see, and each is entitled to her own perspective.

The idea that human beings make even the stars is staggering. At the same time, however, it is important to realize that the thesis is not nearly so radical as it might at first sound. True, the creative antirealist thinks that the stars depend for their existence as such on human conceptual activity. (This is, again, because nothing would *be* a star or have the persistence conditions we associate with stars if human beings hadn't applied the concept *star* to the world. Thus, if Betelgeuse's nature is to be a star—if part of what it is for Betelgeuse to exist is to be a star—then Betelgeuse would not have existed if human beings had never applied the concept *star* to the world. We might still have pointed to the region occupied by Betelgeuse and used the same name to pick out whatever it is that we thought we saw there. But that thing would not have been our star Betelgeuse. It is in just this sense that constructivism implies that the stars depend for their existence on human conceptual activity.) But nobody thinks that the configuration of matter in the regions of spacetime that we take to be occupied by stars is the way that it is because of human conceptual activity. Our thoughts did not *move* matter into the regions occupied by our sun or Betelgeuse. So in that sense we do not at all make the stars or much else in the world beyond what comes into existence as a result of the movements of our bodies.

But why would anyone endorse constructivism? In motivating his own brand of the view, Nelson Goodman starts with the observation that "The sun always moves" and "The sun never moves" are *equally true*, though incompatible. He notes that we don't worry much about this fact because we typically view these statements as shorthand for longer statements that relativize the claim to a frame of reference—statements like, "Under frame of reference A, the sun always moves" and "Under frame of reference B, the sun never moves," which are not incompatible. But, he asks, "if I insist that you tell me how it is apart from all frames, what can you say? We are confined to ways of describing whatever is described. Our universe, so to speak, consists of these ways."

That is the first step: We are confined to a perspective; we have no access to how things might be "in themselves"—independently of all perspectives. Moreover, he says that his observations about alternative descriptions of motion

> provide only a minor and rather pallid example of diversity in accounts of the world. Much more striking is the vast variety of versions and visions in the several sciences, in the works of different painters and writers, and in our perceptions as informed by these, by circumstances, and by our own insights, interests, and past experiences.

Perspectives abound, in other words. And, again, we have no perspective-independent way of gaining access to how things "really" are.

We might strengthen this point as follows. In our efforts to produce theories about the world, we are confined to the resources afforded by our sensory apparatus, our concepts, and our language. Very different creatures—creatures the size of atoms, or creatures with different sensory faculties, like sonar—would tell very different stories about what kinds of things inhabit the regions we take to be inhabited by cars, cattle, planets, and so on. We can *hope* that they would tell the same story about the "fundamental level," the most basic facts about particles and their movements that explain the great diversity of phenomena in the world. But even this hope might seem ungrounded in light of the fact that, for as long as we have been engaged in the scientific enterprise, it has always been true that multiple different (and incompatible) theories equally fit the data. Some persist in their optimism, attributing objective structure to the world despite the fact that multiple accounts of what there is and how things behave are compatible with our data. Others, however, move in the direction of constructivism, arguing that not only can we not *detect* the objective structure in the world, but we do not even have reason to think that there *is* objective structure to the world.

And this is precisely where Goodman's reasoning ends. Ultimately, he argues, we face a choice: (1) we can suppose that what we have in the diversity of "accounts" are just *multiple versions of a single world*; or (2) we can give up the idea that there is a single world and concede that we who offer different accounts from one another genuinely inhabit different worlds. Against the first option he offers the following remark: "The world thus regained [by taking that first option] is a world without kinds or order or motion or rest or pattern—a world not worth fighting for or against." His point isn't, of course, that realists who take option 1 have to give up their commonsense beliefs in motion, pattern, and familiar kinds, such as *cat*, *airplane*, and so on. Rather, the point is just that they have no basis for thinking that their commonsense categories correspond to the objective structure of the world; they have no reason to think that the mind-independent facts about what kinds of things inhabit the world that underlies all of our varying accounts is a world of moving cats and airplanes and so on rather than a world vastly different from what we are presently able to conceive. If your goal is to save the familiar objects, if what you are fighting for in defending commonsense realism is the familiar causally and spatiotemporally ordered world of biological kinds and human artifacts and so on, you would actually do much better to abandon metaphysical realism and to say that all of these different things are indeed mind-dependent. The consequence, however, is Goodman's multiplicity of worlds.

Constructivism is a fascinating view. I see its attractions, though I cannot ultimately accept it. I will not try to argue against it here, however. Rather, in closing, I want simply to make an observation that will bring us back to issues raised in Chapter 1. As you might gather from the argument sketch I have just presented, constructivism is born out of the conviction that our theoretical faculties and our available sources of evidence are not sufficient to enable us to discover the world's intrinsic structure. This is a fundamentally antimetaphysical conviction. It is one that is shared in some form or other by the various critics of metaphysics that we discussed in Chapter 1, and it is a conviction that more or less drives their criticisms of metaphysics. Answering the constructivist and answering the antimetaphysical skeptic, then, are very similar tasks. Both involve explaining why it is reasonable for us to proceed under the assumption that our theoretical faculties and available sources of evidence *are* adequate to the job of putting us in touch with the world's objective, intrinsic structure. Executing this task, however, is not the business of a metaphysics textbook. Here we simply proceed in optimism.

FURTHER READING

On the topic of parallel universes, a good starting place is Max Tegmark's "Parallel Universes," reprinted in *Arguing about Metaphysics*. For discussion of parallel universes in connection with the fine-tuning argument, see John Leslie, "World Ensemble, or Design," reprinted in *Arguing about Metaphysics*; Robin Collins, "A Scientific Argument for the Existence of God," in Michael Murray, ed., *Reason for the Hope Within* (Grand Rapids, MI: Eerdmans, 1999), pp. 47–75; and Stephen Barr, *Modern Physics and Ancient Faith* (Notre Dame, IN: University of Notre Dame Press, 2006). My discussion of the many-worlds interpretation of quantum theory is indebted to Jim Baggott, *The Meaning of Quantum Theory* (Oxford: Oxford University Press, 1992).

On the topic of possible worlds, the best entry points are John Divers, *Possible Worlds* (London and New York: Routledge, 2002), and the superb introduction to Michael Loux, ed., *The Possible and the Actual* (Ithaca, NY: Cornell University Press, 1979), to which my own discussion here is heavily indebted. Also in *The Possible and the Actual* are quite a few of the most important articles from the discussions of modality taking place in the 1970s in the wake of the publication of Kripke's 1963 article, "Semantical Considerations on Modal Logic," *Acta Philosophica Fennica*, vol. 16 (1963), pp. 83–94.

I cited David Lewis's book, *Counterfactuals* (Oxford: Basil Blackwell, 1973), but the most important place to look for his views about modality is his *On the Plurality of Worlds* (Oxford: Basil Blackwell, 1986). I have also found Philip Bricker, "David Lewis: On the Plurality of Worlds," in John Shand, ed., *Central Works of*

Philosophy, vol. V: *The Twentieth Century: Quine and After* (Chesham: Acumen Publishing, 2006) to be very useful; and, as I mentioned at the end of Chapter 2, Daniel Nolan's *David Lewis* is a helpful overall guide to the philosophy of David Lewis.

Alvin Plantinga's views about modality can be found in *The Nature of Necessity* (Oxford: Oxford University Press, 1974) and in the essays helpfully collected in Alvin Plantinga, *Essays in the Metaphysics of Modality*, ed. Matthew Davidson (Oxford: Oxford University Press, 2003). *Arguing about Metaphysics* reprints an excerpt from Lewis's *On the Plurality of Worlds*, as well as an article by Plantinga: "Two Concepts of Modality"—that highlights the differences between his own views and those of Lewis.

On worldmaking, my source for Goodman's views was primarily his "Words, Works, and Worlds," reprinted in *Arguing about Metaphysics*. There is a volume devoted to discussion of his brand of antirealism entitled *Starmaking: Realism, Anti-Realism, and Irrealism*, ed. Peter J. McCormick (Cambridge, MA: MIT Press, 1996). Hilary Putnam's antirealist views appear in a variety of places. For a fairly recent statement, see his *Ethics without Ontology* (Cambridge, MA: Harvard University Press, 2005). Michael Devitt's *Realism and Truth*, 2nd edn. (Princeton, NJ: Princeton University Press, 1997) is an excellent resource for discussion of realism and antirealism generally. The term "creative anti-realism" comes from Alvin Plantinga's *Twin Pillars of Christian Scholarship* (Grand Rapids, MI: Calvin College and Seminary, 1990).

GLOSSARY

a priori   Justified for a believer independently of sense perception or other modes of experience. (NB: A belief or proposition may count as *a priori* for a person even if her ability to understand it is somehow derived from experience.)

A-series   A series of events whose members have properties like "being past," "being present," and "being future."

A-theory of time   A theory of time according to which time is both an A-series and a B-series.

Agent causation   Causation by the direct, immediate activity of an agent, neither by way of choices, beliefs, desires, or other events, nor as a matter of pure chance.

Analytic   All definitions of "analytic" are controversial, but the term usually applies to sentences that are commonly said to express conceptual truths or to be true by definition or to be such that their truth is grounded solely in the meanings of the terms involved.

B-series   A series of events whose members are ordered by simultaneity and temporal priority (earlier-than and later-than relations).

B-theory of time   A theory of time according to which time, if it exists at all, is just a B-series.

Class   A collection of objects.

Compatibilism   The thesis that freedom is compatible with determinism.

Constituent   A rough synonym for "part," which, in philosophical contexts, is often used to signal that the things to which the term applies do not obey the axioms of standard logics of parthood.

Contingent   Not necessary, so a contingent truth is a proposition that is true but not necessarily true, and a contingent falsehood is one that is false but not necessarily false.

Determinism   The thesis that there is, at any given moment, one and only one physically possible future.

Empirical   Empirical claims are claims that one can be justified in believing only on the basis of observation or experience.

Empiricism   The view that all justification for nonanalytic truths ultimately derives from experience rather than *a priori* reflection.

Frame of reference   An object's frame of reference is a coordinate system that takes the object as a stationary origin point.

Fundamental   Fundamental things are the things out of which all others are made or the things without which nothing else could exist.

Hard determinism   Hard determinism is the thesis that (1) determinism is true and (2) incompatibilism is true. Hard determinism implies that no agent acts freely.

Immanent universal   Something that is located in spacetime and has multiple instances. Properties and powers, such as humanity or negative charge, are often (controversially) taken to be immanent universals located exactly where their instances (for example, individual humans or negatively charged particles) are located.

Incompatibilism   The thesis that freedom is not compatible with determinism.

Indeterminism   The thesis that determinism is false. Indeterminism might be true even if much in the universe is wholly determined by local causal factors.

Intrinsic property   A property that something can have regardless of what the rest of the world is like.

Intuition *see* **Rational intuition**

Irreflexive   A relation R is irreflexive if, and only if, nothing bears R to itself. In other words: R is irreflexive if, and only if, aRb implies $a = b$.

Libertarianism   The thesis that (1) some agents act freely and (2) freedom is incompatible with determinism.

Material constitution   Material constitution occurs whenever an object *a* and an object *b* share all of the same parts in common.

Mere plurality   Some objects that do not together compose anything even if, for the sake of convenience, they are collectively referred to by a term – like "football team" – that looks like the name for an individual thing.

Metaphysically possible   Possible in the broadest sense of the term.

Modal expressions   Expressions that communicate possibility or necessity, for example, "may," "might," "must." Talk about modality is talk about what is possible or necessary in various different senses. The different forms of modality include metaphysical, physical or nomological, logical, epistemic, and deontic.

Modal property   Modal properties are properties that have modality built into them, properties like *being able to survive being squashed* or *being possibly made of wood*.

Nominalism   Commonly, nominalism is identified either with the view that everything is particular (i.e., there are no universals) or with the view that everything is concrete (i.e., there are no abstract objects). This book takes the former position.

Nomological   Of or pertaining to the laws of nature.

Ontology   Commonly characterized as the study of what there is. It is the branch of study that focuses on existence claims of the sort studied by metaphysics and on the logical consequences thereof.

Persistence condition   Persistence conditions are modal properties of a certain kind, namely, facts about what a thing can and cannot survive.

Physical constants   Physical constants are universal and unchanging physical quantities like the speed of light in a vacuum or the gravitational constant.

Physicalism   The view that all properties and objects are reducible to the properties and objects posited by our best theories in physics.

Proper part   A proper part of a thing *x* is a part of *x* that is not an improper part of *x*. An improper part of *x* is any object that shares all of its parts with *x*.

Rational intuition   Rational intuitions are intellectual experiences (as opposed to perceptual or sensory experiences) of the sheer obviousness or necessary truth of various claims.

Realism   For any kind term "F" (e.g., "dog," "material object," "property"), realism about Fs is the view that there are Fs, and that something's being an F does not depend on human mental activity, for example, human beliefs, opinions, or concepts.

Reflexive   A relation R is reflexive if, and only if, everything in its domain bears R to itself. In other words, R is reflexive if, and only if, for all x in the domain of R, xRx.

Relata   The relata of a relation are the things that stand in that relation.

Relational property   Relational properties are properties of an object that involve relations to other things.

Spacetime   A manifold of points or regions or locations that can be broken up into spatial and temporal dimensions.

Sparse theory of properties   A theory of properties that places substantial restrictions on which predicates correspond to properties.

State of affairs   A state of affairs is a circumstance a situation or a way things are.

Substance   Substances are property-bearers, subjects of predication. Sometimes the term is used simply to draw a contrast with attributes. More often, substances are construed as independent and unified things on which other things depend for their existence.

Sum   A sum of the xs is an object that has all of the xs as parts and which is such that all of its parts overlap at least one of the xs.

Symmetric   A relation R is symmetric if, and only if, aRb implies bRa. The *resembles* relation is symmetric; the *is smarter than* relation is not.

Thick particular   A state of affairs which has only non-relational properties as constituents. (Non-relational properties are properties that do not involve relations, e.g., properties like having 2 kilograms mass.)

Thin particular   A state of affairs considered in abstraction from its properties.

Transitive   A relation R is transitive if, and only if, $a\mathrm{R}b$ and $b\mathrm{R}c$ together imply $a\mathrm{R}c$. The *is in the same room as* relation is transitive; the *loves* relation is not.

Trope   Abstract particular entities like the particular whiteness of my shirt, the particular tomato-basil flavor of this spoonful of pizza sauce, Socrates' humanity, etc. Tropes are typically referred to as "property-instances" because they are tokens of particular property types.

Universal   A universal is an abstract object which, in the paradigm case, either has or can have instances, or is either located or locatable in multiple places at once.

INDEX

Lightning Source UK Ltd.
Milton Keynes UK
UKHW051527061219
354798UK00011B/87/P

9 780415 574426

CORIOLANUS

Bruce King

HUMANITIES PRESS INTERNATIONAL, INC.
Atlantic Highlands, NJ

First published in 1989 in the United States of America
by Humanities Press International, Inc.,
Atlantic Highlands, NJ 07716

Library of Congress Cataloging-in-Publication Data
King, Bruce Alvin.
    Coriolanus / Bruce King.
        p.   cm. — (The Critics debate)
    Bibliography: p.
    Includes index.
    ISBN 0–391–03643–2. — ISBN 0–391–03644–0 (pbk.)
    1. Shakespeare, William, 1564–1616. Coriolanus.   2. Coriolanus.
Cnaeus Marcius, in fiction, drama, poetry, etc.   I. Title.
II. Series.
PR2805.K56   1989
822.3'3—dc19   88–38994
                                                        CIP

Printed in Hong Kong

THE CRITICS DEBATE

General Editor: Michael Scott

The Critics Debate
General Editor: Michael Scott
Published titles:

Contents

6

General Editor's Preface

OVER THE last few years the practice of literary criticism has become hotly debated. Methods developed earlier in the century and before have been attacked and the word "crisis" has been drawn upon to describe the present condition of English Studies. That such a debate is taking place is a sign of the subject discipline's health. Some would hold that the situation necessitates a radical alternative approach which naturally implies a "crisis situation." Others would respond that to employ such terms is to precipitate or construct a false position. The debate continues but it is not the first. "New Criticism" acquired its title because it attempted something fresh, calling into question certain practices of the past. Yet the practices it attacked were not entirely lost or negated by the new critics. One factor becomes clear: English Studies is a pluralistic discipline.

What are students coming to advanced work in English for the first time to make of all this debate and controversy? They are in danger of being overwhelmed by the cross-currents of critical approaches as they take up their study of literature. The purpose of this series is to help delineate various critical approaches to specific literary texts. Its authors are from a variety of critical schools and have approached their task in a flexible manner. Their aim is to help the reader come to terms with the variety of criticism and to introduce him or her to further reading on the subject and to a fuller evaluation of a particular text by illustrating the way it has been approached in a number of contexts. In the first part of the book a critical survey is given of some of the major ways the text has been appraised. This is done sometimes in a thematic manner, sometimes according to various "schools" or "approaches." In

the second part the authors provide their own appraisals of
the text from their stated critical standpoint, allowing the
reader the knowledge of their own particular approaches from
which their views may in turn be evaluated. The series therein
hopes to introduce and to elucidate criticism of authors and
texts being studied and to encourage participation as the
critics debate.

Michael Scott

A Note on Text and References

ALL REFERENCES to *Coriolanus* are to the Macmillan Shakespeare edition, edited by Tony Parr (London and Basingstoke, 1985). References to secondary material appear with the date of publication on the introduction of each such work. Details may then be found in the References section where secondary works are listed in the order of first citation in the text.

Introduction

EARLY IN THIS century A. C. Bradley claimed that *Coriolanus* was seldom acted and that except for educational purposes it was seldom read. Taste has changed and *Coriolanus* is now often seen on stage and has received considerable critical attention; but it remains a problem to many people because of its lack of an obviously sympathetic character or cause with which the reader or spectator might identify. Whether we speak of distancing, epic theatre or use the Brechtian notion of alienation, *Coriolanus* seems very modern in its unwillingness either to take sides or offer much sympathy for its characters. We are given an excess of information without guidance as to how we are to view what we learn. Its central conflict between individual aspirations and communal cohesion has been at the centre of our culture since the Romantics, and is often interpreted in contemporary terms as some version of the political right against the left, but could as easily be seen as individual freedom versus social control. *Coriolanus* has another claim to be considered modern or even post-modern in its self-reflectivity and self-consciousness of the art of making fictions. The concern in the play with acting, role-playing, persuasion, directing scenes, rhetoric and trials, seems to call attention to the falsity of theatre, and questions the premeditated use of language. The characteristics that make *Coriolanus* contemporary for us confuse those who prefer texts more straightforward in their attitudes or which can be translated into obvious sympathies. Many people are so surprised by the distancing and by disagreeable characteristics of Coriolanus that they dislike the play; but eventually they become convinced that it is one of Shakespeare's greatest works.

Criticism should address problems of the kind of play

Coriolanus is, how we see or read it, what is the effect of the
distancing on our response, how does this play fit into
Shakespeare's work, what kind of social and political pressures
have gone into it, and what it is like in the theatre. Self-
awareness of the basis of criticism is of particular relevance
now that Critical Theory is in fashion and has challenged
pragmatic, empirical, practical criticism. Practical criticism
and the analysis of patterns of imagery, or the New Critic
emphasis on tensions, irony and ambiguity reflected the
modern literature of the time; they were useful methods for
reading T. S. Eliot, James Joyce and Dylan Thomas as well
as Shakespeare. Recent theoretical approaches came into
fashion along with the post-modernism of Alain Robbe-Grillet,
Jorges L. Borges and the view that literature is concerned
with the processes and nature of literature, rather than the
imitation of reality. As literature and culture change so does
criticism; our vocabulary, understanding of technique, our
way of conceptualising, will have different built-in assumptions
than in the past. Indeed, there is a school of reception criticism
which argues that the interpretation of literature is the history
of interpretation – the meaning of a text is how it is viewed
at various times.

We need not become lost in problems of whether such a
history is not itself a fiction; there are surprising consistencies
in the history of the interpretation of *Coriolanus*. The same
questions recur. Does the play have a moral concerning
obedience to government? Is the hero so disagreeable and
excessive in his warrior values as to be the villain of the piece,
or is he admirable for his attempt to live up to an heroic ideal?
What does Shakespeare think of the citizens and the tribunes?
Why does Coriolanus turn from a patriot defending Rome
into someone intent on destroying it? And why does he relent?
We have an idea how the last two questions can be answered.
In terms of plot, Coriolanus seeks revenge and is then
persuaded by his mother that to destroy Rome would both
destroy his reputation and lead to the destruction of his own
family. But we want better, more satisfying answers, perhaps
from psychology or political theory. The imagery and subtexts
push us away from mere narrative towards other kinds of
readings; the distancing requires a conceptualisation of our

response. What kinds of questions are we asking and why?

In the following pages I am not primarily interested in listing the sympathies and opinions of critics towards the characters in *Coriolanus*. Such readings are predictable: each critic claims that the previous one wrongly assumed that Shakespeare was a liberal, socialist, fascist, when in fact he held similar views to that of the critic you are reading. It seems to me more useful to understand how kinds of critical discussion are generated, what light they throw on *Coriolanus*, their limitations, and what other approaches or analyses might be useful.

Part One: Survey

CRITICISM is shaped by conventions or the prejudices of those who criticise. Because of their assumptions some critics will only see class warfare in *Coriolanus*: still others will construct a novel involving the emotions of the characters as they interact on each other. The main critical approaches to literature are contextual, formal or textual, sociological, religious, and interdisciplinary (Marxist, psychological, etc.). While political, social and religious studies can be contextual, they are approaches on their own if distinguished from simple historicism. Each extended work of art depicts or reflects some society, shows or assumes some religion or cosmology. Theatre and production studies might be regarded as textual or formal approaches, but I will treat them separately as they are central to my discussion of *Coriolanus*.

Contextual approaches

Biographical and topical

Contextual criticism is usually some version of historicism and the main question is the kind of context constructed in which to see the work or author. Biographical criticism, which is a version of historicising a context, is of little use for discussing Shakespeare. We know a number of facts about Shakespeare's life but not enough about him as a person to guess what emotions might have gone into his play and poems. For *Coriolanus* the only connection is that Shakespeare's mother died the year we think the play was written. It is possible that this found its way into Coriolanus' affection for his mother; but as can be seen by *Hamlet* and *King Lear* Shakespeare was for some time writing plays about the destructive effects of excessive emotional attachments between children and parents.

Possible parallels between the rebellious heroism of Coriolanus and the lives of such Elizabethans and Jacobeans as the Irish Earl Tyrone, Essex and Sir Walter Raleigh are discussed by Holt (1976). They are too vague to be more than examples of Renaissance individualism. Holt also summarises the arguments of Pettet (1950) and others who argue the relationship between the play and the Jacobean enclosure riots. This obviously is a source for the emphasis Shakespeare gives to drought and shortage of grains in *Coriolanus*. More important it seems the start of Shakespeare's imagery concerning food, nourishment, care, and love. Information about enclosure riots can be found most conveniently in Bullough (1964). Source studies may at first appear convincing, but they are of limited use. The mutiny over grain is significant in Shakespeare's play as an example of inequalities of Roman society; but once the people have been given representatives they forget the grain shortage.

Critics have not found much of interest in Shakespeare's use of his classical sources, although it is sometimes suggested that the classicism and artistic restraint of *Coriolanus* owes much to the closeness with which the dramatist followed Plutarch. An interest in Rome was, however, part of an antiquarianism or historicism which was developing at the turn of the century. Perhaps the leading scholar who did most to show a Roman presence still visible in England was William Camden (Ben Jonson's teacher) from whose *Remaines of a Greater Worke concerning Britaine* (1605), Bullough says, 'Shakespeare took a point or two . . . for Menenius' fable of the belly and its members'. That Shakespeare wrote three Roman plays at this time (the others being *Julius Caesar*, *Antony and Cleopatra*) and Ben Jonson wrote two Roman plays (*Catiline* and *Sejanus*) seems significant to Spencer (1957) and Honig (1951) who examine the Jonsonian context while Huffman sees Jonson and Shakespeare both influenced by James I's use of Roman analogies in his political theories.

Political

Although the political context has been discussed at length, such studies seem barely to touch the play. Having with detail tried to put *Coriolanus* in a political context through the study of the writings of James I, Huffman (1971) claims: 'Shakespeare the dramatist of the King's Men who had already deliberately written plays that spoke to James's interests, had in the court climate itself not only the subject of a political drama but also a clear indication of the treatment he ought to give.' Huffman then offers a reading of *Coriolanus* to prove that a play put on at the Globe and Blackfriars theatres by the King's Men necessarily opposes political innovation and is conservative in tendency. Writing about early Rome, Shakespeare chose one consonant with King James' royalist view of it as a rivalry between absolute monarchy and democracy, between rule and misrule, between order and chaos. Huffman treats each detail as having such a significance. 'The presentation of the now-evil tribunes who continue to demonstrate their evil though the rest of the play corresponds to King James's view of his opponents in the House of Commons.' A footnote remarks that Plutarch contains nothing of Coriolanus' extreme dislike of seeking the people's votes; 'there may be in this characteristic a reflection of James's well-known dislike of crowds of commoners'. It is unconvincing to argue from such weak evidence that *Coriolanus* was written to James' taste. Huffman goes further. Coriolanus' extreme attitudes are wrong because the Stuart king would not approve. 'Coriolanus is the only patrician who cannot respond to the ideal of Temperance, which is the more important not only because of its place in the Graeco-Roman and Christian traditions, but also because King James so strongly urged it.' Huffman claims to understand how Shakespeare's audience might have understood Coriolanus' banishment and revenge. 'In Shakespeare, then, approval is accorded foreign invasion only if it has positive, even religious, associations and does not thereafter harm the country.' Elaborate research here produces commonplaces, triviality, or fog. Huffman neither suggests enough parallels between the play and the politics of the time to show a topicality, nor does he try to examine how the social and political tensions of the period might have been transformed into the Coriolanus story through the mediation of Roman history. Instead we have the crude assumption that the play was written to James' taste and that when in doubt we must ask what James would have thought. James becomes a master myth, which explains everything.

History of ideas

Coriolanus should yield easily to historical contextual approaches. Its themes of revenge and mercy, use of the grotesque, its satiric main character, the shift in perspectives, the lack of compassion and sympathy, the way everyone seems wrong and we end baffled, has many similarities to Jacobean drama by Marston, Middleton, Tourneur, while the wry use of historical materials is Jonsonian. Yet there has been little critical discussion of the play in the context of specifically Jacobean theatre conventions, although we will later find Dollimore offers a Marxist perspective on the drama of the period. Siegel (1968) examines *Coriolanus* within 'The Neo-Chivalric Cult of Honor'. He is concerned with a supposed conflict between two major ethical systems, Christianity and a revived Graeco-Roman humanism. The Christian humanist comes into conflict with an ideal of the medieval knight as expounded by the Tudor aristocracy; an older feudal idea is in conflict with capitalism. According to Siegel, Coriolanus suffers from an obsession with honour, not of pride. At the end of the play, not abiding by the dictates of the neo-chivalric cult of honour which call for revenge even against one's country and parents he is transformed into a god of forgiveness: 'like Christ, he dies as a result of treachery on the part of one of his associates'. As Siegel's methods seem to require him to offer a unified interpretation – pride *or* honour – this gets a bit confused, although he has interestingly teased out the mercy-Christ analogy from the play.

That there was a sharpened notion of honour in the sixteenth and seventeenth centuries is clear from the plays and poems of the time. That it necessarily resulted from two major ethical systems coming together is questionable; ethical systems themselves are influenced by social or political changes. The commonplace that the change is between feudal and capitalist systems is about as useful as fate, destiny or the rise of the middle class. It would be better to look for specific social changes, such as the rise of a European high court culture with the end of Feudalism and the centralisation of the state. Another possible context is instability of the English nobility in the Jacobean period. The Tudors did what they could to lessen the strength and number of lords. James I rapidly increased the number of lords and sold titles. Jacobean England was an unsettled society with anxieties about identity, honour, title, and manliness.

Textual and formal approaches: character and imagery

Fictionalising Coriolanus

Contextual studies have been of little use to understanding *Coriolanus*. Better criticism has been concerned with matters directly arising from the reading of the text of the play (character, images, themes, irony, form, structure). Modern Shakespeare criticism begins in the study of character. The study of character itself developed out of the nineteenth-century focus on the individual, unity of selfhood, a belief in the sense of self which is the heart of nineteenth-century fiction. Jane Austen expects consistency of the self as a moral quality: D. H. Lawrence, Proust and twentieth-century novelists generally see the self as unstable, influenced by emotions, context, the irrational, the repressed. Much twentieth-century Shakespeare criticism works through alternative ways of regarding the self and the world. What is Coriolanus? A patrician warrior true to himself and the code he has been taught? Why is he rejected by the community he claims to represent? Why, having refused to humiliate himself before the Roman citizenry to be elected to the highest office, does he at the end of the play seek to win over the enemy Volscians by the very rhetorical tricks he disdained before?

The classic and most important treatment of *Coriolanus* as character study is A. C. Bradley's lecture (1912). It is significant that Bradley feels uncomfortable with the play and thus looks forward to the need for other approaches to examine the problems he raises. He begins by noting that the play is not popular. The main character's faults are repellent; there is no compensating imaginative effect, such as the supernatural. Shakespeare has totally secularised the world. He has also avoided that other source of pleasure, the 'exhibition of inward conflict', those outbursts of passion when a character, such as Richard II or Hamlet, becomes a great poet. Coriolanus is passionate but not imaginative; he transfigures nothing with the magic of poetry. His eloquence is vituperation and scorn. His deepest feelings are almost dumb; they govern his life but he does not speak about them. When he gives in to his mother and his own fate is decided, he hardly says anything; his inner emotions are hidden from us.

Bradley claims that while political conflict is never the centre of interest in Shakespeare's play, here is a play in which a prominent element is conflict between democracy and aristocracy. He tries to excuse Shakespeare of undemocratic views in portrayal of the citizens. There is no reason to ascribe to Shakespeare any particular politics (i.e. he is not anti-democratic) since the representation of the people is part of 'a dramatic design'. As Bradley develops the notion, it sounds too much like a 'heads I win, tails you lose' argument; there must be sympathy and faults on both sides in drama. If the hero is to be given a reason why he feels he must destroy Rome then there need be strong provocations.

Bradley's character studies of the citizens, Coriolanus, Aufidius and others reveal a wish to avoid controversy or conflict with public opinion. The citizens 'are fundamentally good-natured, like the Englishmen they are'. (But they are Romans!) Bradley notices that Coriolanus' politics are not shared by other patricians. The patricians will reluctantly accept the tribunes; Coriolanus will not. Coriolanus' view of the state is such that it would be 'dangerous' to appoint him consul as he does not acknowledge the political rights of the people. Bradley, however, is soon off in the realm of comforting platitudes. His Coriolanus seems a nineteenth-century English gentleman: Coriolanus is not a tyrant; he is really an aristocrat. Coriolanus treats his fellow patricians as equals because they share his breeding and values. By contrast the plebeians do not share his values 'and they do not even clean their teeth'.

Fictionalising versus epic distance

Bradley constructs an old-fashioned novel, filled with easy psychology and moral judgements. Coriolanus is unjust and narrow, but magnificently true to his ideals. He reminds us of a huge boy with a fine sense of honour who is too simple and noble to explain himself. He is ignorant of himself, and proud but unaware of his pride. When Coriolanus is exiled, he 'is still excited and exalted by conflict'. But 'Days go by, and no one, not even his Mother hears a word'. 'As time passes, and no suggestion of recall reaches Coriolanus, and he learns what it is to be a solitary homeless exile, his heart hardens, his pride swells to a mountainous bulk, and the wound in it becomes a fire. The fellow-patricians from whom he parted lovingly now appear to him ingrates and dastards, scarcely better than the loathsome mob.'

This is pure speculation as to time and motives. It is a fiction created by the critic. Worse, it completely ignores what makes *Coriolanus* so effective; as there is a gap where Coriolanus' character seems to change, we never do understand him, just as we never exactly understand why he later gives in to his mother and spares Rome. Where Shakespeare offers ambiguity and unexplained depth of human character, Bradley wants to explain.

What happens to Coriolanus off stage we do not know. That is inherent in the epic theatre Shakespeare inherited from the medieval mystery play; but it is also a technique he developed further in his later plays. *Hamlet* has a similar gap in the centre. We do not know what motivates the Duke in *Measure for Measure*. Iago gives so many motives for his behaviour that we believe in none. Why cannot Cordelia speak? Some of Shakespeare's great tragedies foreground psychology – *Othello*, for example – others purposefully obscure motivation. Whatever the reason, several of the tragedies, especially the Roman plays, take epic distancing further, making it almost a new technique. *Coriolanus* takes this very far. Bradley by trying to explain character in terms of commonsense psychology reduces Coriolanus to a hurt school-boy. But he embodies social tensions, repressed primitive emotions, communal rituals and more. Bradley reduces complexity into one easy judgement. 'Though this play is by no means a drama of destiny we might almost say that Volumnia is responsible for the hero's life and death.' 'Her sense of personal honour ... was less keen than his; but she was much more patriotic.' In Bradley's lectures on Shakespeare we see an acute mind, an accurate reader, turning complexity into easily manageable cliches, reducing the ambiguity of art into commonplaces. But because he was intelligent, observant and aware that the play was not giving him what he expected, Bradley raised many of the problems which later criticism would discuss. Like Samuel Johnson he often seems to be at his most useful when we disagree with his judgements.

Many later critics follow in Bradley's footsteps, novelising Shakespeare's play, and less consciously seeking simple explanations, assuming a unity of character, confusing the text with what the reader wants and demanding sympathy with the hero. When that does not exist in a simple way, the critic creates either an interpretation which offers a sympathetic Coriolanus or a likeable mob. There is a failure here in accepting the epic mode, in accepting the nature of Shakespeare's experiments with distancing in his tragedies, an unwillingness to accept that Shakespeare's view might be highly pessimistic, cynical, cruel or that he might even have no views which he tried to offer. Bradley assumes a direct relationship between what is seen and Shakespeare. There is no mediation, no mirror or indirect reflection. If the mobs in the play are unfair, Shakespeare must dislike democracy and as, of course, we cannot accept that this is so, it is necessary to find reasons which explain why he shows mobs as unfair.

One reason why Bradleyism continues beyond our desire for characters we can sympathise with is that readers of literature create fictions, we create narratives to explain what is unexplained. We find it difficult to live with chaos, with the fragmentation of life, so we create patterns, stories, myths, allegories, narratives which give meaning to what otherwise lacks meaning or is unmanageable. Shakespeare, in these later plays, exploits our instinct to make fictions by leaving spaces, by offering contradictory explanations, using juxtapositions. He has learned to show not explain; he does not include the connections.

Character, narrative and practical criticism

Bradleyism, the creation of a simple character to fill in what Shakespeare left unsaid or what he showed to be complex and multilayered, and perhaps unexplainable, is the staple of most practical criticism interpretations. Practical criticism does not necessarily lead in that direction but once critics feel the need to explain each line of a poem or play they are likely to seek consistency, unity, and create versions of a story about a patrician and his relationship to his mother and the people; why he seeks and does not carry out his revenge. The better critics, like Vickers (1976), understand that the story is sophisticated by ironic contradictions and parallels, that we see characters through different eyes and therefore the motivation of the speaker must be taken into account. But essentially, practical critics offer a better version of the same kind of fiction, the complexity of life reduced to a manageable narrative with simple psychology and unity of character (although a unity which now includes paradoxes). An effective way for such a critic to operate is to reverse whatever the consensus is at the moment.

Bayley (1981) shows how the game is played. 'Coriolanus could be said to be far more successful in the role of husband and lover than he is in that of soldier and statesman.' 'Like all men who back into the limelight Coriolanus is genuinely embarrassed and miserable when surrounded by an admiring crowd.' Menenius 'has a genuine love for Coriolanus; it is one of the most attractive things about him.' 'Coriolanus is lovable, except to his own mother, whose egotism is proof against any capacity to be really aware of him as a person.' 'Shakespeare here is portraying a kind of class inflexibility common in various ways in all ages and societies. It is even necessary, even beneficial: the self-respect of both parties may depend on it.'

Bayley's remarks are Bradleyian fictionalising, the making up or explaining of character, plus simple judgements and class prejudices disguised as appeals to commonsense. He assumes unity of character, is not much interested in technique, the art of the play or the context which produced it. The play is a comedy, a 'reassertion of human weakness and the tolerations it needs'. 'Coriolanus is human, after all.' Bayley assumes that Coriolanus has backed into the limelight, that someone of that sort is 'genuinely' embarrassed when admired, that Coriolanus is lovable, that Coriolanus does not brag of his ancestry and achievement, and that 'class inflexibility' is good. This sounds more like the expected behaviour of a Tory leader or someone who might be elected master of an Oxford college; it better describes a member of the British upper middle class than the insulting, abrasive, often angry victorious warrior seen in parts of the play. Shakespeare's complex, fragmented unknowable Coriolanus has been turned into a caricature Englishman, even with a recognisable upper-middle-class English mother. The defence of 'class inflexibility' is worthy of Menenius. Bayley's analysis of Coriolanus' character seems a typical blow in the push and shove of English class attitudes.

Imported assumptions and prejudices

Coriolanus brings out class prejudices. John Palmer's (1945) voice of consensus belongs to the early years of the Labour government after the war. 'Second Citizen pleads for Marcius with a magnaminity which is very creditable in a hungry man.' The citizens accept Menenius 'a noble Roman who has a decent regard for their interests'. 'There is no bad blood between them, and, on the popular side, a readiness to consider the other fellow's point of view.' Palmer's interpretation of Shakespeare's play assumes that the world he knows is the world of the past and that Shakespeare's attitudes or beliefs are directly available through a character. 'Menenius is Shakespeare's portrait of an average member of the privileged class in any community, the speaking likeness of an English squire removed to a Roman setting.' Palmer obviously has not known members of privileged classes outside England and other western democracies. But in any case the original Menenius in Plutarch is liked by the labourers because his origins were in that class rather than the patricians. Palmer however says Menenius can 'talk to the people as one man to another because he is entirely assured of his position'; by contrast Coriolanus is 'an aristocrat . . . who has a blind contempt for the common man and is impatient of any claim to consideration or fair dealing put forward by persons not of his own class.' If Coriolanus is not someone whom you would wish to have in your club, the tribunes are Shakespeare's 'counterfeit' presentation of two labour leaders 'they have neither the wish, training nor ability to discuss the quality or intention of their activities. In working for their party they do not claim to be working disinterestedly for the nation. In resorting to the lawful and customary tricks of the political trade they neglect the noble postures and impressive mimicries adopted by persons with a longer experience of public life and of the deportment which public life requires.' In Palmer's battle of polite snobberies you show your superiority by understanding the reasons for the other side's faults. Poor Coriolanus is not going to be much respected by such alliance of patrician noblesse oblige with Labour government.

It would be dangerous if at the end of the day *Coriolanus* turns out really to be about politics, so instead it is neutered. Palmer concludes 'that Shakespeare, who gave to the stage a gallery of political characters unequalled in any literature for their historical veracity, had no great interest in public affairs. He was interested in persons and many of them just happen to have been public persons.' And that whimper is the final reason to suspect character analysis, at least as practised in English criticism, as unable to see cultural products in any depth or to look behind them to what produced them. Palmer and Bayley tell more about expected behaviour in England among the middle and upper classes than about *Coriolanus*. 'Shakespeare had no particular admiration for success in public life.' How does Palmer know? Palmer claims 'Shakespeare had no political bias.' How does he know? This is not criticism. From Bradley's struggle with a play that is contrary to what he wants I learn much about the play. From Palmer and Bayley I learn about the way British social attitudes shape what people want to see when reading a play.

Imagery – textual

The most important literary critic in Shakespeare studies after Bradley was G. Wilson Knight, who influenced both criticism and productions for two decades from the mid-1930s on, both through his own writings and through his influence on L. C. Knights and other critics associated with *Scrutiny* including F. R. Leavis. Knight believed a Shakespearean play was an expanded poetic metaphor. As he was not interested in the historical context, narrative, characterisation, and treated literature as patterns, especially of images and themes, Knight has been called a structuralist ahead of his time. There is certainly that side to Knight's criticism. But there were other interesting aspects that are now neglected. Knight acted, wrote of acting and production, and he had notions about rhythmic body movement and the reduction of the stage to a plain but highly symbolic set. There is also the spiritualistic side of Knight which he hid but which emerged in his criticism as large philosophical themes and in rejected romantic Christ-like heroes who struggled with evil. His artist-hero-devil had to do evil to bring about a greater good. So each work of literature consists of patterns of images and themes and a deeply structured allegory.

In the 1951 edition of *The Imperial Theme* (1931) Knight says he favoured a new precision in the handling of imagery and symbol, an 'insistence on the unity of the Shakespeare play', and that he is concerned with poetic interpretation as distinguished from criticism. Knight saw himself as studying Shakespeare's work as an organic whole, as poetry in its totality, in contrast to those who reduced analysis to one aspect such as characterisation, technique, or some historical context. In particular he objected to those who by studying minor writers attempt to define the probable Shakespeare world view. It is easy to see Knight's limitations. He had no interest in historical, political or social context. His theory of organic form belongs to the nineteenth century. But when all is said and done, Knight understands the imaginative nature of literature in contrast to Caroline Spurgeon (1935), for example, who assumes that lists of images tell us about Shakespeare himself.

Knight claims that in *Coriolanus* War and Love are in opposition. While War in the play signifies power, ambition, nobility and efficiency, nearly all the positive qualities of life, it ignores Love. Because of this war becomes contradictory, self-poisoning, as will any value that does not include love. Knight comments that the style is bare and that we are in a world of civil strife, quarrels over grain and corn, hard weapons, the contact of battle. There is little light, little colour; life seems provincial, limited, with war the only relief. The imagery is metallic. Even the fishes 'swim with fins of lead' [I.i.182]. We hear of 'leaden spoons, Irons of a doit' [I.v.5–6]. (It is a fault of Knight's way of arguing and the selectivity of his approach to spatial patterns that he ignores the contrasting 'cushions' in the same speech.) Another pattern of related images concerns architecture and building, images of a state built on hardness. 'Such references often derived from the essentially "civic" setting. And the present civilization is clearly a hard one, a matter of brick and mortar, metals and stones.' Knight develops a contrast to *Antony and Cleopatra*. There civilisation catches fire, harvests are rich, people form friendships. Here in Rome the city walls limit, the world is constricted. 'Hostile cities are here ringed as with the iron walls of war, inimical, deadly to each other, self-contained.' (Knight works by contrasts, his generalisations are based on details, images, from the text; the generalisations are argued from an imaginative entering into the text, so that city, hero, commercial norms seem one, not opposed as in most readings.) 'Thus our city imagery blends with war imagery, which is also "hard" and metallic. And that itself is fused with the theme of Coriolanus' iron-hearted pride.' In Menenius' speech we can see the associations of building with Coriolanus' hardness of spirit:

MENENIUS.   See you yond coign o'th'Capitol, yond corner-
    stone:
SICINIUS.   Why, what of that?

MENENIUS.   If it be possible for you to displace it with your
little finger, there is some hope ladies of Rome, especially
his mother, may prevail with him.   [v.iv.1–6]

In *Coriolanus* there is no romance of war; none of the
attractions Othello or Antony have as famous conquerors.
The play is not even filled with horror and 'portentous'
warnings. Coriolanus and others fight, break through city
walls, are violent, bloody, harsh, clamorous: 'make you ready
your stiff bats and clubs' [i.i.161]. That is Rome. In Antium
Coriolanus worries that 'thy wives with spits and boys with
stones In puny battle slay me.' A serving man says 'This
peace is nothing but to rust iron, increase tailors, and breed
ballad-makers' [iv.v.230–1]. We hear of weapons, hardness,
violence, impact. When Aufidius and Coriolanus demonstrate
their mutual admiration and loyalty to the code of warriors:

> Let me twine
> Mine arms about that body, where against
> My grained ash an hundred times hath broke
> And scarred the moon with splinters. Here I clip
> The anvil of my sword. . . .
>
> [iv.v.110–14]

Although it might have helped his structural contrasts,
Knight is one-sided in his selection of images. The speech
goes on to refer to the hot, noble love of the two warriors for
each other. Instead Knight again picks up images of violence.
He notes suggestions of infinity in the warrior images ('And
scarr'd the moon'), the images of blood and the emphasis on
violence. 'Here human ambition attains its height by splitting
an opponent's body.' Analysing the Cominius description of
Coriolanus' valour in ii.ii.109–24, Knight says:

Notice the metallic suggestion: the city 'gate', 'din' which 'pierces' his
sense, the fine hyperbole of Coriolanus 'striking' the whole town with
planetary impact. All this blended with 'blood' – he is 'a thing of blood',
'painting' Corioli with its people's blood, himself 'reeking'. There is, too,
'death'. His sword is 'death's stamp', he runs over 'the lives of men',
and dying cries punctuate his advance. Iron, blood, death. But the price

of this excessive and exclusive virtue is that Coriolanus becomes a blind mechanism, ruthless as death itself.

Knight shifts from focusing on images to constructing a character and psychology which will explain the narrative. 'His wars are not for Rome; they are an end in themselves. Therefore his renegade attack on Rome is not strange. His course obeys no direction but its own; he is a power used in the service of power.' He is 'a blind mechanic, metallic thing of pride and pride's destiny'.

Such an interpretation is reinforced by sound patterns: 'a violent and startling polysyllable set amid humble companions', 'two thunderous words in one line', 'strange polysyllables' such as conspectuities [II.i.66], empiricutic [II.i.122], cicatrices [II.i.156], carbonado [IV.v.195]. Such words and sounds reflect the whole play where Coriolanus strides gigantically, thunderously above the multitude.

The nature imagery is usually in pairs of strong weak, suggestive of the inborn inequality of Coriolanus and others: osprey fish, eagle dove, lions and hares, foxes and geese, oaks and rushes, boy and butterfly, eagles and crows, cat and mouse. Such images prepare for the victory of love while showing the natural excellence of the hero. At the climax Volumnia is strong because she 'pits his filial love against his pride'; love is a force of nature stronger than others:

> What's this?
> Your knees to me? To your corrected son?
> Then let the pebbles on the hungry beach
> Fillip the stars; then let the mutinous winds
> Strike the proud cedars 'gainst the fiery sun,
> Murdering impossibility, to make
> What cannot be, slight work!
> [v.iii.56–62]

Through imagery we examine character and psychology. Coriolanus' pride and virtue are twined and intrinsic to each other. They are dedicated to honour as a good in itself. As he fights for honour's sake, not Rome, honour became disassociated from love. That is why Coriolanus insults others using images of curs, rats, scabs. His few patriotic phrases sound trite, hollow, glib; he is dearer to himself than is Rome. His moments of sympathy with other soldiers are exceptional; he is an automaton concerned with war and honour. His relationship with Aufidius shows him in a true light. (Because Knight is still stuck with a Bradleyian concept of character he does not allow for contradictions.)

Knight then turns to Volumnia 'the iron mother of an iron son. She has no interests, no sympathy, no understanding, save in one direction: her son's honour.' This is a play of irony as well as iron. She loves to picture Coriolanus bloody, embattled, scorning others, fighting for her. But she will cause his death.

Knight examines the disease imagery and suggests that in terms of the body politic metaphor, Coriolanus, not the citizens, is the disease which must be cast out. He is the irritant which provokes anger and civil war. As he becomes monstrously mechanical killer, or dragon, he lacks mercy and love. He is power, valour, pursuing its own course. Neither he nor his mother have shown any real love; they have been concerned with honour. Love is impossible without community. As mother and son follow their own pride in seeking honour they find themselves facing each other as opponents, she for Rome, he for himself. 'No Shakespearean play drives its protagonists to so bitterly an ironic climax.' Faced by mother, wife and child, the love he repressed proves stronger than he expected. Coriolanus cannot be author of himself. Examining the imagery of the meeting between Coriolanus and his family in Act v.iii Knight shows its lyricism, and softness which dissolves 'the metal of his fierceness'. In Volumnia, Virgilia and Valeria, Coriolanus' pride is 'opposed by three forms of feminine beauty: motherhood, wifehood, maidenhood'. Love is found after all to rule the world. 'Now as Rome celebrates, we find images of music and the sun dances.' Coriolanus, however, must be sacrificed 'that communities may remain in health'. Knight's criticism has an anthropological side; he shares with T. S. Eliot and Kenneth Burke assumptions of common myths and rituals which are the substructures of social and dramatic forms.

Knight gives a surprising reading to the end of *Coriolanus* which he finds triumphant. Allowing himself to be conquered by love Coriolanus has been purified. He could not have lived uprooted from community; through love he earns our sympathy and has a new source of pride. By sacrificing honour to love he for the first time can boast 'with reckless joy'. His speeches in Corioli, which many critics regard as an attempt to cover up a disaster or even suicidal, Knight sees as a liberation. Though vanquished Coriolanus triumphs, 'infinity now aureoles' him: 'his fame folds in / The orb o'th'earth' [v.vi.125–6]; he is in his splendour, 'Alone I did it' [v.vi.116].

This is an interesting reading, original, and along with Bradley is the basis of most future discussion of the play; but it is a selective, limited consideration of evidence. Knight's patterns seem to overwhelm the evidence; his imagination rather than Shakespeare's might be the text. Patterns of theme and image are superior over characterisation and other approaches which depend on narrative so long as the critic sticks to patterns and does not try to fill in the gaps, cover over ambiguities and contradictions. Knight becomes unsatisfactory when he tries to tidy up events and images into a tight package, a package which requires consistency of character, emotion, dramatic argument; such consistency returns us to pre-modernism, to classical rationality. There seems to be a lesson; avoid tidiness. Let the work explain itself. Having accepted that spatiality is itself a means of organisation do not impose moral or psychological structures on the events.

The slide from imagery to moral judgement and narrative

L. C. Knights follows on from G. Wilson Knight but is more conservative in approach as he relies more on characterisation, narrative and moral judgement. The Foreword and opening chapters to *Some Shakespearean Themes* (1960) claim that Shakespeare's plays form a coherent whole, express an evolving attitude towards life and that the essential structure of the plays is rather to be found in their poetic drama than in plot or character. The verse is the centre of the vitality of the plays, or how we respond to the plays, and the verse not only is a clue to the themes associated with the characters but shapes the figures in the carpet, the themes or attitudes in the canon as a whole. Imagery is the basis of interpretation; when the reader is awakened to significances deeper than plot and character the plays seem living structures of recurring and inter-related imagery. Knights, however, brings moral judgement to bear on what is revealed by a reading of themes and images. Where Wilson Knight wants life and love L. C. Knights shares some of Bradley's commonsense moralism. 'There is also the tragedy of the divided and mutilated city; and a fundamental insight that what this play embodies is that political and social forms cannot be separated from, are in fact judged by, the human and moral qualities that shape them, and the human and moral qualities that they foster.' This insistence on moral judgement distinguishes Knights and Leavis, and other *Scrutiny* critics, from Wilson Knight.

Traversi is another critic influenced by Wilson Knight who finds it difficult to stay with imagery. In *An Approach to Shakespeare* (1969) Traversi recalls Knight when noting that the imagery of *Coriolanus* is 'rigid and unadorned, more appropriate to a village or a country town than to a capital of historical significance'. The society is faced by a 'struggle for power in a world once restricted and pitiless'. Commenting upon Menenius' parable Traversi says 'images of food and digestion answer to the real state of the Roman polity. Stagnation and mutual distrust, mirroring the ruthlessness of contrary appetites for power, are the principal images by which we are introduced to the public issues of *Coriolanus*.' This is excellent criticism as is the identification of heroism and glory with a cult of masculinity. Volumnia's description of her grandson having 'mammocked' a butterfly is 'comment on the deadly lack of feeling which has surrounded' Coriolanus from birth and which he shares. Coriolanus is both a hero and a childish undeveloped human being. While Traversi continues to quote a few images, he drifts back into characterisation, psychology and narrative. Coriolanus' 'true enemy lies finally, not in those around him, but in himself'. 'The demagogic demands of the tribunes are balanced by an unreasoning obstinacy in the warrior.' When Coriolanus, faced by his mother's pleading, attempts to smother his instincts, he is renegade to 'his own being' as well as his family and city.

Visual imagery

Charney (1961) notes in *Coriolanus* little figurative language of fancy; when Coriolanus uses figurative language he prefers simple similes rather than metaphors. Such similes add vividness of force rather than convey new areas of significance. The style of the play reflects Coriolanus' attitude towards speech. He has an aversion to words as they represent flattery, eloquence, politics; for him an inability to speak is 'a claim to integrity'. The style of *Coriolanus* is not so much 'Roman' as 'objective and public'. If the verbal imagery is disappointing, the play is filled with visual imagery as, for example, when we see Coriolanus standing in his robe of humility, or the way the yielding of Coriolanus to his mother's plea is shown by the stage direction *'He holds her by the hand'*. Except for kissing Virgilia, 'this is the only physical contact between Coriolanus and another human being in the entire play, and it indicates a climactic moment of reconciliation.'

Religious, sociological and anthropological approaches

In Shakespeare's plays there is usually some religious allegory or some Christian dimension which is applied if only intermittently to the narrative, usually towards the conclusion. The usurpation of Richard II, God's representative on earth, unleashes a long period of political instability and civil war, a national curse. Shakespeare may or may not have believed this explained the wars between the houses of York and Lancaster as secular explanations are given as well; but the religious vision is there as a perspective which allows the plays to be read as a homily on the need to obey divinely approved monarchy. Hamlet faces a conflict between the secular and the religious, and learns to resign himself to divine providence. Some of Shakespeare's characters' suffering and sacrifice may recall Christ's passion and death. Some plays, such as *Measure for Measure*, are capable of being fully allegorised as we become aware of biblical echoes, allusions, parallels and symbols.

Simmons (1973) claims there is an unspoken ironic contrast in *Coriolanus* between Roman virtue and Christian love. Roman virtue as defined by Plutarch was 'valiantness'. 'Now in those dayes, valiantnes was honoured in Rome above all other vertues: which they call *virtus*, by the name of vertue it selfe, as including in that all name, all other special vertues besides. So that *virtus* in the Latin, was as much as valiantnesse.' (The 1595 version of Plutarch's 'Life of Ceisi Martius Coriolanus'.) Coriolanus embodies such virtue to the extreme and has been raised in it by his mother. Others assume that such virtue will be put to the use of Rome, but the election to the consularship and the creation of the new office of tribunes sullies the notion of pure virtue; they demand that other currencies – popularity, willingness to court the people, love of others – be used to pay for honour rather than honour being 'valiantness'. Coriolanus' notion of honour is independent of public payment, whether by the spoils of war or by office, and is therefore dirtied by the demand that he be political, accommodating, ingratiating, elected. Viewed in other ways we may say Coriolanus is being adolescent, acting from class prejudices, or has sexual fears of contamination, but within the perspective that Simmons examines, a perspective which is unquestionably in the play, Coriolanus pursues a notion of virtue with a purity beyond that of the other characters. The pursuit of Roman virtue brings him into conflict with the flawed Rome he serves, exiles him, and, ironically, appears only to find possible fulfilment in his valiantness in destroying Rome. Roman virtue thus turns against itself. It is an impossible ideal of virtue.

Simmons assumes that 'in his Roman tragedies Shakespeare is at one and the same time recreating the historical reality of the glory that was Rome and perceiving that reality in a Christian perspective.' Although the Roman heroes can only play their parts within their vision of the world, the reader, supposedly, is aware of the limitations of the vision and sees the events through a Christian perspective. The Rome of the play is set within the vision of St Augustine's *The City of God* where the earthly city is contrasted to the Heavenly City. This is a flawed contextual reading in which it is assumed that some position shapes the creation of the work of art and can be used to interpret its details.

Simmons' argument is methodologically weak since *Coriolanus* offers few biblical echoes or Christian symbols and the argument can only be sustained by the claim that the lack of such evidence is proof of the need for an ironic vision of events. Coriolanus' refusal to show his wounds can be seen as part of 'typological parody of the reverence and love behind Christ's stigmata and open hands'. Simmons argues the Third Citizen's 'we are to put our tongues into those wounds and speak for them', and other wound-mouth-tongue imagery implies 'a ritual in which the outward sign transubstantiates the inner grace. This action, in which the hero must show his wounds in the spirit of humility and self-sacrifice, begs with tragic operative irony the blessed "other case" – mankind's accepting, and therefore participating in, the benefits of Christ's Passion.'

There is one passage in *Coriolanus* which has sometimes been suggested as Christ-like: when his mother convinces him not to sack Rome, Coriolanus foresees his death as a result of making peace. His 'let it come' might be viewed as Christ's acceptance of his destiny to die to reconcile man with God. While the text must be pressed hard [v.iii.187–91] to carry the significance, supporting evidence is the theme of mercy which appears towards the end of the play. 'He wants nothing of a god but ... mercy' [v.iv.24–6]; 'thy mercy and thy honour' [v.iii.200].

By arguing for irony (the saying of the opposite) Simmons has allegorised the play. Like a biblical interpreter he uses scraps of evidence as proof of a theological doctrine which supposedly has shaped the narrative and which the story is said in some way to illustrate. This is no different from a Marxist interpretation or any interpretation which reads a work of art as a metaphoric extension of some master trope or supreme fiction – Christianity, Marxism, The White Goddess, or Progress. At his worst Simmons' offers improbable allegorisations, such as interpreting *Coriolanus* in terms of John Calvin's *Commentaries on the Book of the Prophet Daniel*: Shakespeare's imagery of iron, dragons, and love between men is explained as deriving from the Bible and explicated with reference to Calvin's marginalia. If such excesses of scholarship and Christian allegorising make Simmons' readings appear special pleading he shows why the Roman plays seem so futile; a pagan world in which action can only be referred to secular social norms lacks purpose and is disillusioning. There is no suggestion of a dimension that would give life purpose, meaning, consolation. While the plays with Christian dimensions may show a futile secular world there are symbolic patterns which offer consolation – confession, repentance, restoration and an afterlife. There is in *Coriolanus* a Roman concept of the city as a mother, the city as in itself the ground or ultimate end of activity; but Shakespeare does not recreate a Roman mythology as an alternative dimension to Christianity. There are allusions to Mars, Diana and other classical gods, but they offer no coherent picture of a cosmos. When, however, Coriolanus seeking revenge is referred to as god-like, a view of the cosmos is implied. The gods seem all-powerful, but without care, pity or mercy for humanity.

Coriolanus as sacrificial scapegoat

From an anthropological standpoint communal ritual is the foundation of religion. If we see Coriolanus as a sacrificial figure it might better explain his function in the play than by transforming him into an ironic Christ. Burke (1966) assumes that tragedy is a secularisation of ancient ritual; a tragic play should have at its core 'some kind of symbolic action in which some notable form of victimage is imitated, for purgation, or edification of an audience'. The character or hero must be suitable to be a sacrificial victim and the situation or plot must be plausible in such a way that the audience will accept (and participate in) the 'victimage'. The symbolic dimension in the play will be relevant both to the topics or themes of the play and to the society for which the play has been made.

The class struggle

Burke sees Shakespeare projecting social problems from the London of his day on to ancient Rome. This creates an acceptable 'distance'. He assumes that *Coriolanus* has behind it the suffering of the poor as a result of the Enclosure Acts which dispossessed many tenants from the land and he refers to the riots which others sometimes see as the topical source of the plays; he sees an analogy between the plebeians of Rome and the under-privileged of England, and between the patricians and the privileged; he assumes conflict between the haves and the have nots. Coriolanus as hero dramatises this conflict; his pride as warrior and his belief in the rights of his class bring out conflict rather than glossing over it the way Menenius does. From his first entrance on stage Coriolanus heightens class conflict. He is excessively proud, excessively truthful, excessively representative of the values which Rome thought necessary for virtue. There is no temperance, no middle way for Coriolanus. His virtues and vices are similar and make him a potentially tragic figure, a sacrifice to relieve social tensions. Like Cordelia, another tragic sacrificial figure, he cannot speak well, he cannot pretend. He therefore cannot be accommodated in a complex society with its division of labour since he brings out the divisiveness which is part of the social system. His death following the raising of tension is cathartic.

Ritual has a function within society; ritual is a structure or gesture, to use Burkean terminology, which might have various purposes but here has a psychological-sociological content. In particular, Burke suggests that the possible context is a period when 'many *nouveaux-riches* were being knighted . . . it is *new* fortunes that people particularly resent'. He sees the social context as part of a change from feudal to class factionalism; a transvaluation has taken place from the religious to national-ism and with this there is a new kind of factionalism, the class struggle. However, various kinds of motivation are present in the play: the family factionalism that was part of feudal relations, the class motivation that is part of the new national order, the motivation of nationalism and individualism. Burke does not claim individualism is a unique post-medieval system;

rather he sees individualism as universal. We are biologically individuals. In most societies, the individual has a sense of himself, a name, private pains. Individual-family-class-nation are tangled and become knotted when Coriolanus, the individual, sees himself as part of a family which is part of a class which in his mind is the nation. He is manoeuvred by his mother, the patricians, and the tribunes into a position where he in revenge is going to attack the nation. The situation has become grotesque, how does it contribute to the medicinal?

Coriolanus as satyr

Here Burke has a brilliant insight. Coriolanus is like a figure from a satyr play who rails at and lampoons others. From his first appearance on stage, he is a master of vituperation; he stirs up the political system and keeps the play active. Unlike Timon of Athens, Coriolanus is disrespectful and scurrilous to the plebeians only, not to the patricians. His rages are infantile. His is a child's invective; it is the rage of those who are powerless. Whether or not we agree with his views we take pleasure in expressing what is socially repressed. Coriolanus provides an outlet, an outlet which while medicinal is also dangerous. Coriolanus' suitability for the role of scapegoat is his excessiveness, the way he brings out the conflicts between self, family, class and nation. His excesses, while purging our repressions, are punished, and thus a promise of general peace. Burke's title is 'Coriolanus – and the Delights of Faction'.

Burke's study of Coriolanus is brilliant in its fullness of vision and analysis of many different but related kinds of behaviour. The scapegoat ritual has a different social dimension in the modern world of the nation state and within a society organised by classes. The curious richness of motivation in the play shows differing kinds of society – feudal notions of family loyalty sitting alongside class notions and loyalty to state. Coriolanus' railing and insults bring social tensions to a head and make him the focus for resentment – a figure whose death will be felt as cathartic. He speaks the resentments of his class towards the lower orders. As he is resented by those he insults, his death is a promise of reconciliation between classes, between family and state. Individualism is seen as biological, not a social construct; it is therefore likely to be in conflict with family, class and state. The play ennobles the individual while sacrificing him to larger social groups.

Burke's theoretical approach anticipates yet is fuller and more satisfying than that of recent theorists. Its weakness is a lack of relationship to details of the text and to a specific context. Why is this a period of the *nouveaux riche*? Is Coriolanus really motivated by feudal family values rather than by his dependency on his mother? Burke's ideas have some of the inclusiveness and therefore unprovableness of comment about the rise of the middle class. If the death of Coriolanus is medicinal why do so many critics record a sense of futility at the end? Comprehensive theorisation bringing in many realms of human activity is desirable, but the study of literature also needs the concreteness of, say, Brecht's analysis of the first scene of *Coriolanus* and a demonstratable relationship between an art object, social group, ideology and historical context.

History as the absurd: Coriolanus in Eastern Europe

The assumption that *Coriolanus* is about class warfare informs much criticism of the play. Kott (1964) looks at the class struggle and historical developments in the play from the perspective of a disillusioned Marxist, someone who had seen the Communist Party as the main barrier against the triumph of Fascism and as the liberator of Eastern Europe. Subsequently the Russian occupation of Poland and Stalinism leads to loss of faith in the notion that history is evolving towards some better future. Instead of the death of God, Kott's view is shaped by the death of purposeful History. There is a process, the process is perhaps predictable, but the results are cruel, disillusioning. Kott offers an Eastern European, post-Marxist vision of The Absurd. The Absurd results from incongruity, or what Kott calls contradictions. Instead of Marxist contradictions working themselves out into a dialectic of progress, there is a grotesque dialectic of mean, brutal, unsatisfying change. Kott praises Shakespeare for offering a realistic view of history as purposeless, absurd, rather than as a comfortable ideology. Thus Shakespeare becomes our contemporary.

Unlike many critics who only treat *Coriolanus* as a struggle between the hero and the people, Kott discusses the second half of the play after the banishment. The first half has 'a republican moral'. An ambitious general who despises the people aims at dictatorial power, is banished and betrays his country by going over to the enemy. The second half of the play has a contradictory message. Having driven out its military leadership the city has no defence and is 'doomed to destruction'. The people 'can only hate and bite', but are unable to defend their city. Among the nameless crowd 'only Coriolanus was a great man. . . . History is cruel and abounds in traps. The great ones fall, the little ones remain.' Shakespeare in *Julius Caesar* and *Coriolanus* has introduced Republican Rome into tragedy, and history has now become ironic. Coriolanus is marked by greatness but is crushed by history. The play reveals a bitter, pessimistic, cruel philosophy of history.

Kott sees three basic notions of society in the play. Two are of classes; the plebeians hold an egalitarian version of it. Coriolanus holds a hierarchical view. The third notion is that of solidarity, the organic body metaphor used by Menenius. Each contains a vision of how society should be organised, each is a reflection (an ideology) of the group or person using it, and each proposes to explain or organise the world. Shakespeare holds the three systems – egalitarian, solidarity and hierarchic – to criticism, confronting them by history. The war with the Volscians is the first contradiction, making egalitarianism foolish. The plebeians act like rats, are only interested in looting the dead. Hierarchy seems proved as the way of history. But even in victory there are reminders of the cost. Titus Lartius in Corioli is 'Condemning some to death, and some to exile.' When his wife weeps Coriolanus reminds her and us that 'Such eyes the widows in Corioles wear and mothers that lack sons.' History consists of losers as well as victors. Cruelty is required by such an heroic, hierarchical society. However, by an irony of history Rome has now become 'the people'. Sicinius says 'What is the city but the people?' and the Citizens reply 'The people are the city'. Once the consciousness of the people has entered history it may be repressed but it cannot be driven out. From now on such values as patriotism and public fame must co-exist with those of egalitarianism. Regardless of being stupid or stinking, 'the people are Rome, and Coriolanus is a traitor to his country'.

Where can Coriolanus go? The world is not empty. He will be a revenger, a Tamburlaine, a scourge who will cleanse the city by destroying it. But the days of divine scourges are over. This is not a play of divine providence. History 'has caught' Coriolanus 'and driven him into a blind alley; has made a double traitor of him'. He will betray his country and then betray himself and his own sense of himself by giving in to his mother's pleas. Kott, like Burke, finds a sublime, absurd but not to be despised, individualism in Coriolanus after his banishment. Kott sees in Coriolanus' god-like inhumanity, in his dismissal of his former friends and loves, a wish to destroy an unsatisfactory, contradictory world. 'Coriolanus opposes the world with his own absurd system of values.' The patricians, with their ideology of social solidarity (in which they are the favoured stomach) and the plebeians have demanded compromise from Coriolanus and by trying to accept such demands he has been destroyed. Now at the end of the play when he appears to rise once more and become 'an avenging deity' he finds himself again defeated by history. He has become a traitor and must now perjure himself to the Volscians if he is to get out of the role of avenger. He must be false to himself to be true to himself as a Roman noble. To save Rome is to destroy himself. Coriolanus suffers an ignoble death and, ironically, is then praised by the man who plotted against and killed him, the one warrior whom he respected as an equal. Kott says that *Coriolanus* is not popular as a play since it offers no solution to the contradictions of history, no shared system of values for the city or state and the individual. The fact that one does not love the people is not reason enough to be declared the enemy of the people; that is the real bitter drama of humanism.

False analogies and lack of psychology

Such a brilliant essay is persuasive rather than convincing.
What is to stop Coriolanus and his friends from repressing
the plebeians? Why assume that class only came into being
with the early modern period? There is also the avoidance of
psychology. How can we understand why Coriolanus does not
destroy Rome without discussing his relationship to his family
and especially to his mother? Coriolanus cries when rejected
by his mother. The text several times mentions it: 'it is no
little thing to make / Mine eyes to sweat compassion'
[v.iv.195–6], 'At a few drops of women's rheum . . . he sold
the blood and labour / Of our great action' [iv.v.436–48], 'For
certain drops of salt' [v.vi.93], 'at his nurse's tears / He
whined' [v.vi.97–8], 'thou boy of tears:' [v.vi.101]. Coriolanus'
relationship to his mother ironically fulfils what the tribunes
earlier say about him. They seem to know him better than we
may at first be willing to accept in the light of their mean-
spirited attitudes. Another issue that Kott and Burke avoid is
how Volumnia persuades Coriolanus to change his mind.
Exactly what does she say, what is effective?

Attempting to avoid the self-determinacy of Marxist history,
Kott has created an absurdist version in which history
determines itself without any purpose. He allegorises *Coriolanus*
into a version of Polish twentieth-century history. The way
Kott's essay on *Coriolanus* concludes, celebrating the individual
as victim of the people, seems strangely romantic. It signifies
more than it says, and I suspect what it means has much
more to do with Kott's Poland than with what we both might
agree to find in Shakespeare's play. In my 'reading' or
interpretation of Kott's criticism, his *Coriolanus* seems a
metaphor for Stalinism, for the Leninist idea of the party as
vanguard. If I ask myself about the hero who defends the
state but who is trapped by the corridors of history, I recall
the Polish old order, the aristocracy.

Those who see *Coriolanus* as a metaphor of a class struggle
too often rapidly move away from the text. When Kott refers
to anything with a direct bearing on the play it stands out as
having a different, stronger interest. He mentions in passing
that Livy's version of the history of Coriolanus has a different

conclusion from the Plutarchan version Shakespeare uses. According to Livy Coriolanus retired peacefully and lived long afterwards among the Volscians. That Shakespeare ignored this story and chose a more bloody, cynical version tells me more about the imagination which shapes the play than most criticism.

Social anthropology

Every clan, tribe, society, nation has means of binding its members into believing they can only be human if they belong to it and that others are inferior: every society makes unreasonable demands on the individual. What is this society that uses, abuses, and finally brings about the death of Coriolanus? Paster (1985) discusses the conflict between the notion of the city as a means towards individual perfection and the reality in which 'perfection comes only through death'. 'The social mandate for heroic self sacrifice collides with the heroic mandate for self-realization conceived in civic terms.' Roman politics are predatory, savage, and destroy the hero.

In *Julius Caesar* and *Coriolanus* Shakespeare shows a real city; in each the governing order is challenged and the city is in crisis. The plays are concerned with the question of what a city is or should be. The patricians identify Rome with themselves; the tribunes see the city as its citizens. In the play as a whole 'Rome' occurs 86 times but almost always by the patricians. The tribunes use it six times; the citizens never. Identification with the notion of Rome is therefore patrician, although the idea of the city is claimed for the citizens. Rome is a patrician standard of conduct, an idea of how to behave, a concept of greatness which, as is shown by the plebs in battle, the poor do not share. Since the idea of Rome, of contributing to its greatness, works against including the plebs, they become outsiders, the opposing, despised Other. Coriolanus, who believes the ideology of his class, wants to rid Rome of the citizens as if 'they were barbarians'. They are less than human: 'Though in Rome litter'd; not Romans'. Romanness also means the civic obligation to sacrifice family to the honour and protection of the state. There is a conflict between the notion of equality of patricians and the fame and honour they seek. Within the communality not all patricians are equal. The more successful you are at being a Roman the more you threaten the balance of the state.

Food is an image of unity. In *Coriolanus* cannibalism, eating, feeding, are recurring images. The plebs are starving and demand cheap grain; this is granted by the patricians rather than risk revolt. Coriolanus would refuse the plebs cheap grain; they should fight the Volsces to take their grain. You only join Coriolanus' community as a soldier. But Rome devours its heroic sons to purge the city of its tensions. If Rome is identified with monuments, buildings, roofs, walls, the life of the city is associated in the imagery with animals, eating, parts of the body, violence. The plebeians see Coriolanus as a dog; Aufidus says Coriolanus is to Rome 'as is the osprey to the fish, who takes it'. Coriolanus wants the plebs to be lions and fox in battle; but instead they are hare and geese. Menenius says they are a wolf and describes Coriolanus as a lamb. Coriolanus calls Rome a 'city of kites and crows'. People symbolically eat people. Battle, war, is usually associated with eating. Coriolanus sees war as a means 'to vent our musty superfluity'.

Volumnia has nourished Coriolanus to be a Roman 'Thy valiantness was mine; thou suck'st it from me'. He has been nourished to be sacrificed. The blood images in the play link with the food images: blood is family, wounds, the life one gives for others. The plebs want to see blood from the hero, that shows he has symbolically died for them. Coriolanus will not show his wounds; he has died for some other cause, not for them.

Volumnia saves Rome by becoming the 'embodiment of mother Rome'. To march on Rome is to march 'on thy mother's womb'. Having made Coriolanus choose between shedding the blood of his family or giving up his revenge Volumnia speaks of her self as 'thy dear mother' [v.iii.161], a 'poor hen' who 'clucked thee to the wars, and safely home'. As Paster says 'to march against Rome is to turn against the sources of his life'. The fame and honour he sought can only be achieved in Rome through Romans; he cannot be author of himself. Volumnia has become that Roman dam that eats its young. Coriolanus dies so that Rome can live. When he tells his mother he will die for compromising, she makes no comment. He loves her; she loves Rome. I had better quote Paster who offers a more feminine vision than I naturally would:

> Shakespeare cannot deprive Rome of its central importance. It is worth saving because the city as mother is the source of nuture, training, and ideals, the achievement of common humanity, and the seat of the heart's affections, which it is impious, unnatural, and perhaps impossible to deny.

Because of the nature of the city, fragile, made up of class conflicts, the fickleness of the populace, the inevitable conflict between its best and the rest, such harmony can only come about through an endless process of violence and regeneration, comedy and tragedy. The community goes on; 'in the endless tragic comic cycle of regeneration, devouring the heroes it nurtures and immortalizes because it is in its nature to do so'. Yet by surviving at the cost of Coriolanus 'it survives diminished, starved by such feeding'.

Paster shifts the class conflict from a Marxist vision of history to the social structure of cities and communities, as likely to be found in ancient Rome as the present; she approaches the structure as an anthropologist might. The community must sacrifice its best if it is to survive since community requires both harmonious egality and inharmonious achievement. For the sake of the harmony the hero, while necessary, must be sacrificed. The food metaphor points to the predatory nature of life and cannibalism as part of survival. Nurture, community are feminine, the mother, the continuity of birth and regeneration in contrast to the masculine warrior, achiever, individual, son.

Interdisciplinary approaches

Many recent critical theories are basically interdisciplinary approaches to literature. While structuralism and deconstruction are textually oriented, they evolved from a theory of language which is seen as self-referential systems loosely linked to reality. Thus for both, and for most post-modernist theory, language or kinds of discourse is the focus of discussion, and literature is no longer culturally privileged. Cultural materialists (usually Marxists), feminist, Lacanian and other critical approaches are perhaps only different from other interdisciplinary approaches – such as literature and philosophy, literature and the Fine Arts – in that their methodologies dominate the text, bringing, as in contextual approaches, assumed meanings or attitudes to bear. They, and the deconstructionalists, would argue that other approaches are shaped by unrecognised ideologies, such as patriarchy, capitalism, liberalism, empiricism, etc., and conclusions are inscribed in the assumptions which shape the methods.

Marxist

Older Marxists saw literature in relation to the class struggle over ownership of the means of production – the struggle to determine who distributes the social product. Such Marxist analysis was largely sociological; literary production and the themes of literature were understood directly in relation to class. Thus Burke and Kott assume *Coriolanus* portrays or reflects a class struggle although they seem to differ about who represents whom. Burke sees Coriolanus as having the pride and self-assertion of a rising class or newly rich whereas Kott seems to find him representative of some older order of individualism or perhaps even the last of the aristocrats overtaken by the working class. It is of interest that Burke and others, such as Eagleton, seem to detect behind the character of Coriolanus bourgeois individualism rather than a dying feudal order. This is curious as the most obvious way to read the play in socio-economic terms would be to regard Coriolanus as part of an older feudal order, the patricians, being challenged by new urban bourgeoisie of shop keepers, lawyers, traders, and other citizens. This is how Shakespeare's plays were understood by orthodox Russian Marxist critics such as A. A. Smirnov who claimed that Shakespeare criticised both social classes but was sympathetic to the citizens in *Coriolanus*.

Post-structural Marxist

The shift from older to new Marxist approaches came as a result of the fusion of Marxism with semiotics, structuralism, or other linguistically based theories of analysis. Instead of ideology being a kind of propaganda by which a class defends its values, a class remaking history, truth, nature and other values according to its own convenience, ideology now became encoded in the very structures by which we perceive and understand reality. Thus all vision has to be both ideological and part of some structure of language (using the term broadly to mean a system of signs). Various fusions of this kind dominate modern critical theory with the intent of the critic now being to unmask, demystify or show the operation of ideology in a text.

Eagleton (1986) begins by arguing that linguistic stability is a sign of social order, but as Shakespeare is highly productive of puns, metaphors, riddles and other word play which unsettles a stable language his creativity is at odds with his political ideology and the plays are 'devoted to figuring out strategies for resolving' this contradiction. Rather than focusing on class struggle Eagleton's interest is 'the interrelations of language, desire, law, money and the body' in Shakespeare's plays. Coriolanus is 'though literally a patrician, perhaps Shakespeare's most developed study of bourgeois individualist, those "new men" (for the most part villains in Shakespeare) who live "As if a man were author of himself and knew no other kin".' (In view of most psychological readings it is doubtful many will agree that 'Coriolanus is as superbly assured in his inward being as Hamlet is shattered in his'.) Linguistic theory seems to have replaced Volumnia when Eagleton claims 'Coriolanus confers value and meaning on himself in fine disregard for social opinion, acting as signifier and signified together'. 'Coriolanus is nothing *but* his actions, a circular, blindly persistent process of self-definition. He cannot imagine what it would be like not to be himself.' He is 'a kind of nothing . . . because he is exactly what he is, and so a sort of blank tautology' who will not 'engage in reciprocal exchange or submit to the signifier'. He looks forward to a time 'when a whole society will fall prey to the ideology of self-authorship, when all individuals will be only begetters of themselves, private entrepreneurs of their bodies and sole proprietors of a labour force.'

Eagleton's conclusions are inscribed in his method of analysis, including the assumption that one is shaped by society and its langue. Kott, living in Poland, has more sympathy with humanism; Eagleton welcomes a crisis in the individual and the supposed death of humanism brought about by linguistic theories – itself analoguous to the older Marxist view that people are created by social and historical situations. (One would have thought the expansion of international capitalism, and the cultural relativism created by international communications were better, as well as more Marxist, explanations.) While Eagleton should believe in an economic base with all else superstructure, the precise relationship of the social and linguistic is confused since language becomes the way we conceptualise the historical and economic. His Marx seems rewritten by Borges.

The decentring of man

Dollimore (1984) claims that whereas English and American literary criticism is aesthetically and ideologically obsessed with order many Renaissance writers were aware that ideology is embedded in social practices and institutions. The literature of the Jacobean period was sceptical, showed the collapse of the Elizabethan providential view of the cosmos and is characterised by discontinuity and the decentring of man similar to modern materialist analysis. Dollimore favours analysis which reveals that Christianity and Humanism are ideologies imposed on reality and not virtues. Coriolanus is for Dollimore, as for Eagleton, a prime example of the contradictions of bourgeois humanist essentialism. Coriolanus believes that his virtue is prior to and independent of his social environment. He feels superior by birth and by his actions regardless of what society may think. Volumnia, although educating him to such ideas, knows better; for her fame and reputation derive only from society and state. Where Coriolanus sees the world in terms of absolutes she understands that power is part of a social network 'in which intervention not essence is determining'. Dollimore argues '*Coriolanus* does not show the defeat of innate nobility by policy, but rather challenges the very idea of innate nobility. So when Coriolanus is exiled from Rome he declares confidently "There is a world elsewhere" [III.iii.137]. But it is the world being left which he needs, because it is there that his identity is located.' When Coriolanus arrives muffled to offer himself to Aufidius the latter fails to recognise Coriolanus even though they have many times fought each other. This shows that 'Aufidius loves not the man but the power he signifies; he puts a face to the name, not vice-versa.'

I think Dollimore is off the track here. The scene is meant to be dramatic. Aufidius does not admire Coriolanus as a Roman leader of armies; he admires and dreams of the power of the man Coriolanus who personally beats him in battle. Dollimore's mis-statement of the case is similar to many misreadings, Marxist and otherwise, which seem so antagonistic to Coriolanus that you would never know that he is shown in the play winning a battle alone by himself and that the tide of battle shifts in his favour whenever he appears. His soldiers love him.

As the nature of Dollimore's discourse has been created to unmask power relations in bourgeois society there is predictability in what is offered as insights. 'Essentialist egotism, far from being merely a subjective delusion, operates in this play as the ideological underpinning of class antagonism.' Coriolanus needs the plebeians as 'a class to exploit at home' and as 'objects of inferiority without which his superiority would be literally meaningless'. (Again this ignores what Coriolanus does, there is no evidence of his exploiting of the plebs unless Dollimore is referring to the price of grain; the situation he describes might better apply to the tribunes who need Coriolanus to oppose to have power themselves.) Dollimore's inaccuracies unfortunately undermine the possible insight he offers.

Dollimore's target is what he calls 'essentialist humanism'. Dollimore's hero is the Aufidius of the later part of the play whose speech 'So our virtues / Lie in th'interpretation of the time' shows that virtues are socially constructed. 'With the

dissolution of the universal . . . a new kind of history is
disclosed . . . its focus is unmistakable: state power, social
conflict and the struggle between true and false discourses.'
Shakespeare once more seems to be in full agreement with
the ideology and practice of the critic; he really is our
contemporary.

Psychoanalytical

Some of the most interesting insights into *Coriolanus* have been
offered by psychological and psychoanalytical approaches.
The tradition from Freud onwards of reading Shakespeare's
plays as if they were open to psychoanalysis was continued
by Hofling's (1957) 'An Interpretation of Shakespeare's *Coriolanus*' as a phallic narcissitic character whose narcissism
expresses itself in an exaggerated display of self-confidence,
superiority, and aggressive courage. He sees Coriolanus'
personality formed by his mother, 'an extremely unfeminine,
non-maternal person', who tried to mould her son to fit her
own ideal of masculinity. Her method was to withhold praise
and affection except for aggressive achievements. Not offered
any emotional nourishment Coriolanus is filled with aggression
exhibited through fierceness and his dislike of the plebeians
and his attempted revenge on Rome. The later is interpreted
as revenge on his mother. Viewed in this way, *Coriolanus* is a
play about characters and their relations rather than politics.

Adelman's (1980) study of food imagery, dependency and
aggression in *Coriolanus* builds upon previous studies to incorporate political and other considerations. Using the social
context of enclosures and food riots Adelman claims that
Shakespeare by beginning with the mutiny 'shapes his material
from the start in order to exacerbate these fears in his
audience'. If the portrait of hungry mouths demanding their
own adds excitement to *Coriolanus* the centre of the play is 'the
image of the mother who has not fed her children enough'.
The social image is a projection of Volumnia's lack of
nourishment of Coriolanus as a child. She has created her son
by sending him to war 'at an age when a mother should not
be willing to allow a son out of the protective maternal

circle for an hour'. Blood and his wounds have become his nourishment rather than mother's milk. 'Thrust prematurely from dependence on his mother, forced to feed himself on his own anger, Coriolanus refuses to acknowledge any neediness or dependency'; he must view himself as totally self-sufficient. Praise threatens him as it implies that he is not self-sufficient and has acted to win approval of others. Asking, craving, desiring are the equivalent of eating; Coriolanus would rather starve than admit he wants or needs nourishment and is dependent on others. He wants to be author of himself, a self-creation symbolised by his new name, Coriolanus. His manhood is secure only when he plays the part Volumnia created for him. He must deny the possibility of changing, and refuses to assume different roles, such as flattering the public to become consul. He associates his manhood with being isolated, alone, independent from others. Deprived of nourishment, he seems to find it outrageous that others would not be and resents the demanding mob.

Shakespeare offers in the play a 'hungry world' in which everyone seems in danger of being eaten. Coriolanus is horrified by the mouth of the crowd which, a citizen says, wants to put tongues into his wounds. 'For the phallic exhibitionism of Coriolanus' life as a soldier has been designed to deny the possibility of kinship with the crowd; it has served to reassure him of his potency and his aggressive independence' and he fears collapse into infantile dependency. Having defined himself by opposition to the crowd Coriolanus constructs in Aufidius a likeness of himself, a mirror image of what he wants to be. Aufidius as invented by Coriolanus assures the latter of his 'own male grandeur'; thus he cannot see that Aufidius is a schemer and opportunist. His decision to go to Aufidius and their embrace is a 'flight from the world of Rome and his mother towards a safe male world'. Nourishment can be safely taken 'because it is given by a male'. Coriolanus' rage with Rome is really a hunger directed towards his mother. Rome has re-enacted the 'role of the mother who cast him out'. 'The cannibalistic mother who denies food and yet feeds on the victories of her sweet son stands at the darkest center of the play' as is shown by Menenius' remark about Rome being 'an unnatural dam' which eats 'her own'.

Adelman offers insight into the final scene between Coriolanus and his mother; Volumnia defeats her son by uncovering the defensive system he is using. His fantasies of revenging himself on her by killing her in the destruction of Rome are made explicit when she says she will kill herself and that he can only destroy Rome by treading on his own mother's womb. Her death would no longer be seen as an 'incidental consequence of his plan to burn Rome'. But as his notion of independence depends on the fantasy of being self-created, without kin, when this collapses he loses his defences.

Turning towards the distancing of the play Adelman notes that Coriolanus is as isolated from us as he is from everyone else; we never know what he is thinking. He dies as he has tried to live, alone. Coriolanus gives free expression to our desire to be independent but he also threatens us as we want him to be dependent and like us. If he is defeated by others we must give up our fantasy of omnipotence and independence, but the independence represented by the burning of Rome is intolerable. The kind of dependency shown in the play 'brings no rewards, no love, no sharing . . . it brings only the total collapse of the self'.

By concentrating on the psychological history of Coriolanus and his mother Adelman has provided a brilliant but limited character study. But the kind of approach limits and shapes what can be discussed. For all its brilliance the psychological approach seems unable at present to handle the openness, multiplicity and complexity of Shakespeare's plays.

Theatre approaches: performance

In contrast to literary approaches there are interpretations of drama from the perspective of production, staging, acting, and so on. These include study of the theatrical mode or style of the period – a method I will discuss in Part Two – analysis of Shakespeare's staging, studies of actual performances and adaptations.

According to Berry (1981) performances of *Coriolanus* usually stress either the political aspect or character. In the late eighteenth–early nineteenth century John Philip Kemble strengthened Aufidius' jealousy of Coriolanus, and played the part of Coriolanus as 'a study in marble pride'. This interpretation Berry finds recurring over the past two centuries. The actor aims at loftiness, will, sternness, and austerity. Rigid pride earns an easy pseudo-Romanness while avoiding other issues in the play. By contrast Kean in the early nineteenth century avoided sublime contempt of the people and appeared more frustrated, raging, impotent, even childish. Being small rather than large Kean played to assert an identity. Macready's performances during the first four decades of the nineteenth century were marked by an increase in size of cast, a general expansiveness for the sake of spectacle. He made the mob on stage better dressed, better armed, confident rather than ill-dressed cowards. Possibly influenced by the reform movements of the nineteenth century, Macready sees the plebs as central figures opposed to Coriolanus. F. R. Benson's *Coriolanus* in 1901 gave even more vitality to the crowd and importance to the tribunes. Benson tried to soften the part of Coriolanus by playing him as boyish (the historical Coriolanus must have been in his mid-30s) and somewhat amusing. There was the famous French production of 1933–4 then understood as a right-wing, fascist denunciation of the supposed weakness and corruption of the socialist government. A 1952 Stratford production tried to separate warrior Coriolanus from the patrician to make him rather a tough soldier than a proud aristocrat. This Coriolanus is a likeable human if an aggressive military man. Laurence Olivier's 1959 *Coriolanus* at Stratford put emphasis on the relationship between the soldier and his rival rather than the conflict with the plebs. Private emotions, false modesty, sulky pride, narcissism, public-school self-belittlement, took priority over the fascist-communist interpretations of the 1930s.

Many recent interpretations are psychological rather than ideological. For a time, as in the John Neville–Tyrone Guthrie production of 1983, emphasis shifted towards homosexual feelings between Coriolanus and Aufidius. To view the play as private is radically different from most literary interpretations; literary critics see the play as public, mostly about politics. But acting traditions are different with identity, homosexuality and other private concerns as important as the political. The justifications for a homosexual reading are that Coriolanus is dominated by his mother; he seldom shows affection for his wife; he is chaste in exile and is as obsessed with Aufidius as Aufidius is with him. If physical contact between men in sports is regarded as latent homosexuality, fighting between two warriors carries this even further. Many productions feature a long embrace at iv.v.110–15; there are such revealing comparisons and remarks as Aufidius' claim that he is happier to see Coriolanus 'Than when I first my wedded mistress say / Bestride my threshold'. He dreams that he and Coriolanus are on the ground 'fisting each other's throat'.

In other productions Coriolanus is transformed into a class conscious anti-heroic aristocrat, a petty patrician, someone with an impossible code of honour who goes to pieces. He is varnish rather than a giant, upper-class correctness rather than a potential tyrant. Coriolanus also becomes part of a black-leather myth, the weak-strong boy who wants to be a man, the Roman in love with the foreign Volscians. Berry notes that while the 1970s was a period when British theatre was often political, *Coriolanus* had stopped being a political play on the British stage.

Productions of the play are significant in that various actors and directors put emphasis on psychological aspects that literary critics ignore. There is Coriolanus' possible acting of a role, his boyishness and domination by his mother, the psychology of his relationship with his mother, the psychology and latent homosexuality of his relationship and love–hate bond with Aufidius and what this may tell us about his unease in the civil-political world. In a play where everyone has an opinion of Coriolanus and where there is no one steady fixed perspective on him, why do literary critics accept his assertiveness on face value? Our obsession with equality blinds us to the possible subtexts of Coriolanus' character in the play. We do not see his weaknesses; yet directors find such subtexts and Shakespeare's method creates them.

The significance of performances is not limited to specific interpretations; that actors and directors can find such varied interpretations in each line shows the openness of the text, the possible multiplicity of meanings in the words. If each speech, each scene, every character can have a different, defendable interpretation, how is it possible to insist on one meaning having more authority than another? If readings are based on the discourse of previous interpretations, or on the conventions of contemporary art, or the concerns of our time, they apparently become a matter of preference not fact. The text remains the same but the methods of understanding, and the assumptions which shape them towards an interpretation, change. Put differently, *Coriolanus* is always there, but the nature of the reader changes.

Having taken interpretation of *Coriolanus* apart how can we put it together again? Or must we accept that post-modern criticism will be arbitrary, a deconstruction with no firm basis for reconstruction?

Transpositions

The study of literature has in our time become a self-enclosed world with critic responding to critic. It is a corrective to see *Coriolanus* through the eyes of creative writers. Writers usually transform the play – the way Shakespeare transformed Plutarch – into a version of the tensions of their own age. Nahum Tate, John Dryden, John Dennis, Ibsen, T. S. Eliot, John Osborne, Arthur Miller, and Brecht, each finds in *Coriolanus* some combination of techniques or themes evolving in their own work. To read the play through the perspectives of later adaptations and styles is to see what a complex structure it has, a structure of thoughts, emotions, images, ideas, characters, events open to almost unlimited interpretations. The greatness is in its potentiality for significance.

Some dramatists read the play in the light of the politics of their time. According to Berry, Tate's *The Ingratitude of a Commonwealth or The Fall of Coriolanus* (1682) recommends 'Submission and Adherence to Establish Lawful Power' (during the Exclusion Crisis). John Dennis, after the Jacobite rebellion of 1715, wrote *The Invader of His Country, or The Fatal Resentment* (1719) with Coriolanus transformed into a Stuart pretender. As Dryden tried to move from the artificiality of the Heroic Play (with its epic plots, stylised dialogue and themes of love, honour, conquest) he wanted a drama which was affective and yet universalises. The bond between men of action, the mutual respect of two warriors, between Coriolanus and Aufidius, became an obvious model for Dryden's scenes of two warriors embracing in *All for Love*. Apparently he saw no homo-erotic implications in such mutual admiration. Rather he wanted to filter impurities from a type, and found in Shakespeare's play a partial model for the scenes in Act I, where Antony hugs Ventidius. Even more important was the meeting in Act v.iii with Volumnia; the pure emotionalism, the appeal to ties of family, to bonds between mother and son, wife and husband, child and father, is an influence on the scene in *All for Love*, Act III, where Octavia leads Antony's two small daughters on stage and through an appeal to his emotions and honour, temporarily wins Antony back from Cleopatra. Similarly Dryden's hero, like Coriolanus, is a man of tears. In v.iii Coriolanus is conquered by his mother, the scene is highly emotionally charged. That the scene is one of deep emotion is pointed to (another trick Dryden learned from Shakespeare of the late tragic period) by 'But out, affection! / All bond and privilege of nature, break!' [v.iii.24–5]. The scene would have little purpose, and the irony that results would be ineffectual if it kept the same distance as elsewhere. The focus changes. The language itself points to the emotionality, 'those dove's eyes / Which can make gods forsworn? I melt, and am not / Of stronger earth than Mothers . . . Great Nature cries "Deny not"'. Dryden also learned such expressive rhetorical devices from *Coriolanus* as doubling exclamations and other charged phrases to point to emotion. When Coriolanus holds his mother by the hand he says 'O, mother, mother' and soon after 'O, my mother mother! O!' [v.iii.183–6].

It is useful to see *Coriolanus* through the eyes of Ibsen learning the art that built *A Doll's House*, an art which ensures irony, gaps, ambiguity, slippages, different perspectives. Those domestic realistic tragedies of the middle period are made up from short little scenes placed next to each other much the way Shakespeare constructs his plays. Ibsen's dramas gain their richness from juxtapositions, unexplained information, gaps in explanations, the tantalising subtexts which may or may not throw additional light on the main themes. Often we are given shreds of information about a character's past, which suggest another interpretation on the main action. The distancing, irony and subtexts are part of Shakespeare's method of construction. Ibsen found it particularly useful to demonstrate that what seems willed might be determined by the past (Nora and her father; Coriolanus and his mother).

In the opening scene of the play Coriolanus is described by the First Citizen as the 'chief enemy of the people' [1.i] Enemy of the people. The title of one of Ibsen's plays in which the hero becomes the outcast. In *An Enemy of the People* the chief character is a medical doctor who finds that a local factory has been polluting the water supply. This can result in typhoid. But as the town depends on tourists for its living its leaders, rather than close the baths for two years to improve the water supply, brand the doctor 'An enemy of the People'. The doctor's family suffers as a result. Ibsen has imaginatively transposed the characters and themes of Shakespeare's play to his own time; Coriolanus is now faced with the problems of industrialisation and the environment which conflict with supporting a family.

Ibsen shows that those who rule are self-seeking, ambitious and will harm the community through their decisions. The majority are found to be no better. The theme passed on through Ibsen to Arthur Miller; both those who govern and the majority refuse to face the truth. Instead of warning against Volsces, the modern Coriolanus warns against infections, pollution. Ibsen will return to this idea in *The Wild Duck* with the do-gooder's motives questioned. Does such honesty do as much harm as good? Does it reflect some private desire to triumph over or destroy others? The paradox that the person who is true to some higher code becomes the enemy of the people is directly in the situation of Shakespeare's play. The reversal that takes place between Coriolanus as patriot and standard of Roman virtue and the Coriolanus who is revenger, scourge of Rome, is like the do-gooder who, alienated from a corrupt society, interferes in the lives of others. The Coriolanus who is an archetype of Ibsen's heroes is a romantic individualist, an idealistic product of modern liberal notions of the self and its social duties.

In T. S. Eliot's two 'unfinished' Coriolan poems the hero

with 'no interrogation in his eyes' is contrasted to the common people who 'hardly knew ourselves' as they wait with stools and sausages. The Coriolan poems would appear to contrast the purposeful, cold hero (the indifferent sphinx of Yeats' 'Second Coming') to the purposelessness in modern life as represented by lack of religious faith and by the Statesman's endless, useless, time-wasting, time-consuming committees, rules, subcommittees. It is implied that Coriolanus belongs to some older, ritualistic past or belief. The proud Roman warrior, with his excess of one virtue, has become an 'enemy of the people' first as an Isbenite reformer, then as an Ibsenite troubled protestant do-gooder interfering in the lives of others. Eliot's Coriolanus is a symbol of undemocratic purposefulness and vitality in contrast to the modern age of industrialisation and mass culture. John Osborne rewrote the play under the title of *A Place Calling Itself Rome* where under the guise of Rome it becomes another *Look Back in Anger* at modern democratic England.

Such interpretations are as right or as wrong as most, being projections of contemporary concerns. What interests me is how Coriolanus changes from a romantic hero to a fascist leader. Marxist critics find nothing unusual about this since presumably the individualism of the past which gave birth to modern democratic ideas was bourgeois individualism and the play represents its inner contradictions. The history of ideas is a record of ideologies and their contradictions in relation to changing historical realities. The liberal-humanist critic, while not supporting Coriolanus' outbursts against the mob, is likely to be shocked that this possible symbol of romantic individualism has been condemned without just consideration for his services. We keep coming back to the fact that while Coriolanus represents what society values, society will not accept a leader who insists on disagreeable truths.

Arthur Miller's adaptation of Ibsen's *An Enemy of the People* tones down the anti-democratic sentiments in Ibsen's play. Ibsen finds amusement in Dr Stockmann's belief that the public will welcome his bringing of truth about the pollution of the water supply; he laughs at the comedy of the doctor expecting a testimonial instead being voted an enemy of the people (a reworking of Act III of *Coriolanus*). Miller, writing under the threat of McCarthyism and American pressure towards conformity, turns the play, as Martin Esslin notes, into 'a plea for the protection of unpopular minorities'. *Coriolanus* has been transformed into, to quote Miller, 'the question of whether one's vision of the truth ought to be a source of guilt at a time when the mass of men condemn it . . . there never was, nor will there ever be, an organized society able to countenance calmly the individual who insists that he is right while the vast majority is absolutely wrong.' But even Miller is unwilling to accept that Coriolanus' substitute, Dr Stockmann, might be superior to the masses because better educated, trained and more cultured as a result of being raised as an aristocrat. Miller deletes as 'fascist' Dr Stockmann's claim to superior knowledge resulting from superior culture. This reinterpretation of *Coriolanus* censors the possibility suggested by Ibsen that the elite might be better able to judge. The local newspaper owner and small shopkeeper of Ibsen's play are presented as no better than Shakespeare's citizens; they are ignorant through lack of education and influenced in their evaluation of the truth by economic considerations.

Brecht understood that the power of *Coriolanus* was in its fullness, its objective presentation of historical forces, even though they might contradict Shakespeare's own politics. Speaking of the way the 'plebeians' do not collapse after proclaiming their determination to revolt, Brecht notes that in Shakespeare they are not laughed off stage and indeed become united. Similarly he objects to claims that Menenius' fable of the body and the belly is not convincing; it is world famous and was the ideology of the time. Shakespeare gives the plebeians good arguments in reply. One of the actors comments about Coriolanus: 'It's interesting, this contempt for the plebeians combined with high regard for a national enemy, the patrician Aufidius. He's very class-conscious.' Another participant in the discussion comments on: 'The crystal clarity of Marcius's harangue! What an outsize character! And one who emerges as admirable while behaving in a way that I find beneath contempt!' Brecht replies:

And great and small conflicts all thrown on the scene at once: the unrest of the starving plebeians plus the war against their neighbours the

Volscians; the plebeians' hatred for Marcius, the people's enemy – plus his patriotism; the creation of the post of People's Tribune – plus Marcius's appointment to a leading role in the war. Well – how much of that do we see in the bouregois theatre.

This is excellent criticism. The generalisations are factual without becoming lost in detail and without being led away from the text by theory. The Marxist notion of literature as ideology and a reflection of class conflict strengthens the ability to describe the action and generalise about it; Brecht does not deny Coriolanus' grandeur or try to cut him down to size. Unlike some recent Marxist critics who argue that Shakespeare was the voice of the ruling powers and therefore must be demythified and deconstructed, Brecht's speakers examine the evidence:

> There's another point where Shakespeare refrains from coming down on the aristocratic side. Marcius isn't allowed to make anything of Plutarch's remark that 'The turbulent attitude of the base plebs did not go unobserved by the enemy'. He launched an attack and put the country to fire and sword.

Brecht recognised *Coriolanus* as having the objectivity he sought in his own epic theatre and that such fullness is lacking in modern drama.

Part Two: Appraisal: Methodological Problems

IT IS USEFUL to review some of the advantages and problems of various critical methodologies. Source and contextual studies assume that the background or context cited by the scholar explains *Coriolanus*. If to avoid the crudeness of direct influence we claim that an historical or other context is mediated, we assign the significance of the play to a generalisation or some untestable fiction of the past. If all history is a fiction, being selective or creative narrative, how can we situate *Coriolanus* in a context both specific enough to be probable, yet mediated to avoid topical allegory associating Coriolanus with Essex or Raleigh?

Just as proposed contexts create historical fictions, so interpretation often returns to analysis of character, but character is misleading in Shakespeare's plays as it is a temptation to explain what is not explained or shown. Almost every critic of *Coriolanus*, at some point, falls into characterisation as a means of explaining the story. Characterisation soon leads to psychology. We need to be aware of its dangers as fiction and that our perspective is either through the eyes of other characters or through the eyes of the character. No evidence is unprejudiced; character is not explainable on the evidence presented. The story is also confused and full of gaps. A successful form of interpretation of Shakespeare's plays has been by way of imagery. Study of imagery assumes that spatial structures of themes and symbol are as significant as character or story. Most critics, however, are unable to keep to pure study of structures of imagery and need to relate imagery to story, character and, like most of those who discuss character, moral judgement. In interpreting any theatre analysis of stage craft and visual language is necessary.

Coriolanus is a play about a community as well as its main character. Some of the most interesting interpretations bring out such communal aspects as the class war, the ritualist basis of the hero's death, the social and political changes that require the hero's death. Rome seems a mediation for Jacobean England. That the play has no Christian dimension, makes it a study of the secular world. Shakespeare might have felt that secularity was the only world or he might have felt a world without religion was futile, but the play shows a predatory, dangerous world in which language is used as a weapon for persuasion and for disguise.

Post-modernist theory or Jacobean theatre of mirrors?

We seem to have wandered into post-modern theory with our creation of unknowable characters, fictional contexts and self-referential art. This is to be expected. We read the art of the past according to the conventions of our time. The art that survives such changes in tastes becomes classic. Yet the conventions of the Globe Theatre plays, as explained by Beckerman (1962), are not that different from the post-modern. Beckerman's Renaissance theatre of multiplicity in which independent or semi-autonomous scenes mirror each other, and in which instead of classical unity there is an egalitarianism of plot, character, poetry and thoughts, sounds modernist. Of course it is not; it is of the Renaissance. According to Beckerman, the Globe plays – including *Coriolanus* – are not closely linked by cause and effect; the episodes contrast, echo, illustrate or in some way mirror each other. Each scene is a unit in itself, a unit in which the effect is often disproportionate to the cause. There is seldom a climax concentrated in one place; rather it is spread out or as in *Coriolanus*, multiplies (he is twice tried, defended and judged in Act III). There are also rules which govern the last scene (justice, pronouncement of judgement, the highest figure in authority speaks the final words) but the plays seem open structures or mirrors, organised around some themes, information about characters, loosely related actions, simple psychology, and recurrences.

The difficulty L. C. Knights and others have in locating significance in Shakespeare's narrative rather than in verse and imagery is perhaps explained by Beckerman's analysis of what he terms the dramaturgy, especially the various structural patterns and climaxes in the dramatic narrative. As the plays are episodic and not linked by causation, the action is not linear. Incidents do not follow each other in a succession of closely linked events. Shakespeare likes to alternate scenes to break up continuity. The climax is usually diffuse, a plateau rather than a compressed, intense scene. Because of the episodic nature of the plays and the way character, plot and rhetoric are of equal significance, there is no easily definable theme. Rather there are a number of mirrors which reflect upon each other. While Beckerman does not discuss the mirrors in *Coriolanus* there are obviously parallels between the relations of Coriolanus, Menenius and Volumnia to the community; the various ways Coriolanus, Aufidius, and Volumnia keep or fail to keep warrior notion of private honour; Volumnia's final triumph and Coriolanus' death; the plots of the tribunes and Aufidius' plot against Coriolanus. A Shakespeare play does not say, it offers a series of juxtapositions and contrasts which illuminate each other.

Staging and some conventions

Consider *Coriolanus* from the standpoint of production, as does Styan (1967). The platform stage created intimacy and depth. It was wide and deep, with lots of space, many playing areas. Space was both localised and symbolic rather than realistic. There were two symmetrically arranged doors. Coriolanus [I.ix] is at one gate of Corioli; Cominius retreats at the other. The doors are used to show Coriolanus' valour in contrast to the others. He occupies a different space, has his own focus. The balcony provides other spaces, other places such as the walls of Corioli. Yet space is not distinct. It can be fluid and not realistically observed, more like a child's arbitrary world than the reality we know. Act v.vi of *Coriolanus* seems to be both in Antium and in Corioli, simultaneously; Shakespeare does not here distinguish between them but shifts the references back and forth as desired for the effect. The stage is symbolic rather than realistic. The Romans and Volsces are distinguished by their different costumes as opposing clans; but the costumes are not necessarily historically accurate. The main consideration is to distinguish people or groups visually and to provide a quick symbolical content. Coriolanus the soldier may be bloodied but he is also in a superior military costume. When he stands before the plebs in the gown of humility to ask their vote, we are aware of the gown as a humiliation, a symbol of a proud man being humiliated and ill at ease. Gestures are symbolic and convey a stronger meaning than on our stage. In *Coriolanus*, kneeling, the symbol of obedience, respect and supplication is used forcefully. Cominius, Coriolanus' former general, is reported to have kneeled to beg that Coriolanus not destroy Rome [v.i]. Volumnia again reverses roles by kneeling to her son; then Coriolanus' son kneels to him; finally all four – mother, wife, son and Valeria (symbol of Roman purity) – kneel. The effect is striking, ceremonial and unnatural in that the women and his son represent what Coriolanus most respects about the Roman code he claimed earlier to represent. Here are his bonds to Rome in supplication, unnaturally humiliating themselves (in contrast to his unwillingness to humiliate himself before the plebs).

Another symbolic, visual gesture is when Aufidius stands on the murdered Coriolanus in triumph and disrespect. Visually – gown of humility, women kneeling, Aufidius standing on Coriolanus – the play communicates a concern with domination, humiliation, status, power. Sometimes Shakespeare's stage directions are explicit. We see the 'mutinous citizens' with their 'weapons', then Coriolanus enters, war with the Volsces is announced and in a stage direction which upset Brecht and continues to upset many modern readers we are told 'Citizens steal away'.

In discussing conventions of grouping on the open stage Styan mentions that while Coriolanus is not addicted to soliloquies – he is not introspective like Hamlet – he is isolated from those on stage. He fights alone before the gates of Corioli, stands alone in the gown of humility, appears disguised at Aufidius' banqueting hall, faces his family by himself (with Aufidius looking on) and is dressed like a Roman when among the Volsces. If this heightens the individualism, it shows his alienation, loneliness, and suggests a potential rebel and traitor. He is part of no community.

Another convention is the use of oblique commentary; almost everyone in *Coriolanus* offers an opinion on the hero. There is continuous commentary on him from different perspectives. We do not see him from inside, which would privilege his point of view; we see him in public while others discuss his private emotions (ambition, attachment to mother, pride, etc.). Instead of the hero offering soliloquies to us, the tribunes several times finish a scene alone commenting on him. His character is seen in the round, he is inspected from different points of view and in relation to varied interests. These voices add to the richness of his character, the ambiguity and complexity, the fullness of the part. In keeping with the juxtapositional mode of the epic style, Shakespeare makes effective use of silence. Virgilia, by not speaking, offers a contrast to Volumnia, perhaps disapproving of her notions of dying for fame, perhaps simply showing how Coriolanus has failed to mature beyond his mother's influence into an independent man. Many statements in the play gain their strength by extreme understatement, suggesting irony or further depths. When Aufidius briefly says 'I was moved withal' in reply to Coriolanus' 'would you have heard a mother less?' we feel more is meant than said. Juxtapositions, silence, visual symbols and excessive information do not fit into a single interpretation. Critics too often give a one-dimensional reading, ignoring the richness that the play offers.

The crowd

The ways in which Shakespeare communicates can be seen, as Styan says, by the treatment of the crowd. It is rarely just a mob. The play begins with the mutinous citizens (a reversal of what we would expect and an inversion of Renaissance

notions of stage decorum). They speak first and gain equality,
becoming in our mind a symbol of the community. Moreover
they are individualised, though nameless, and have different
points of view. The first citizen is radical, the second more
conservative and understanding of the problems of the patricians and Coriolanus; the citizens are not on a rampage and
need to discuss what they are doing and why. They even listen
respectfully to Menenius. By contrast it may be felt that
Coriolanus acts riotously when he first appears and begins
insulting them. He may subdue them with contempt, they
may feel defeated by the new situation created by Volscian
attack but they are not contemptible early in the play. In Act
II.iii 'Enter seven or eight citizens'. This is not a mob but
different people who discuss a situation and have different
points of view. They are courteous. They put up with
Coriolanus' insolence and mockery. They discuss the situation
and then, egged on by the tribunes who do seem contemptible,
they become 'a rabble of plebeians with the Aediles' [III.i]. A
reading of the play needs to give attention to such distinctions
and changes in group psychology.

Seven scenes of warfare: Act I.iv–x

Between I.iv and I.x, Shakespeare gives us seven scenes of
warfare. Why not one? As the Romans are being beaten back,
Coriolanus 'enters' separately cursing the retreating: he leads;
the Volsces flee; 'he enters the gates' while the others fall back
in fear. After we are told that he is dead, Coriolanus re-enters
the stage, 'bleeding', 'assaulted by the enemy'. He is superior,
clearly the hero in this world of battle in contrast to Coriolanus
the ranting, dislikeable, proud patrician of scenes in Rome.
But he is also foolhardy, great but likely to end badly. He
takes too many risks. Next [I.v] 'enter certain Romans with
their spoils'. The citizens' view of war! Here we are now on
Coriolanus' side. He is bleeding and they are scavengers.
Then [I.vi] 'enter Cominius, as it were in retire, with soldiers'.
Is Cominius the voice of temperance or another one of
Shakespeare's moderates who says the right thing in a way
that convinces us that moderation is wrong? 'We are come

off / like Romans, neither foolish in our stands / Nor cowardly
in retire' [I.vi–xiii]. He might be right; but I want to be on
Coriolanus' side in any battle. As Cominius pontificates,
Coriolanus enters covered with blood 'come I too late?'
Hearing that Aufidius is near, Coriolanus wants to lead
volunteers against him. Again he is contrasted favourably
with 'the common file' and with Cominius, his supposed
superior. Coriolanus is a charismatic hero. The soldiers 'all
shout and wave their swords'. They take him up in their arms
and cast up their caps. In I.viii Aufidius and Martius engage
in a great slanging match. At the heart of such greatness is
the self not the state. The fight between states, clans, tribes,
classes, is about possessions, security, comfort, property.
Coriolanus is engaged in a personal combat over nobility and
dominance. This is a personal test. Here is the romantic
individual. The duel, one on one between the leaders, is ruined
when Volsces come in to the aid of Aufidius who is 'shamed'
by such help. This is the zenith of the play for both men.
Aufidius, beaten over and over by Coriolanus will in future
try to win by 'shame' and policy; he will become a mean-
spirited but eventually victorious realist, like the tribunes.
Coriolanus will soon be returned to the world of politicians,
words, hypocrisy in which he destroys himself through the
very virtues that make him a great hero.

These scenes, including I.x, are not just about fighting.
They are as rich in meaning as the political scenes. In earlier
societies these scenes would dominate the work of art; but
times have changed and politics now dominate the world of
the warrior. War does not really end, but peace is war in
masquerade, and Coriolanus is not good at such masquerades.
He is a dinosaur from an earlier era and cannot adjust. Or is
he? In *Coriolanus*, *Othello* and *Antony and Cleopatra*, Shakespeare
is interested in the vulnerability of the honest warrior in the
corrupt world of politics, social persuasion and words. But
why should this come up in Shakespeare's work at this time?
What is its context? And might it have some parallel to the
conflict between revenge and Christian mercy in the other
plays of this period? Does *Coriolanus* represent a chivalric
heroic world idealised in court literature, an Orlando Furioso,
an Almanzor, during a time when party, legal training, and

cunning will be more valuable than bravery and physical strength? Might he represent a feudal order remembered with nostalgia?

Distancing

There are few soliloquies in *Coriolanus*. Its effect depends on action and the character in the community, a character with little observable inner life. The interplay between characters has its own complexity as when Aufidius observes Volumnia's pleading with Coriolanus. He brings into the scene other kinds of loyalties, values, dangers, perspectives than that between mother and son, Roman and Roman. It is such juxtapositions, contrasts, multiple perspectives which are the basis of Shakespeare's theatre and which make it epic. The focus shifts from class war to safety of state to personal honour to family to conflict between honouring a warrior and keeping him from political power by banishing him. The tribunes are mean-spirited, calculating, ignoble, ambitious, but they are correct in their assessment of Coriolanus and what he will do and they have as much justice on their side as he does. Aufidius studies him and ultimately wins. Knott and Burke show a hero trapped in the corridors of history, in a dead end; Paster suggests that rather than being a dead end, Coriolanus is the great individual the community needs for its survival. Such complexity and such objectivity need the distance and fragmentary scenes that we find in the epic theatre. It is what Brecht wanted but was seldom able to achieve as he also wanted to control the meaning or created too much empathy for characters.

An historical style: the house of mirrors

Seeing the literature of the past through the eyes of post-modernist literature and recent critical theory, most criticism appears to be a fiction, fictions which seldom seem solidly grounded in much textual evidence. The older critics may have misread or interpreted with naïve assumptions about the unity of the text but the textual evidence was in itself of interest. Increasingly interpretations, contexts, theories seem words, words, words. How to get out of the labyrinth in which one fiction leads to another? Beckerman's analysis of Shakespeare's plays at the Globe Theatre offers a way out. It may be scholarly fiction but the analysis is testable. The notion of an Elizabethan or Jacobean play as a house of mirrors with no clearly articulated central theme and the idea of the equality of the plot, character and imagery corresponds to my experience of *Coriolanus*. It is not a new idea. It is generally accepted that the late Renaissance thought by analogies and constructed works of art with double plots, reflectors, multiple symbols and perspectives. There is a recognisable historical style by which to read *Coriolanus* which corresponds to our notion of openness, decentredness, and post-modernism. It is not a matter of Beckerman being right or wrong. He offers a way to discuss *Coriolanus* which still corresponds to the text and to ways of studying Renaissance art and literature that have in the past proved valuable.

In the house of mirrors called *Coriolanus* certain themes, image patterns, concerns, and kinds of psychology seem foregrounded and predominant, calling attention to themselves, demanding awareness, requiring recognition regardless of how they are interpreted. There are such themes as virtue and pride, self-hood versus community, language and persuasion, planning and deceit, role-playing and directing others, the influence of sexual attraction and of emotional dependency on individual and communal conduct, the necessity and futility of politics (and perhaps all relations). The way Shakespeare builds by juxtapositions, the excess of information provided about characters, the gaps in characterisation and narration, the way a Shakespearean text aims at a multiplicity of significances, the richness of imagery, means that themes multiply from the evidence of the text.

The isolated hero's tragedy

Coriolanus is one of the plays of the tragic period which while showing the hypocrisies and corruptions of the society, reveal the impossibility of living outside social groups. The individual's relationship to society is also explored in *Othello* where the Moor as an outsider to Venice and civilian society is easily misled by Iago. Coriolanus' sense of superiority as warrior and noble, his hatred of the hypocritical politicians and the conniving isolates him from society, makes him a victim of those who are cunning and clever in manipulating others. While many of Shakespeare's plays give us a sense of a Christian spiritual order transcending society, some plays of the tragic period – especially those with classical pagan settings – offer no feelings of spiritual consolation contrasting to the dog-eat-dog savageness of secular life. In these plays the hero is isolated but without hope of moral and spiritual redemption.

Coriolanus is a classic hero of the epic, superhumanly brave, alone, true to himself and his warrior sense of virtue; but his bravery and truth to his code is tragic: it leads him to insult others for their lack of bravery and he appears proud to those who expect leaders to court and flatter them. As a result he damns his own chances to become a leader in his society; such leadership is expected from someone of his achievement and family.

There is no place Coriolanus can live; he is too proud of his achievements as a soldier and noble (in his eyes the two are related; to be a warrior is to embody the ideal of his class) to accept the humiliation required of him in Rome as a necessary part of the political process. Among the Volsces he is easy prey to the manipulations of others and when challenged reverts to the anger and pride which ruined him in Rome and which is even less acceptable among his former enemies to whom he has now broken a pledge. There is no final triumph, reconciliation, confession, forgiveness or self-knowledge at the end of *Coriolanus*. The ending is not even ambiguous; it is perhaps demoralised, 'Let's make the best of it' [v.vi.147].

The hero, society and honour

There is a long literary tradition of the warrior hero who in being true to his own valour and honour spurns the softness, luxury, corruption and hypocrisy of society; he fights for himself not for a master or a state. Eventually, however, he falls in love and is conquered by a woman. As he woos the woman and transfers his personal sense of honour to fighting for her honour, he begins the process of socialisation; his freedom and energy are put at her disposal and then are harnessed to the state through his marriage to her. His male freedom and aggression become channelled through her into socially useful actions; love and marriage redirect his libido, making him part of a community whereas previously he was at war with everyone.

Coriolanus is similar to such a classical hero in his seeming invulnerability, anger, pride, ready tongue, sense of self-hood and belief in the virtue of his warrior code with his proud notion of honour, valour, and so on. War for him is a time when the individual can shine and be true to himself. War and battle destroy the hypocrisies of peaceful society and enable one to be superior over others. The warrior fights for himself and his honour, not for the city and wealth. But this is what irritates the tribunes about Coriolanus. They want a soldier under their command, they want soldiers who claim their fight is for the people and the state. They want a servant who will obey them and those they represent, they want to be top dog; but for Coriolanus war is competition for martial valour and honour, not a fight between two communities for wealth, resources, property. The epitome of Coriolanus' epic code is the man-to-man, hand-to-hand, fight between two great soldiers to prove which is number one, who is the best.

Coriolanus' code goes back before the modern state to a time of independent warriors, who fought for themselves. Coriolanus has been educated to such a code by his mother, who like other members of the nobility holds ideals about a warrior's value; but, in fact, as in shown by the play, his mother sees such virtue as at the service of the state. The difference between mother's and son's view of valour is partly ideological, partly psychological. For the mother there is no conflict between state and self because the state and Roman nobility are one. No contradiction exists for her between fighting for self-honour, fighting for Rome and performing duties as a noble; they are the same. Faced by signs of conflict her instinct is to keep the community together through compromise and hypocrisy. For her there is no difference between war and peace; politics are a kind of war in which words are used instead of arms. She tells her son to win by speech over the commoners what he wants to win by force of arms. Since honour for her means honour by the state, to destroy Rome is to destroy one's name. She will die in suicide rather than share such dishonour. Honour can only come from Rome, it is given by a society of which she sees herself as part despite evidence that the society is severely divided into classes and that a change is taking place which will weaken the dominance of the class to which she belongs and with which she identifies Rome. It is arguable that the values she has taught her son are a confusing mixture of warrior, class and patriotic duties which made sense until they were challenged by the claims of another class to govern and share in the economy. As a mother she fulfilled her duty to her class by teaching her son to be a fearless warrior for Rome; she continues to fulfil her duty and its ideal of dominance through service to the state when she persuades her son not to destroy Rome.

For Coriolanus the situation is different and indeed it has changed. Emotionally Coriolanus is not part of a larger community; he feels himself part of a class which he believes has made Rome. He sees himself born to rule by exemplifying the values of his class, especially those of a warrior. But the more he lives up to the values taught by his mother, the more he will be alienated from others, since others are not the fearless superhero at which he aims. His most brave and characteristic actions are bound to give rise to envy, animosity, and lead to his alienation and isolation by exceeding the behaviour of others. Even the enemy warrior Aufidius, whose hatred of Coriolanus appears a perverted love, so envies him that he resorts to treachery and lies to destroy him.

But as important as Coriolanus' god-like excess of virtue and his overly literal belief in his mother's ideal there is the changed political situation. The lower classes now have a say in government through their representatives and it is clear from the play that this amounts to a controlling interest since the tribunes as voice of the people have veto power. They gain free grain and prevent Coriolanus from consularship in both tests by threatening civil war. As Rome and the nobility are no longer one, there is a contradiction which Coriolanus understands but which the patricians refuse to face and attempt to avoid facing through appeasement and compromise, acts which shift power to the tribunes. The rights of the commoners to deny consularship is an ancient if seldom used right. What is new is the right to elect tribunes. The tribunes create an organised political focus around discontents, economic drives and fears, turning the populace into a class with a consciousness of itself, its demands and its own potential power.

Coriolanus claims for himself the values of the past, especially an older (feudal) code of personal and family honour – nobility expressed in action by soldiership and in conduct by contempt of those who are not nobles or of gentle birth. Coriolanus' code of the warrior's superiority through his prowess has been challenged by the tribunes and commoners – those who claim rights without fighting for them in the field of battle against external enemies. He is like a chivalric warrior who, faced by modern notions of democracy, retreats into a feudal or ancient code of personal glory. If for him the people are the Other, not Rome, the tribunes see him in similar terms as an enemy, who will take away both their new positions in the government and the people's ancient rights. For them Rome consists of the people, a term which seems only to include the commoners they represent but not the nobility. What particularly irritates them about Coriolanus and makes them hate his virtues is that his victories are for himself, his mother and his upper-class vision of Rome. By showing that Rome requires his nobility, his valiantness, Coriolanus implies that the commons, the non-soldiers, are disqualified from rights to dignity and political power.

Coriolanus begins as a Roman and symbolically becomes a child. As the Roman ideal is challenged by class, it shatters and Coriolanus is driven outside society fighting for his own notion of honour and revenge. This is undermined by the effect of his mother on him. A curious situation then develops at the play's conclusion in which Coriolanus is both reduced to the boy who once learned his ideals from his mother and is returned to society to be killed.

Coriolanus, rather than showing how the hero with his masculine values becomes part of society, shows how such values and energy make the hero different, isolated from society. This is the story of the warrior after marriage, of someone who cannot integrate and accommodate, and who in his own view would be humiliated by coming to an arrangement with the existing social situation. He is, however, through his mother temporarily persuaded to attempt to accommodate himself to civil society. Significantly, it is through the love of his mother, rather than a female friend, mistress or wife, that he is persuaded to go before the people to plead for his consularship, and his love for his mother causes him to return again to the people to try to win them; his mother persuades him not to take his revenge on Rome. The result in each case is a disaster, the last of which results in his death. It could be said that Shakespeare shows the impossibility of realisation of the warrior ideals in the political–social world. Surrounded by mother, wife, less heroic nobles, political class pressures, jealousies, the heroic ideal turns out to be disastrous; viewed with a little psychology, the hero is found to be a mother's boy destroyed by momma's ambition to be a respected leader of society.

Shakespeare's recurrent themes and techniques

Most authors have their 'bag' of themes, scenes, characters, obsessions, mannerisms, ideas, structures, which recur throughout their work and which develop, evolve and change in significant ways. *Coriolanus* offers a new treatment of a number of Shakespeare's recurring themes such as the causes of evil, the divorce between language and reality, the destructive manipulation of the naïve by those who can shape social action, the role of hypocrisy in life, the futility yet necessity of political and social action, the dominating role of some women, the alienation of the hero, the self-destructiveness of anger, and so on. The play also is a further development in the ironic distancing inherent to epic theatre, reveals a contrasting development in the use of affective scenes and the linking of domestic and personal with the public. There is a greater individualisation of language and style reflected in new liberties with the iambic pentameter and syntax. There is a further questioning, even a deconstruction of the tragic. Perhaps most significant, acting, directing, writing scripts for others, is treated here as both normal to society and evil. The theatre and language seem to bring destruction.

There are other themes of interest. Coriolanus' relationship with his mother follows Hamlet's intensity of feeling for his mother. (And this is another play with a missing or displaced father.) Like *Hamlet* this is a play where the state becomes a corrupt prison from which the hero is only liberated by exile, while his attempt to return and find revenge ends in his death. Coriolanus' unjust trial by the citizens in Rome and his trial at the end of the play recalls the many trial scenes in Shakespeare's plays ranging from Hamlet's attempt to try Claudius (the play within the play and the prayer scene) to the more relevant scenes in *Measure for Measure* where a corrupt Angelo controls the power of justice and Isabella is helpless, the scenes in *King Lear* where the king tries his daughters, and Gloucester's trial. The total impression is that there is no justice in this world in Shakespeare's plays (and perhaps it can only be found in Christian mercy). *Coriolanus* is in some ways the most horrifying example of justice perverted because the hero is stripped and declared a traitor not by hypocrites but by the mass of the people led by demagogues. Coriolanus contributes to his own downfall, but after seeing this play who would ever trust a trial by one's peers again?

Usually there is some pretence at the end of Shakespeare's plays that suffering has been worthwhile. Cleopatra symbolically triumphs by cheating Ceasar of his triumph, by her death which is viewed as marriage to Antony. Hamlet revenges his father; Fortinbras will rule and set right what appears to have been an injustice caused by Hamlet's father. We may feel that Angelo has not reformed and that Isabella is being pushed into marriage which she may not want, but the three marriages at the end of *Measure for Measure* formally conclude the play with a feeling of renewal and justice satisfied. *Coriolanus* offers no symbolic satisfactions. Coriolanus' life has been wasted for what? Nothing has changed. Rome is neither more unified nor safe. Coriolanus' mother is now a hero but few will feel that the mother's success is admirable. Signs of futility have always been there in the plays and increasingly so in the tragic period but *Coriolanus* appears to be a play which accepts that life has no purpose outside what might be gained in a futile world of corruption, hypocrisy and evil ambition.

Coriolanus shares with many of Shakespeare's plays the theme of wrath (anger or choler). The hero or main character in a moment of mad anger brings down his world, ruins what he has or destroys what he loves. Othello in jealousy killing Desdemona is one version of the theme; King Lear first in anger disinherits Cordelia, then in anger destroys what nest he has left with his two daughters. Coriolanus is a prisoner of wrath, 'wrath overwhelmed my pity' [I.ix.84]. The tribunes know that it is easy putting him into a rage; it is possible to take advantage of his choler to prevent his election. They wait for him 'to fall in rage' and 'anger'. And that is just what happens in III.i and III.iii. So there is no doubt that the audience of *Coriolanus* or the citizens understand what is happening, several speeches prepare us for Coriolanus' self-destructive anger. Menenius warns him to be calm; there is the rather funny exchange:

> MENENIUS.   His choler?
> CORIOLANUS.   Choler!
> Were I as patient as the midnight sleep,
> By Jove, 'twould be my mind.
>   [III.i.82–5]

Menenius warns him 'Put not your worthy rage into your tongue' [III.i.239]. His mother says that he should have a brain as well as a heart and learn like her the 'use of anger' [III.ii.30]. And III.ii concludes with Cominius, Menenius and Coriolanus all supposedly agreed that he must speak 'mildly' to the citizens at his trial. Having twice ruined himself in Rome by displays of anger, he once again falls into the trap in Corioli, giving Aufidius an excuse to kill him. One of the great ironies of the play is that cunning Aufidius not only works Coriolanus into a rage but then pretends rage to kill him. Nothing can be more cynical than Aufidius' 'My rage is gone, / And I am struck with sorrow' [v.vi.147–8]. This is partly a play about the destructive effects of anger.

Language and acting as deception

Since the popularity of post-modern fiction and critical theories which see a text as a construction, it has become commonplace to say that literature can either imitate reality or be concerned with the art of art and that it more likely, or more interestingly, is concerned with the latter. Shakespeare's plays always have a concern with the nature of language, spectacle, playing and directing, treating each as a danger, an untruth, a potential source of evil. Perhaps he had a writer's distrust for words? The villains of his plays – Richard III, Iago, Edmund – are the wordsmiths, the ones who make up the plots, who arrange scenes that deceive. The best speakers, the playwrights, are evil. If they are not (Prospero is a major exception) they are aware of the potential of art to do evil. *Coriolanus* is filled with playlets, rehearsals, roles, acting. It is also a play where Shakespeare does not fall back on a possible devil theory of evil. Richard III and Iago are in part traditional vice characters. Iago gives many explanations for his conduct but he is finally someone whose malcontentedness seems devilish rather than of human origins. In the case of the tribunes, the nobles, Aufidius, there are no devils; they are driven by recognisable human ambitions, the desire for power, fear, envy. The self-referentiality of the play is not therefore an abstract theoretical concern with the art of drama; rather the play questions whether language, the ability to deceive others, the art of falsifying may in itself be a moral danger, not only untrue but evil in origin because false and most likely used to deceive the innocent. Consider that opening scene in *King Lear*. Language is used to lie, truth cannot flatter. Coriolanus' best quality is that he cannot lie. What he says may be dislikeable, hateful, but it is not flattery, does not cover secret aims.

Revelations of character

Characters appear to change during the course of the play – as in Coriolanus' case because of circumstances – or because we are given more information and see in new ways. Characters are either unstable or unlikeable. Aufidius is perhaps too much of a function to be regarded as evidence but there is the obvious case of Menenius. At first we are told that he is 'honest' and 'one that has always loved the people'. But the people do not seem to realise that his speech to them about the state as a body and his blaming the drought on the gods is patrician ideology and propaganda. Part of his effectiveness is the bubbling, old honesty he pretends. He tells the tribunes 'what I think, I utter, and spend my malice in my breath' [II.i.55]. Later, however, whatever he says is likely to be a lie or premeditated for political effect. He is like the tribunes, Aufidius and Volumnia, in trying to use Coriolanus for his own ends. Like many moderate figures he is made a bit absurd by Shakespeare. He is convinced that the world consists of people like himself who are governed by simple comforts and desires, and that all he needs do is to appeal to Coriolanus after the latter has eaten and is 'dieted to my request'. It is difficult not to see either Menenius' predatory nature or Shakespeare's ironic attitude towards him in the language 'then I'll set upon him' [v.i.58]. Before the Volsces, he speaks of Coriolanus in such a way that detracts from the warrior's achievement and makes us wonder if Menenius always lies. He claims he has always amplified and 'varnished' Coriolanus. He appears absurd when he asks 'has he dined?' Where is the spontaneous, honest tongue he claimed? The speech to Coriolanus is such an awkward clumsy artificial mess that it seems likely Shakespeare has the knife into Menenius and is making certain that we judge him. It will be noticed that most of the characters except Coriolanus are made less attractive after Act III.

Coriolanus and his mother

At the core of each of Shakespeare's plays is some fundamental

human problem, a failed rite of passage such as the unwillingness of a father to give up his daughter's love (*King Lear*) or
the way jealousy turns into destructive rage (*Othello, Winter's
Tale*). Hamlet although 30 years old seems immature in his
idealisation of his father and his emotional attachment to his
mother.

Early in the play the First Citizen says the services Coriolanus has done are not for his country but 'to please his mother'
[i.i.39]. His mother speaks of him both as a husband and as
someone she would sacrifice for the fame it brought: 'If my
son were my husband I should freelier rejoice in that absence
wherein he won honour, than in the embracements of his bed
where he would show most love' [i.iii.2–6]. Coriolanus says
his mother 'has a charter to extol her blood' but this 'grieves
me' [i.iv.16–18]. Her praise and his embarrassment seem
revealing of an adolescent's relationship to a parent from
whom he has not become emotionally independent. Volumnia
calls him 'my boy' [ii.i.105], 'my son' [142], 'my good soldier'
[ii.i.105] and when they first are together in the play she needs
remind him of 'thy wife' [ii.i.183] to whom Coriolanus says
only 'O my sweet lady, pardon' [ii.i.188].

Coriolanus is dominated by his mother who persuades him
to seek the consularship she wants for him. 'Why force you
this?' [iii.ii.51]. She replies 'I am in this your wife' [iii.ii.65],
'My son, go to them' [iii.ii.72–3], 'Go and be ruled' [iii.ii.90].
He becomes her performing dog: 'My praises made thee first
a soldier, so, / To have my praise for this, perform a part'
[iii.ii.108–9]. Volumnia can win any argument by rejecting
him: 'Thy valiantness was mine, thou suck'st it from me, / But
owe that pride thyself'. To which he replies 'Mother, I am
going to the market place: / Chide no more' [iii.iii.129–30,
131–2]. A leader of the army, a man-killer who single handed
conquers a city and he pleads 'Chide no more'! When
Coriolanus loses his temper before the crowd Menenius says
'Is this the promise that you made your mother?' [iii.iii.85].
Later, after he is banished from Rome and taking farewell
from his mother he tells her to cheer up and implicitly
compares himself both to Hercules and to a husband:

Resume that spirit you were wont to say,

> If you had been the wife of Hercules,
> Six of his labours you'd have done, and saved
> Your husband so much sweat.
>
> [IV.i.16–18]

Later Volumnia recommends to Virgilia that she imitates her in lamenting 'in anger, Juno like' [IV.ii.53]. Juno is both goddess of Rome and the wife of Jupiter.

Coriolanus seeking revenge on Rome claims 'wife, mother, child, I know not' [v.ii.74], but as soon as he sees his mother, wife and his child he fears he will be 'tempted to infringe' his 'vow / In the same time 'tis made' [v.iii.21]. His mother bows and he is disturbed, feeling a reversal of the universal order, 'As if Olympus to a molehill should / In supplication nod' [30–1]. He is so stirred that he must attempt to harden himself in his will (a sign, of course, that he is likely to reverse himself):

> . . . I'll never
> Be such a gosling to obey instinct, but stand
> As if a man were author of himself
> And knew no other kin.
>
> [v.iii.34–7]

Despite his assertions that he is an individual with a strong sense of himself, Coriolanus has strong ties to his family, especially to his mother, which undermine his claim to selfhood. His mother is the focus of his feelings. She persuaded him to stand for consul, to stand trial by the people and now she persuades him to give up his revenge. Rather than the great hero who said he will banish Rome by going into exile, he is found to be a tearful boy unable to resist his mother's scolding. He cannot even follow his own self-interest. She is 'the most noble mother in the world' [v.iii.49] to whom he kneels in homage. She needs only to kneel in supplication before him for him to be disturbed and find the situation unnatural, although as a powerful conqueror he is to be supplicated. That he is disturbed by the symbolism shows that under the god-like public aspect remains an immature child. Except for minor interjections from the other characters the remainder of v.iii takes place between Volumnia and Coriolanus. Their relationship is one play, a drama between a dominant mother and a rebellious but dominated son. Her principles have made him what he is; he lives by her words. She will destroy him now rather than let him ruin her vision of herself as a superior patrician mother who sacrifices her sons for Rome. Having no other son to sacrifice to the country, she can only sacrifice him. Nobility is birth, manner, conduct, position. She increases her nobility (fame in Rome) by destroying his nobility (valiantness as soldier; truth to his integrity of self and class).

Cominius and Menenius could not persuade Coriolanus to listen to their pleas; but Volumnia plays on him as son, lover, ungrateful son; 'Thou art my warrior / I holp frame thee' [v.iii.62–3]. Coriolanus hardly has a chance and is already weakening: [v.vi.78–86] 'I beseech you . . . tell me not . . . desire me not / T'allay my rages and revenges with / Your colder reasons'. Volumnia's speech [v.iii.94–125] with its 'we' merges Coriolanus' wife and child with herself in a more sophisticated appeal than Menenius' awkward, trite claim upon his relationship ('O my son, my son') [v.ii.73]. Where Menenius cries and supplicates, Volumnia, having first established an emotional bond between the family and Coriolanus, now indicates that her loyalties to Rome are as great as, even greater, than her love for her son. The situation is tricky since outright rejection of Coriolanus could lead to one of his rages; she leads him on, slowly breaking down his resolve to be independent. Then when his family emotions have returned, she starts turning away from him until he gives in. She involves him in her dilemma, rather than showing interest in his hurts, so that she can threaten him. She fudges and blurs boundaries between Rome and family ('whereto we were bound . . . the country, our dear nurse'). As she does this it first appears that she will not choose between son and country (or . . . or, either . . . or else) and that whether he is victor or loser he is a humiliation in her eyes. He will either 'be led with manackles through our streets' as a loser (which we know is unlikely) or if he wins he will be celebrated for 'having bravely shed / Thy wife and children's blood'. Having portrayed victory over Rome as equivalent to bloody murder of his family she further works on his emotions by threatening suicide. She begins this part of the persuasion with 'son' and with reference to herself. 'For myself, son / I propose not to wait.' After the mocking of him in 'bravely' ('bravely shed / Thy wife and children's blood') the use of such phrases as 'For myself', 'I', 'son', personalises the situation, making Coriolanus' revenge not on Rome but on his family and especially on her:

> . . . thou shalt no sooner
> March to assault thy country than to tread
> . . . on thy mother's womb
> That brought thee to this world.

The image of 'tread' which occurs in key moments of the play shifts here from 'tread on the country's ruin' [v.iii.116] to 'tread . . . on thy mother's womb'.

His son's 'A shall not tread on me' [127] provides another mirror, supporting the notion that war on Rome is war on his family; he cannot take revenge on one without warring with the other.

Persuasion and dependency

As in the history plays civil war becomes war between members of a family. This does not imply that Shakespeare believes what Volumnia argues. He is dramatising someone persuading another person, and we are made conscious of this as a scene of persuasion. It is preceded by two similar attempts to change Coriolanus' mind and by parallels to Menenius' speech. Moreover we recall earlier scenes in which Volumnia worked on his emotions, turning him into a dependent child. And we are aware of her willingness, even eagerness to sacrifice him, for her reputation in Rome: 'his good report should have been my son; I therein would have found issue . . . had I a dozen sons . . . I had rather had eleven die for the country' [I.iii.21–6].

The second part of Volumnia's speech [v.iii.131–82] uses many of the same tricks, complaining and scolding, that she had used in Rome when persuading Coriolanus:

> . . . There's no man in the world
> More bound to's mother, yet here he lets me prate
> Like one i'th sticks. Thou hast never in thy life
> Showed thy dear mother any courtesy,
> When she, poor hen, fond of no second brood,
> Has clucked thee to the wars, and safely home
> Loaded with honour.

As the scene continues the three women and the son kneel in a striking image of supplication. But Volumnia's words are not those of a supplicant. As often in the play the visual and the aural offer contrasting messages. She both reminds him of family ties and rejects him:

> So, we will home to Rome
> And die among our neighbours. . . .
> This fellow had a Volscian to his mother;
> His wife is in Corioles, and his child
> Like him by chance.
>
> [v.iii.122–5]

Faced by rejection, curses, sentiment, motherly appeals, Coriolanus is conquered and after a long dramatic silence typical of his truth to his inner self, he breaks down in tears and cries 'O, mother, mother: / What have you done?' [v.iii.182–3]. He knows this will lead to his death, 'Most dangerously you have with him prevailed'. She says nothing. It is typical of Shakespeare's technique that there should be this silence where we might expect the mother and Virgilia to respond or show some concern about the danger they have brought on Coriolanus, some celebration of their victory, or an attempt to persuade him to go back to Rome with them. We can make up fictions, assume it is Coriolanus' sense of honour which leads him back to Corioli rather than Rome but in fact we know nothing, the focus shifts away from the relationship between Coriolanus and Aufidius.

Crying

Even more striking than the kneeling and the holding of
Volumnia by the hand is the information that Coriolanus is
crying: 'it is no little thing to make / Mine eyes to sweet
compassion' [v.iii.196]. This echoes the tears of Menenius in
v.ii.74 ('here's water') which may or may not be spontaneous.
It is characteristic of Shakespeare's objectivity that we do not
know if Volumnia is any more sincere than Menenius – she
indeed may be less – or just a better, more skilled pleader.
(When we learn that the citizens in v.iv are now attacking the
tribunes they formerly worshipped, we know what Shakespeare
probably thinks of their inconsistency. The Third Conspirator
tells Aufidius the people are only interested in results and
accept whoever is in power [v.vi.17–18].) But those tears are
extraordinary and will be recalled several times in the final
scene by Aufidius. They suggest Coriolanus' immaturity. Here
is a warrior who has killed men crying at his mother's claim
that he never does what she wants (which we know is false)
and that she will kill herself if he takes his revenge on Rome.
How does this differ from an immature, childish quarrel and
its threats? Shakespeare's magic is to ground themes of mercy
and honour in such psychology. Various parallels and mirrors
occur in v.iv when the tribune Sicinius says that Coriolanus
'loved his mother dearly'. 'There is no more mercy in him
than milk in a male tiger' [v.iv.29–30].

Masculinity is a theme of the play. The Roman notion of
maleness is of hard, unflinching, bloodiness. Volumnia claims
that blood 'becomes a man' [v.iii.42–3], in 'cruel war' Coriolanus 'had proved himself a man' [v.iii.19]. Significantly, when
he is beginning to crack under the emotional assault of
Volumnia, Virgilia and his son, Coriolanus says 'Not a
woman's tenderness to be / Requires nor child nor woman's
face to see' [v.iii.129–30]. The shift into rhyme is a convention
of Jacobean drama used for scenes of emotional heightening,
formality, symbolism, comments to the audience, another
departure from realism.

Volumnia enters Rome [v.v] in triumph, recalling Coriolanus' triumph in ii.i. This contrasts with v.vi where Coriolanus
attempts to enter Corioli (another parallel) in triumph and

will die for having betrayed the Volsces for 'a few drops of women's rheum' [v.vi.46]. 'For certain drops of salt' [93] 'At his nurse's tears / he whined' [97]. He is 'a boy of tears' [101]. It is the word 'boy' which Coriolanus cannot bear. This sets off his rage. If he entered Corioli knowing the situation was dangerous, he now explodes through all his caution and repeats his former self-destructive behaviour, bragging how he killed Volscians: 'Boy!! O Slave!' [60], 'Boy! False Hound!' [111], 'Alone I did it. Boy!' [116].

The hero lives in a world of lesser people with petty ambitions and ugly plots who gang up to exile and kill him. His mother for all her pride turns out to be like them.

Sex, love and bonding

Coriolanus is not mature; he is emotionally still a boy. This implication is furthered by sexual imagery which is rather focused on the relationship between the soldier and other men than on him and women. Wilson Knight felt that Coriolanus as a killing machine was conquered by love, a force of good. I see love in the play as something demanded by society, by Coriolanus' mother and as an immature weakness of Coriolanus. Aufidius sticks to his desire for revenge and emerges victorious over his rival at the play's end.

Shakespeare early establishes the use of sexual imagery in treating the relationship between the two warriors. They are like lovers. When Coriolanus (who is still Martius) sees Cominius on the battlefield:

> O, let me clip ye
> In arms as sound as when I wooed; in heart
> As merry as our nuptial day was done,
> And tapers burned to bedward.
>
> [I.v.29–32]

Shakespeare will not treat the relationship between Coriolanus and his wife Virgilia with such sexual emotion, indeed she is so silent in the play as almost not to exist. In his relationship with Aufidius, Coriolanus uses the language of hate as if it were intense love: 'I'll fight with none but thee', 'We hate alike' [I.viii.11–13]. In their fight for dominance, they stimulate each other to excitement: 'Let the first budger die the other's slave, / And the gods doom him after!'

> Alone I fought in your Corioles walls,
> And made what work I pleased: tis not my blood
> Wherein thou seest me masked. For thy revenge,
> Wrench thou thy power to th'highest."
>
> [I.viii.8–11]

(This looks forward to 'Alone I did it' [v.vi.116].) Later, defeated by Coriolanus, Aufidius says 'If e'er again I meet him beard to beard, / He's mine, or I am his' [I.x.11–12]. He wants to 'Wash my fierce hand in's heart' [I.x.29]. Suggestion of the sexuality of battle is also seen in Cominius' description of Coriolanus 'When he might act the woman in the scene, / He proved best man i'th'field' [II.ii.98–9]. Within Roman values to be a victorious fighter is to be a man. A boy is a woman until he has proved himself as Coriolanus did although he still had an 'Amazonian chin' [II.ii.93].

The virgin warrior: fear of contamination

Coriolanus objects to putting on the gown of humility, he says he cannot 'stand naked' and entreat the people [II.ii.139]. The imagery of sexual modesty is continued with 'It is a part / That I shall blush in acting' [147–8]. Sexuality, besides being part of fights for dominance, is part of acting, playing roles, persuading others, especially in politics or in relationships. Coriolanus feels playing to the public is prostitution of his truth to himself; it spoils his integrity. To entreat others is to buy votes. It also transfers power to them. Your value is no longer what you do; it is what others say you are. The themes of power, domination and origins of value keep being expressed in images of food, money and sex. How you love and are loved is how you are nourished, paid, valued and nourish, pay, value. Coriolanus believes his right to be consul by his 'own desert' [II.iii.68]. He has made himself on the battlefield. He lives by an image of himself. To stand before the people means he is for 'hire' [ii.ii.152]. The citizens also see their power as sexual: 'We are to put our tongues into these wounds' [iii.i.6]. Images of tongues link speaking to the sexual and the many blood images in the play (blood as breeding, as self, as what makes him a man, and which the public wants revealed to it almost as looking at his private parts). When Coriolanus first appears in the gown of humility, he objects: 'I cannot bring my tongue to such a place' [ii.ii.55]. His mockery of the citizens is in sexual terms. When they object 'you have not loved the common people', Coriolanus replies that he is 'the more virtuous that I have not been common in my love' [ii.iii.98–9]. If common here links the love of the people and the commoners and prostitution, there is exhibited, as elsewhere in the play, a strong attraction–hate relationship in dependency. Coriolanus loves–hates his mother on whom he is dependent. Aufidius will come to hate Coriolanus on whom he becomes dependent as a warrior. The people want to be loved. Menenius tells the people 'most charitable care / Have the patricians of you' [i.i.67–8]. The First Citizen replies 'care for us? . . . They ne'er cared for us yet. Suffer us to famish' [i.i.81–2]. To love and care for is to protect, to nourish, be intimate with. The people are attracted to Coriolanus as a victor, but when he spurns them they want to kill him. His fear of contamination by the people is almost sexual; but he needs them if he is to be consul, so his own dependency on them may explain the intensity of his hatred.

The price of love: unclean mouths

Coriolanus' unwillingness to reveal his wounds makes him seem an innocent guarding virginity. The terms he uses to describe the citizens refer to their lack of cleanliness, their bad breath. This may well have been a fact of the time; but Coriolanus seems as obsessed as if contact were sexual intimacy. When the citizens ask for his love, Coriolanus mocks 'I will counterfeit the bewitchment of some popular man and give a bountiful to the desirers' [ii.iii.106–7]. He will only show his wounds in private [ii.iii.80–1,172]. The wound,

blood, sexual imagery becomes degraded into prostitution and
is linked with the imagery of money, price, cost, reflecting the
citizens' perspective but also associated with the futility of
life. Exchanges are often treated as the buying of sexual
favours:

> THIRD CITIZEN.   You must think, if we give you anything,
> we hope to gain by you.
> CORIOLANUS.   Well then, I pray, your price, o'th'consul-
> ship?
> FIRST CITIZEN.   The price is, to ask it kindly.
> CORIOLANUS.   Kindly, sir, I pray let me ha't. I have wounds
> to show you, which shall be yours in private.   [II.ii.73–
> 81]

Throughout the play the relationship between Coriolanus
and Aufidius is tinged with mutual admiration that borders
on the sexual. Coriolanus asks whether Aufidius discusses
him: 'Spoke he of me?' No teenager could be more eager:
'How? What?' 'He would pawn fortunes . . . so he might / Be
called your vanquisher'. 'I wish I had a cause to seek
him there' [III.i.12–19]. The ironic foreshadowing of how
Coriolanus' wishes will be fulfilled should not distract from
the contrast between Coriolanus' attraction towards Aufidius
(which is mutual) and his hatred of 'The tongue o'th'common
mouth' [III.i.22].

Coriolanus does not like speech and associates defilement
with tongues, stinking breath, prostitution of honour through
words and hypocrisy. His words are direct, like blows, honest,
and often angry. He seems to view the tribunes especially in
sexual terms as a contamination: 'sedition' has been 'ploughed
for, sowed / by mingling them with us' [III.iii.70–1]. Since the
'tribunes are the people's mouth' [III.i.269], the mutual hatred
of Coriolanus and the tribunes is to be expected. Coriolanus
is not the first to feel that mixing of the classes, races, castes,
clans, of self or identity with others is sexual defilement. His
vocabulary mingles the sexual and physical with many other
themes of the play such as the body politic and images of
feeding: 'How shall this bosom multiplied digest? / The Senate's courtesy?' 'Thus we debase / the nature of our seats.' The

rabble 'will in time / Break ope the locks o'th'Senate' [III.i.130–6]. Those who 'love the fundamental part of state' will want to 'pluck out / the multitudinous tongue, let them not lick / The sweet. . . . Your dishonour'. [III.i.150, 154, 156]. The associations between tongue, sexuality and masculinity are obvious. 'Put not your worthy rage into your tongue' [III.i.239]; 'His heart's his mouth / What his breast forges, his tongue must vent' [254–5]. Cominius who is always calculating and lacks daring sees this as 'manhood' turned into 'foolery' [266].

Pretending love: inconstancy

Even Volumnia speaks of winning over the crowd in terms of pretending to be in love:

> Say to them
> Thou art their soldier, and being bred in broils
> Hast not the soft way which, thou dost confess,
> Were fit for thee to use, as they to claim,
> In asking their good love; but thou wilt frame
> Thyself, forsooth, hereafter theirs.
>
> [III.ii.80–5]

(This is what Coriolanus does at the play's conclusion when he returns to Corioli: 'I am returned your soldier, / No more infected with my country's love' [v.vi.71–2].) Coriolanus feels prostituted, humiliated, soiled.

> Must I go show them my unbarbed sconce? Must I
> With my base tongue give to my noble heart
> A lie that he must bear?
>
> [III.ii.99–101]

He feels 'possessed' with 'Some harlot's spirit', his 'throat of war' unmanned 'an eunuch or the virgin voice' and speaks as if winning over the crowds to his side were like 'schoolboy's tears', a 'beggar's tongue', 'inherent baseness' [III.ii.111–22]. The sexual analogies continue when a Roman speaking to a

Volscian about the banishment of Coriolanus says: 'the fittest time to corrupt a man's wife is when she's fallen out with her husband' [IV.iii.32–3].

Changing loyalties is sexual; Coriolanus speaks of his allegiances in terms of love. Sexual feelings, affections and social ties are intertwined. Thinking on the strange turn of fate that has led him from fighting for Rome against the Volsces to offering his services to the Volsces, he muses:

> Friends not fast sworn,
> Whose double bosoms seem to wear one heart,
> Whose hours, whose bed, whose meal and exercise
> Are still together, who twin, as 'twere, in love
> Unseparable, shall within this hour,
> On a dissension of a doit, break out
> To bitterest enmity. So fellest foes,
> Whose passions and whose plots have broke their
>   sleep
> To take the one the other . . .
> . . . shall grow dear friends
> And interjoin their issues. So with me:
> My birthplace hate I, and my love's upon
> This enemy town.
>
> > [IV.iv.12–24]

The sexuality of battle

When Coriolanus reveals himself to Aufidius the imagery is erotic. The scene shows the bond between the two warriors but the sexual content is unmistakable; the admiration of the two warriors for each other is charged with homo-erotic feelings:

> Let me twine
> Mine arms about that body, where against
> My grained ash a hundred times hath broke
> And scarred the moon with splinters. Here I clip
> The anvil of my sword, and do contest
> As hotly and as nobly with thy love

> As ever in ambitious strength I did
> Content against thy valour. Know thou first,
> I loved the maid I married – never man
> Sighed truer breath; but that I see thee here,
> Thou noble thing, more dances my rapt heart
> Than when I first my wedded mistress saw
> Bestride my threshold.
>
> [iv.v.110–22]

They have been dreaming of each other in images of violence
which approach sexual fulfilment:

> And I have nightly since
> Dreamt of encounters 'twixt thyself and me –
> We have been together in my sleep,
> Unbuckling helms, fisting each other's throat –
> And waked half dead and nothing.
>
> [iv.v.126–30]

The line 'Your hand – most welcomed!' [iv.v.151], which
many actors and directors have treated as the climax of the
play, may be seen as Coriolanus' betrayal of Rome and
himself; but it takes on a possible sexual significance as
well. It is further foregrounded when the second servingman
immediately says 'By my hand' [iv.v.153]. Thus we remember
it when the third servingman soon says: 'Our general himself
makes a mistress of him, sanctifies himself with's hand, and
turns up the white o' th'eye to his discourse' [iv.v.203–5]. The
notion of war as sexual energy can be seen in the remarks of
the servingmen: 'Peace is . . . a getter of more bastard children
. . . peace is a greater maker of cuckolds' [233–40]. War makes
men bond together whereas peace makes men hate one another
[241].

The sexuality of domination

Aufidius' relationship to Coriolanus seems sexual not only in
admiration but also in the desire to dominate. Whereas
Coriolanus in his innocence and directness regards his relation-

ship to Aufidius as that as a superior among equals, Aufidius is watchful, studying the Roman, waiting for a chance to reverse the defeats of the past. His language of dominance and conquest is sexual: 'When, Caius, Rome is thine, . . . then shortly art thou mine' [IV.vii.56]. If such sexuality is violent, predatory or part of admiration, love often implies influencing someone. When someone must persuade Coriolanus not to destroy Rome, it is someone who can use love to stop him. Affection has become a lever, a tool. Cominius is 'his general, who loved him' [v.i.2]. When the tribunes appeal to Menenius to plead with Coriolanus they say 'make trial what love can do' [v.i.40]. Why someone who loves Coriolanus would want to defend Rome is not clear. Menenius, however, has no hesitation to go on such an errand and brag to the Volsces that Coriolanus, 'is my lover' [v.ii.14]. Coriolanus admits 'I love thee' [v.ii.91], says that Menenius 'was my beloved in Rome' [v.ii.95] and speaks of the 'old love I have' for him [v.iii.12]. Whether or not such references have latent homosexual content, Coriolanus does not seem obsessed with sexual desire for women; he remains chaste in exile. His only tenderness towards Virgilia occurs in v.iii where we learn 'my true lip / Hath virgined it ever since' [47–8]. He is more concerned with his relationship to his mother than to his wife.

After Volumnia has conquered Coriolanus, Aufidius plays a similar role as conquerer. He has 'raised him' [v.vi.20] and claims Coriolanus has seduced his friends [v.vi.24], although Aufidius admits that he 'gave him away / In all his own desires' [33]. After Aufidius kills Coriolanus he 'stands on him' and is told 'tread not upon him' [v.vi.134], which while symbolic of dominance and a reversal of previous humiliation might – especially as we are told that Aufidius has drawn his sword – be seen as sexual.

Power

Coriolanus shows power changing and the psychology of power – particularly how power reflects the needs of the people and society in different times and situations. Power is not stable, it shifts between the mob, Coriolanus, the tribunes, and Volumnia and finally, Aufidius. Power is sometimes gained by threats, by conquest, by demagoguery, by persuasion, by trickery – but inevitably power is created by men and women in specific situations and is not directly based on tradition, although ideas about institutions and traditions are part of the battle for power. Consider how power shifts. At first the dominance of the elite is challenged by the mobs who have been driven nearly to mutiny by the scarcity and cost of grain. This is an economic matter upon which the survival of the citizens depends. Faced by a possible revolt which would destroy their property and position, the nobility capitulate; they try to save what they can by compromise, offering cheap grain and the right of the commoners to have representation in the government. The compromise reveals weakness. Power cannot be shared unless there is a common interest, ideology, rhetoric, will, and so on. Protection of the state is such an interest in time of war; shared economic well-being is another.

Despite Menenius' claim that the state is an organic whole there is little reason to think many Romans in the play recognise shared class interests. At one extreme the tribunes only recognise the rights of the people (actually this means the tribunes' own status and power as elected representatives) while Coriolanus only recognises the rights of the nobles as the class which has built Rome in the past and which provides leadership in defence against enemy states. Power has shifted to the tribunes more than most of the nobles realise – although Coriolanus, who is blind in other ways, instinctively sees what has happened. The weakness of the nobles is soon proved when they are willing to sacrifice Coriolanus, their main hope of regaining power, rather than risk civil war. Before that, however, Coriolanus is momentarily brought close to power by single-handedly leading the troops to victory over the Volsces. His soldierly abilities are needed as long as there is an outside threat; short of taking arms and conquering Rome, he can govern only as part of a political process.

The tribunes, like Coriolanus, understand that there is an unfinished revolution in progress and that the nobles will not risk losing all their possessions in civil strife. Coriolanus sees what is happening and is unwilling to accede quietly to the change. Thus, Coriolanus' attempt to be approved to consularship brings to a crisis the implicit war between nobles and other classes. The tribunes know that they must by any means keep Coriolanus from the consularship as he is likely to lead a reaction. The conflict between the two major groups of the Romans is represented by the conflict between Coriolanus and the tribunes. Political conflicts and tests of strength are not abstract but are between individuals who in the historical process represent opposing groups. The tribunes know that the defence of their own power requires them to destroy Coriolanus; his unwillingness to compromise, his clear understanding of how power shifted with the creation of the tribunes, his popularity, strength of character and ability to unite men as soldiers make him dangerous, someone who by instinct and ability will defend what he considers a threatened older order. Coriolanus will fight for what he considers right. But his rigidity, his excess of virtue and his inability to use language hypocritically causes his downfall as it allows others to manipulate him into public displays of anger that alienate the populace.

The tribunes save and extend their power by persuading the citizens that their own liberties and rights are threatened. Faced by possible revolt, the nobles agree to deny Coriolanus the consularship; they agree to his trial and exile. The tribunes can convince others that Coriolanus is a threat because they and others think Coriolanus is no longer needed to defend the state; they want to believe that the Volsces, having been defeated, will not fight again. In their blindness to outside threats, they reveal a parallel one-sidedness to that of Coriolanus. He can understand only the world of war; they can imagine only a time of security. He despises those who will not fight; they imagine people naturally forming a community, protecting each other collectively through political rights, and they hate assertions of superiority. Although the action of the play would appear to support Coriolanus' view of the world, it also bears out that of the citizens. Or it could be said that both are wrong.

Power in the play shifts to the tribunes who have tested the nobility and found them without the will to resist. We learn, however, at IV.iii.20–7 that the banishment of Coriolanus has pushed some nobles to their limit and there is a possibility

that if the tribunes go much further, the nobles might fight to
restore the old order. The tribunes now appear conciliatory.
When we next see them [IV.vi] they are being treated by the
populace as their gods; the citizens kneel to them (the visual
symbol of obedience) and pray for them. Their power,
command of the political order and backing by the populace
is only possible as long as it is not challenged by force since
they and the citizens are not good soldiers. When Rome learns
that Coriolanus is leading a foreign army, the tribunes
immediately lose their power which shifts wildly among those
nobles who are perceived as capable of persuading Coriolanus
not to revenge himself.

In *Coriolanus* as in *Antony and Cleopatra* and in *Hamlet*, there
is always an enemy army waiting to pounce on weakness; life
is brutal, conquer or be conquered. These are not pacifist
plays. Richard II's kingship is not able to resist Bolingbroke's
greater will and force; legitimacy needs something more than
right and justice if it is to govern. It requires the power to
enforce its will and order. The nobles lacked such will before,
now the tribunes lack power. When Coriolanus is persuaded
by his mother not to attack Rome, power shifts to her and,
ironically in the light of Coriolanus' failures, there is talk of
making her consul. A parallel shift in power occurs among
the Volsces. Aufidius, beaten in battle by Coriolanus and
pushed aside from his leadership of the army, finds that after
the compromise with Rome, he can now claim that Coriolanus
is a traitor and then kill him with the aid of conspirators.

Shifts in power and tensions between legal authority and
the actual force which governs is a central theme of the history
plays; in *Coriolanus* the situation is more complex as popularity,
legitimacy, loyalty, and power keep changing from moment
to moment. In the tragedies, especially the Roman plays,
people are mostly governed by self-interest; those who are not
are usually the victims of others.

Act v.vi

The conclusion of *Coriolanus* is curiously flat. Coriolanus, the
only innocent among the leading characters, is savagely

murdered and life goes on in its tasteless, base way. Aufidius, betrayer and murderer, rapidly says he is sorry (which we may doubt and think is another act of policy), reminds everyone that Coriolanus 'in this city. . . . Hath widowed and unchilded many a one' [151–2], 'Yet he shall have a noble memory', which grudging praise is depressing after we have watched Coriolanus for five acts. Even a villain deserves more sympathy. We know that historically the Volsces did indeed celebrate Coriolanus as a hero and honoured him after his death. Shakespeare purposefully played down those facts which might have given the play an up-beat ending and celebrated Coriolanus; he has denied the audience the feeling of satisfaction we expect at the end of tragedy. The ending of *Coriolanus* takes further the deflation and scepticism which Shakespeare has been practising in his tragedies. After Cleopatra's apparently triumphant death ('she looks like asleep / As she would catch another Antony / In her strong toil of grace'), the concluding speech by Caesar suddenly deflates what we have seen: 'her physician tells me / She hath pursued conclusions infinite / of easy ways to die'. After we have seen him plotting against Coriolanus, and indeed been warned earlier that he will use any means possible to 'potch at him' [I.x.15], it is hard to believe that Aufidius' 'rage is gone', or he is 'struck with sorrow'. But this takes us back to the whole dangerous problem of developing subtexts and character study, a method which Shakespeare's technique, with its excess of material supplied and lack of linkage between bits of information, invites. In the case of Aufidius we have enough information that a further novelisation of motives and psychology is likely to be in the realm of probability. From Act I.x onward we have been warned he wants to conquer Coriolanus by any means and we may assume that his behaviour from Act IV.v onwards is partly governed by craft. That would not prevent such emotions as the desire to beat Rome, admiration and homo-erotic feelings for Coriolanus, bitterness and resentment that Coriolanus has become the hero of the troops, outshines him as a leader of the Volsces soldiers, and treats him with less respect than he feels he deserves. In fact we are given information that Aufidius is awaiting his chance for revenge (a revenge that mirrors

Coriolanus' revenge against Rome). At the end of Act iv.vii there are two speeches in which Aufidius darkly says about Coriolanus that he has found means to 'break his neck' [iv.vii.25]. In the concluding speech of the scene Aufidius makes an analysis of Coriolanus' conduct in Rome and announces that when Coriolanus succeeds in defeating Rome he will soon be destroyed, 'then shortly art thou mine' [57].

We are not surprised when Aufidius turns from Coriolanus' rival into an Iago-like villain, directing a play in which Coriolanus finds himself, as in Rome, acting a dangerous part prepared for him. The ending might lead us to agree with Vickers' view that Coriolanus will 'destroy our complacency about politics forever'.

Coriolanus' death

Is there any reason to assume that Coriolanus has no subtext, that he remains innocent about the ways of life, that he goes to his death like a charging bull that has not learned the cause of the moving cape? In Act v.iii when he gives in to his mother, he says that while she has won a victory for Rome:

> But for your son – believe it, O believe it –
> Most dangerously you have with him prevailed,
> If not most mortal to him. But let it come.
>   [187–9]

The way he appeals to Aufidius for approval indicates feelings that he has done wrong. 'Let it be' is Hamlet's phrase for accepting his fate. Why does Coriolanus return to face the Volsces in Corioli rather than go safely to Rome? He knows that trouble is expected and now behaves exactly as he should have in Rome when standing for the consularship. He knows how to use words and display to plead favour. He returns to the sound of drums and trumpets, and makes a speech which [v.vi.71–84] interprets his conduct in a more favourable light than is perhaps accurate. He made a 30 per cent profit in the campaign and shamed the Romans and has gone as far as the gates of Rome. This sounds good unless like the spectator and

Aufidius you know the truth. Coriolanus would not be doing this unless he too has learned cunning, policy and hypocrisy. You may feel he has now become human, that for the first time in the play you like him. Or you may feel this Coriolanus is just another politician, a former hero who soils the mad idealism of his past. Shakespeare's technique is such that he leaves the question open. After Aufidius calls him a 'boy of tears' Coriolanus reverts, as expected, to his enraged, insulting behaviour as he did twice in Rome. And as in Rome the people start to demand his death. History repeats itself.

Or does it? There is a strong possibility that Coriolanus expected this to happen and actually welcomes a chance to die. 'Cut me to pieces. . . . Stain all your edges on me.' He sees himself as a figure in history: 'If you have writ your annals true, 'tis there . . . I fluttered your Volscians in Corioles' [111–15]. 'Alone I did it.' Suicide? Someone like Othello trying to provide a last minute self-justification before death? The speech may at first look like the heroic stoic self-sufficiency of Act III.iii ('I banish you'); but it can equally be read as a bit of play-acting by someone determined to control his own death, someone working on those whom he knows plan to kill him. I do not say this must be so. This is a possible reading, a reading either created by Shakespeare's technique – which allows multiple interpretations – or a reading sensitive to implications of the text, implications which suggest a new, emotional development in Coriolanus since his exile. There is Aufidius' odd claim that Coriolanus 'with dews of flattery seduced his friends' [v.vi.23]. Critics find this so unlikely of Coriolanus that they assume Aufidius is making excuses. But it could be true. At the play's end we still know little about Coriolanus' inner life or his life in exile. We really do not need, like modern Theorists, to deconstruct the text to be free from 'dead' readings. A Shakespearean play is so open in its possibilities that critics who claim a need for the freedom to deconstruct must be driven by other motives than the supposed prison of the text.

In many of Shakespeare's plays, especially in the tragic period, there is towards the end a suffering Christ-like figure. This may be a sacrificial woman, such as Desdemona or Cordelia, or a character who recalls Christ perhaps, like

Richard II, by some analogy formed in their own mind. The play may seem to reach towards an allegory or perhaps only recall a providential view, as in *Hamlet*, which some character comes to accept. In the Roman plays such a dimension is missing, as it should no doubt be. Yet if examined closely *Coriolanus* shows a few surprising traits at the conclusion in common with *Measure for Measure*, *King Lear*, and other plays with Christian themes. I am thinking of the importance of mercy and the way Coriolanus accepts his fate, 'let it come'. There is the possibility, as Kenneth Burke and others have suggested, that we regard Coriolanus as a sacrificial figure. This is in contrast with the cool pagan god-like revengeful Coriolanus, who is uncaring, unmerciful and bent on destruction. The gods in the play seem distant, cold, without mercy. They look down and laugh. We might say that Christianity is in the play as an erasure, a presence that has been removed but which is still felt by not being there:

> MENENIUS.   He wants nothing of a god but eternity, and a
> heaven to throne in.
> SICINIUS.   Yes, mercy, if you report him truly.
>
> [v.iv.24–7]

Comedy?

Ibsen referred to his *An Enemy of the People* as a comedy and G. B. Shaw, perhaps influenced by Ibsen, called *Coriolanus* a comedy. The play is not a comedy in the conventional sense of having an amusing, happy ending – unless you are a Roman – but there is an insight here that needs to be considered. Except for Coriolanus, this is not a play in which significant characters die. After an immense expenditure of energy in plots, attempted revenge, plans, nothing much changes. It is a play of repetition and anticlimax and people have been shown to be proud and vain; it is a demonstration of the vanity of human wishes and politicians and heroes.

The people, whether Roman or Volscian, one moment want to kill, the next worship, then soon again want to kill Coriolanus. Coriolanus enters Rome a conquering hero and is soon sent into perpetual exile; he enters Corioli a hero and is soon killed; the man no one can defeat in battles keeps giving in to his mother and even cries when she threatens to disown him. Volumnia raises her boy to be a hero, but she is finally the hero. The tribunes want Coriolanus banished so they can rule, but no sooner has he turned against Rome than they cannot defend the city and call him their countryman (instead of the enemy of the people). Menenius is so confident of his ability to win Coriolanus from destroying Rome that when he fails, he is unwilling to accept that Volumnia may have succeeded. But then the tribunes are unwilling to accept that Rome may be in danger; they are so proud of themselves that they want to whip the messenger rather than listen to the truth. Everyone of any importance in the play, except Coriolanus, is busy manipulating others, with usually what turns out to be disastrous effects. Nothing succeeds. Coriolanus does not become consul. Coriolanus does not destroy Rome. The tribunes find that political power is not finally true power. The one man whom Coriolanus admires turns out to be the most base of the lot. Farce? Cynicism? Disillusionment? Realism? It is a matter of tone. The tone is cool, distanced, epic, but the elements are indeed there for Ibsen's comedy.

The politics of neo-classicism

Coriolanus was written during the early years of the formation of English neo-classicism, when Ben Jonson and others explored what use could be made of the classics for improving literary style, understanding human nature and political wisdom. The neo-classicism of the Stuart period was not merely cultural – architecture, literature and portraiture in painting – but also political. This is obvious later in the century when Roman analogies are invoked as often as biblical parallels to argue political positions by both Royalists and Republicans. The stereotypes of the later seventeenth century were being formed in the early Stuart period. Behind such a mode of imagination was the start of modern British history studies in the form of the antiquarianism of William Camden, the great scholar who was Ben Jonson's teacher. Camden attempted to collect information about English history with an awareness of its Roman period. (Camden's 1605 *Remains of a Greater Worke Concerning Britaine* is the basis of a few points in Menenius' fable of the belly.) The effect of this was to make modern Britain appear continuous with Rome; England now had a classical past, rather than the crazy quilt of late medieval English monarchy, an historically recognised past, a legitimacy (remember the tribunes anticipate that Coriolanus will claim his ancestors built Rome), and was part of Europe (a Stuart policy in contrast with Tudor isolationism). England was viewed as a continuation of Roman politics and rituals.

If Rome provided a model for the state, its laws (James was obsessed with Roman law) and the duties of the citizen, it also provided an historical model – examples of the dangers of republicanism, the fall into anarchy and tyranny. Such conservative ideas were in formation, being used, explored, but perhaps had not reached the clarity and fixedness they would achieve by the second half of the century. This does not mean that *Coriolanus* must be interpreted in a specific way. The play has a political context, but the context does not impose a specific argument on the text. A work of art reflects, mirrors is Shakespeare's word, social and political tensions, it seldom votes for a party.

Neo-classical influences can be seen in many of Shakespeare's plays, such as in *Othello* and *The Tempest* which concentrate the action in place and time, a concentration which contrasts to Shakespeare's manner in his history plays and *Antony and Cleopatra* or the highly formalised artifice of romance, as in *The Winter's Tale*. Superficially *Coriolanus* lacks classical unity; the location changes and covers an expanse of time. But the play feels classical and that has to do with something besides the setting. The focus on the main character and his obsession with virtue which destroys him is an adaptation of the Aristotelian notion of tragedy being about some good characteristic taken to an extreme which becomes a cause of tragedy. Coriolanus embodies too well values of his society: masculinity, valour, warfare, bravery. His tragedy is his truth to such virtue, his lack of moderation. In this play there is no secondary plot, rather there are plots by secondary characters which advance the main action and cannot be kept distinct from what Coriolanus does as he is often involved with or reacting against them. The restricted canvas space feels classical as it approximates the aim of classical unities.

Besides the focus on the hero there is the matter of tone, the play's distancing of its characters from our sympathy. Such distancing is inherent to epic technique and was learned from Shakespeare by Ibsen and Brecht; but there is a difference between such effects as inherent to a form and the conscious exploitation of distancing. Here distance and irony may at first appear objective until you realise that Shakespeare undermines (through what they say and what others say about them) every significant character in the play. What looks like objectivity is actually satiric. Satire was the main mode the Elizabethans learned from Rome.

The two plays Coriolanus most resembles are Ben Jonson's Catiline and Sejanus. They have a similar concentration on Roman politics, a flat, objective tone, a possible satiric intent. Shakespeare is not Jonson and there is evidence that his play was written and performed first; but we should see Coriolanus in the context both of Shakespeare's plays on classical, especially Roman history, and Jonson's satirical histories of Rome. There is a distinct Jacobean literary kind to which Coriolanus belongs and which is part of the English revival of interest in Roman culture and history.

Social context

It is tempting to find analogies between the events of Coriolanus and late sixteenth–early seventeenth-century English history. The play concerns city mobs, the urban mobs that threatened Parliament throughout the seventeenth century, and which were led by dissenting members of Parliament. The characters on stage are mechanics, apprentices, shopkeepers, traders, not farm workers. The enclosure riots were the result of larger changes within the structure of English society and economics; they were part of the rationalisation of farming, which was in itself part of a movement towards greater centralisation in tax collecting, government, and so on. The kind of urban mutiny shown in the play belongs to the early modern world. The tribunes who represent the people have become a class in themselves. The situation in the play where no one class dominates, but in which there is unresolved potential civil war, is like early seventeenth-century England in which feudal power had been destroyed and the question remaining is whether the court or Parliament will rule.

Coriolanus mirrors the conflict between Parliament and court by showing a shift of power, a new class of people's representatives which threatens authority, a situation that is still unclear, and that the threat of mutiny has scared those in power. A state without clear leadership is in a bad condition and eventually the issue of dominance must be resolved one way or another. Coriolanus recognises there is a revolutionary situation and the granting of the tribunes is different from the ancient rights of the past to which the tribunes appeal. Coriolanus does not understand that his own appeal to tradition might be as revolutionary and modern as that of the tribunes.

But who are the rabble and their tribunes? Not who do they allegorise, but what social forces are mediated through them? While it is wrong to apply a modern class system to early seventeenth-century England, these citizens are probably the new petit bourgeoisie, the shopkeepers, tradesmen, craftsmen, of rapidly growing London. Then who are the tribunes? There is little evidence in the text but as they are familiar with law, history, the lives of the nobles, they are likely to be the new class of Inns of Court lawyers, who emerged in the century and who would lead the parliamentary forces in questioning the power of the king and the nobles. Such people were usually from landed families, younger sons, small farmers, freemen, those who had been excluded from nobility but who were better educated and of a higher social class than the mechanics and small shopkeepers. Such lawyers formed a definite block in Parliament.

This leaves such questions as what kind of political and social tensions found expression in Coriolanus? Why is he so aggressive about his rights as a noble? Why are they so specifically tied up with being a warrior? What social tensions are being mirrored or mediated? There are two distinctive themes here. Coriolanus feels he is part of a family that created

Rome, part of a group deriving from the founding fathers. Very few British nobles in the Jacobean period could in truth claim such a history as old nobility. The Tudors had a policy of eliminating the feudal lords through not naming new lords. Everything possible was done to diminish the number of lords so that by the time James I was crowned there were few titled nobles in England. Given early deaths, poor survival rates from illness, financial bankruptcy, it was sufficient merely not to appoint new lords to bring a class near extinction. Regarded in this way Coriolanus if he were British would have belonged to an endangered species around 1603. Coriolanus is concerned with his honour, his class, his freedom from contamination by those who lack his blood. If Coriolanus lived in a settled society where worth and title were recognised, he would not need to assert his class privileges and try to convince other nobles to fight to preserve their rights. Under Shakespeare's portrait of Rome are the social tensions of seventeenth-century England. Many of the Jacobean nobility had purchased or simply taken on themselves the titles of families that had died off or been ruined. A false pedigree purchased from those in charge of recording titles and a good marriage was enough to make a rich merchant into a noble within a generation. No wonder the nobles in *Coriolanus* are more familiar with the use of words than swords and when threatened by mob violence will compromise or sacrifice Coriolanus, the only real warrior among them.

The insecurity of the new class of nobles is reflected in the themes of the play, in the particians' claim to have a function whether as Menenius' belly or in the case of Coriolanus as warrior. The insecurity of the nobles is even more obviously reflected in the unsettled political situation of the play with its revolution in progress which challenges the nobles' right to power and the curious refusal of the nobility except Coriolanus to do more than temporise. There is no evidence from the play that this is a ruling class. The tribunes seem to have their own way throughout as do the Volsces except when Coriolanus fights for Rome. There is a gap. Where there should be a class and its instruments and its means of power, there is Coriolanus versus the mob and Coriolanus versus the outside enemy.

What begins as a play about food riots involves, I have suggested, a struggle between the urban mob plus the petit bourgeoisie led by a class of lawyers united against one man who represents the values of the nobility. The kind of political issue raised by the play would seem to refer to the relations between the king and Parliament. Both Coriolanus and the tribunes speak about the ancient rights of their class but in the situation as depicted in the play there are no real ancient rights at stake; there is a new conflict between the tribunes' desire to rule in the name of the people and Coriolanus' wish to destroy the power of the tribunes before they can extend their power to governing. This becomes clear after Coriolanus is exiled. The citizens pay the tribunes the respect and homage given to governors. The tribunes know from the first that if Coriolanus is given a consularship they are doomed and a counter-revolution will take place destroying their new power. Either he governs or they govern. The situation is clear when Coriolanus leads the Volscian army against Rome. No one can stop him. More important, he, unlike the historical Coriolanus, makes no distinction between the plebs and the nobility in his revenge.

Coriolanus and monarchy

There is an important issue involved in Coriolanus' claim that government cannot be mixed and that someone must rule. English monarchy had traditionally been understood on the model of the king's two bodies. The king is more than a person. The king or queen rules in and only with the approval of Parliament. The Stuarts, however, had a continental notion of kingship and claimed a divine right to rule. Indeed they often ruled without Parliament, which they avoided calling. Kingship was looked upon by the Stuarts as an inheritance.

Coriolanus embodies the new Stuart notion of patriarchical rights of the king. The ancient rights he claims were in Stuart times new claims to supreme power; just as the ancient rights of the people as expressed by the tribunes turn out to be a new power. The tribunes claim a right to veto and a right to arrest anyone who defies them, as representatives of the people. In practice this is the right to govern, or at least to stop others governing. Coriolanus is like an early Stuart king denying the rights of Parliament to any say in government. Why are the other nobles in the play so unwilling to risk war? Because for them the distinction between ruler and ruled is less clear. They are more political than Coriolanus, but in their mind the question of who rules is not an either/or situation. They have no plans to reverse the new situation – beyond putting Coriolanus on the consul – because for them the government is either mixed or as true conservatives they can live with changes. Coriolanus cannot. For him government is inherited and is a right to be supreme.

The play as a mirror of the time has at its core the supreme issue of seventeenth-century politics, who will rule. The nobility do not count except as supporters of Coriolanus. Either the people's representatives will rule or this one man will rule in the name of inherited right. *Coriolanus* is a mirror of the times, an embodiment of political tensions which will be played out clearly within forty years.

Conclusion

I began with problems raised by the distancing effect of *Coriolanus* which prevents sympathy or empathy with any character or group. While each person in the play has qualities possible to like, or at least agree with, they have stronger characteristics or views which audiences will hate. Moreover our perspective keeps changing or the character changes; but the changes take place outside our vision so that we only see the results, not the reasons for them. Such distancing is inherent to the epic sweep that the Elizabethan theatre inherited from the Mysteries; but it is also clear that during the late tragic period Shakespeare was experimenting with theatrical form, pointing to effects he wants, using verbal pictures, shifting the perspective through the eyes of a character (such as Cordelia in the division of the kingdom scene in *King Lear*). There is also the classicism; this is a play without subplot, without clowns and without addresses to the audience.

One effect of such distancing and classicism is to reduce

the spiritual ring around the play; it has no cosmology, offers no sense of the purpose of life. It is a play in which life is secular, materialist, a struggle for power and goods. Essential values, the individual, honour, virtue, pride, selfhood, are called into doubt and shown not only to be useless in the predatory world in which people gang up to get what they as a group desire, but the victors gain little. If Shakespeare in *Coriolanus* could be said to offer proof of the logic of cultural materialism, he could also be said to show why such a view is demoralising. This has led some critics to speculate whether we should not turn the play inside out and say that because the pagan world is awful *Coriolanus* indirectly preaches Christianity. It could, however, be argued that the scepticism and futility carries further a vision found in the tragedies of this period, that it is no different from, say, *King Lear*, as a statement about the terrors of reality.

A secular modern view is seen in the political focus, the class struggle, the way the play shows Rome divided and constantly threatened by others. In such a world, Coriolanus' pride is almost surreal, he is a Martian from another planet or era, an old-fashioned warrior hero in an age and culture of materialism. Yet this materialism is called into doubt as a final end of existence by the way the characters and mobs are driven by the need for love. The crowds want to be loved, and when not loved become murderers, just as Coriolanus has been made a warrior by his cold mother. This relationship of love to hate, of care and aggression seems at least an equal fact of life as the material world. If it is tempting to construct fictions about the relationship of *Coriolanus* to Jacobean politics and culture, the text is capable of a complexity of interpretation and yet is grounded in the most basic, most universal of emotions, our desires for love, our feelings of dependency, our anger and rage when care is denied, our need to be fed both food and affection. The moral tale we might want to construct remains open, but this most distant and cold of plays recounts the story of a society and a great man driven by lack of love.

Art depends on the renewal and progress of conventions. In *Coriolanus* Shakespeare has updated what Waith (1962) calls the Herculean Hero – Tamburlaine, the untamed, all-conquering warrior – put him in a society and examined such unbridled individualism and primitive virtue in political society. In the process the warrior has become a victim of psychology as well as, by a reversal of historical roles, representative of both modern individualism and the absolutism of James I. Interpretations can and will pile up relentlessly as we move, or history moves, Shakespeare's play through other contexts and further new cultural perspectives. Its greatness is its inner richness of imagery, political debate, irony, suggested characterisation, theatricality – a richness which is bound to result in multiple perspectives since the text will offer evidence to support many readings and methodologies. The mirroring, parallels, cross-cutting, changing focus and distance are characteristic of much late Renaissance, early Baroque art and especially of Jacobean drama; but we readily find such characteristics in *Coriolanus* because modernist and post-modernist styles have taught us to seek open, unstable texts. It is agreed that the Roman plays lack a religious dimension, but Cavell's (1985) brilliant essay worries the text to discover a radical inversion of the rituals of communion, a tell-tale erasure so strong that it will be difficult to ignore in future criticism of the play, especially as it can be linked to earlier insights by Siegel, Simmons and Burke. Having pressed the text so hard there is no way we can stop, no return to innocence. That is the glory, frustration and absurdity of criticism, especially of interpretative criticism. Formalist criticism is also influenced by the approach brought to the text, but as can be seen from the criticism of Wilson Knight, is more likely to be objectively descriptive. Objectively descriptive. An impossibility as words can never imitate what they describe.

There is no one correct interpretation of *Coriolanus* or any text. We cannot know the author's intent, what his age understood by the play, or even expect most other readers or stage-goers in our time to agree as to its significance. Such a bleak view assumes that the language of the text is there, but it has no fixed relationship to some original significance. What relationship it might have had is made more unstable by historical changes and the various conflicting elements (word play, politics, psychology, relationships to other texts, etc.) within the text. We can even question is there a text? What exactly did Shakespeare write? Who wrote the stage directions?

How accurate and accurate of what is the first printing?

If radical scepticism destroys the text, leaving nothing but scepticism, literary life goes on and most interpretations of *Coriolanus* seem to refer to the same play and use the same or similar evidence, even though the data are differently interpreted. Unless we are committed to radical scepticism, a text is there, but the questions we ask of it change what we read. Our answers are inscribed in our questions. If words can never precisely describe *Coriolanus* – just as we cannot precisely describe a landscape or an emotional experience – there is no description without the attempt. Each critic has a responsibility to work towards clear accurate descriptions of the play and its elements while being aware that any copy or analysis of reality is bound to be limited. If interpretation is a form of fiction-making at least we can try to be accurate and humble. If our maps of reality are bound to be wrong they benefit by being made with an awareness that the critical methods we employ are themselves sources of distortion while being necessary. That's life in the post-modern age.

References

Contextual approaches
Leigh Holt, 'From Man to Dragon: A Study of Shakespeare's *Coriolanus*', *Salzburg Studies in English Literature*, LXI (1976).
E. C. Pettet, '*Coriolanus* and the Midland Insurrection of 1607', *Shakespeare Survey*, III (1950) 34–42.
Geoffrey Bullough (ed.), *Narrative and Dramatic Sources of Shakespeare: The Roman Plays. Vol. V* (London, 1966).
T. J. B. Spencer, 'Shakespeare and the Elizabethan Romans', *Shakespeare Survey*, X (1957), 27–38.
Edwin Honig, '*Sejanus* and *Coriolanus*: A Study in Alienation', *Modern Language Quarterly*, XII (1951), 407–21.
Clifford C. Huffman, '*Coriolanus' in Context* (Lewisburg, Pa., 1971).
Paul N. Siegel, *Shakespeare in His Time and Ours* (London, 1968).

Formal approaches: character and imagery
A. C. Bradley, 'Coriolanus' (1912) in *A Miscellany* (London, 1929).
Brian Vickers, *Shakespeare: Coriolanus* (London, 1976).
John Bayley, 'The Thing I Am: *Coriolanus*' in *Shakespeare and Tragedy* (London, 1981) pp. 147–63.
John Palmer, *The Political Characters of Shakespeare* (London, 1945) also in: John Palmer, *Political and Comic Characters of Shakespeare* (London, 1965).
G. Wilson Knight, 'The Royal Occupation. An Essay on *Coriolanus*' in *The Imperial Theme* (Oxford, 1931; 3rd edn, London, 1951).
Caroline Spurgeon, *Shakespeare's Imagery and What It Tells Us* (New York, 1935).
L. C. Knights, *Some Shakespearian Themes* (Stanford, 1960).

Derek A. Traversi, *An Approach to Shakespeare* (1938 2nd edn 1956; Garden City, 3rd edn 1969).

Maurice Charney, *Shakespeare's Roman Plays: The Function of Imagery in Drama* (Cambridge, Ma., 1961) pp. 142–97.

Religious, sociological and anthropological approaches

J. L. Simmons, *Shakespeare's Pagan World: The Roman Tragedies* (Charlottesville, Va., 1973; Brighton, 1974).

Kenneth Burke, *Language as Symbolic Action* (Los Angeles, 1966).

Jan Kott, 'Coriolanus or Shakespearean Contradictions' in *Shakespeare Our Contemporary* (Garden City NY, 1964) pp. 133–62.

Gail Kern Paster, 'To Starve with Feeding: Shakespeare's Idea of Rome' in *The Idea of the City in the Age of Shakespeare* (Athens, Ga., 1985) pp. 58–90.

Interdisciplinary approaches: Marxist and psychoanalytical

Terry Eagleton, *William Shakespeare* (Oxford, 1986).

Jonathan Dollimore, *Radical Tragedy: Religion, Ideology and Power in the Drama of Shakespeare and his Contemporaries* (Chicago, 1984).

Charles K. Hofling, 'An Interpretation of Shakespeare's *Coriolanus*', *American Imago*, 14 (Spring 1957) 411–31.

Janet Adelman, 'Anger is My Meat: Feeding, Dependency, and Aggression in *Coriolanus*' in *Representing Shakespeare* eds Murray M. Schartz and Coppelia Kahn (Baltimore, 1980) pp. 129–49.

Theatre approaches: performances and transpositions

Ralph Berry, 'The Metamorphoses of *Coriolanus*' in *Changing Styles in Shakespeare* (London, 1981).

John Dryden, *All for Love* (1678).

Henrik Ibsen, *An Enemy of the People* (Preface by Martin Esslin) English adaptation by Max Faber (London, 1967).

T. S. Eliot, 'Coriolan' (1931).

Arthur Miller's adaptation of *An Enemy of the People* by Henrik Ibsen (New York, 1951).

Bertold Brecht, 'Study of the First Scene of Shakespeare's

Coriolanus' in *Brecht on Theatre* ed. John Willet (London, 1964).

Appraisals

Bernard Beckerman, *Shakespeare at the Globe: 1599–1606* (New York, 1962).

J. L. Styan, *Shakespeare's Stagecraft* (Cambridge, 1967).

Eugene M. Waith, 'Coriolanus' in *The Herculean Hero* (New York, 1962) pp. 121–43.

Stanley Cavell, 'Who Does the Wolf Love? Coriolanus and the Interpretations in Politics' in *Shakespeare and the Questions of Theory*, eds Patricia Parker and Geoffrey Hartman (New York, 1985) pp. 245–72.

Selected Bibliography

B. A. Brockman (ed.), *Coriolanus: A Casebook* (London, 1977, reprint 1982, 1983).

Reuben A. Brower, 'The Deeds of Coriolanus', *Hero and Saint* (New York, 1971) pp. 354–81.

David Daniell, *Coriolanus in Europe* (London, 1980).

Alan Dessen, 'Shakespeare and Theatrical Conventions' in *The Cambridge Companion to Shakespeare Studies* (Cambridge, 1986).

Bruce King, *Macmillan History of Seventeenth-Century English Literature* (London, 1982).

James E. Phillips (ed.), *Twentieth Century Interpretations of Coriolanus* (Englewood Cliffs, NJ, 1970).

Stanley Wells (ed.), *The Cambridge Companion to Shakespeare Studies* (Cambridge, 1986).

Index

Page numbers in italics indicate the main discussion of a critic or theme.